The Story of
Ray Davis

RTP
Research Triangle Publishing

Research Triangle Publishing
PO Box 1223 Fuquay Varina, NC 27526
Published 1995 in association with
Korean War Veterans Memorial Dedication Foundation, Inc.

ISBN 1-884570-29-1

Library of Congress Catalog Card Number: 95-68482

Grateful acknowledgment is given to
Col. Wm. J. Davis in the publication of this book.
Typesetting and interior design by Atlanta Asian News.
Cover design by Corporate Solutions.

Printed in the United States of America
10 9 8 7 6 5 4 3 2 1

The Story of
Ray Davis

General of Marines

World War II, Navy Cross

Korean War, Medal of Honor

Vietnam, Distinguished Service Medal

"Lessons Learned in War and Peace"

For Knox

WARRIOR

MEDAL OF HONOR

NAVY CROSS

DISTINGUISHED SERVICE
MEDAL (2)

SILVER STAR MEDALS (2)

LEGION OF MERIT (2)

BRONZE STAR

PURPLE HEART

PRESIDENTIAL UNIT
CITATION (5)

NAVY UNIT CITATION (3)

CAMPAIGNS (14)
WORLD WAR II
KOREA • VIETNAM

FOREIGN AWARDS (7)

SERVANT

CONGRESSIONAL
MEDAL OF HONOR
SOCIETY

1ST & 3RD MARINE
DIVISION ASSOCIATION

MARINE CORPS LEAGUE

MARINE YOUTH
FOUNDATION

MARINE SCHOLARSHIP
FOUNDATION

EXECUTIVE: GEORGIA
CHAMBER OF COMMERCE

BOARDS:
BERRY COLLEGE
MARINE MILITARY
ACADEMY

SCHOLAR

ATLANTA TECHNICAL
HIGH SCHOOL

GEORGIA INSTITUTE
OF
TECHNOLOGY

BASE DEFENSE
WEAPONS SCHOOL

AIR-INFANTRY
SCHOOL

NATIONAL WAR
COLLEGE

MARINE CORPS
EDUCATION CENTER

MARINE CORPS
BASIC SCHOOL

CONTENTS

INTRODUCTION

Raymond Gilbert Davis, General, U. S. Marine Corps, Retired, is a man of relatively few words. The fact that in three years the following could be extracted from this authentic hero is a living monument to what this writer originally deemed impossible.

We had discussed such a project back in 1954 in a chance meeting in Marine Corps Headquarters. As a Tactics Instructor at The Basic School in Quantico, I had sold articles to the *MARINE CORPS GAZETTE* and *NAVAL INSTITUTE PROCEEDINGS* about "our" battalion, the lst Battalion, 7th Marines. At the Chosin Reservoir, Korea, he was the CO (Commanding Officer), and I was in one of his rifle companies. At that time Colonel Ray Davis' reply had been: "Bill, if you think such a book would tell the real story about what a great job our troops did in that terribly difficult environment, I'm available."

It all came back in late November, 1987, when he sent money for another copy of my book, *CHOSIN MARINE*--which he termed "the worm's eye view." Someone borrowed the copy I gave him at the 35th Anniversary of The Chosin Few in San Diego in 1985, and lost it. "Besides, Bill," he wrote, "you talked about getting together on a book. Perhaps now is the time."

Originally, after discussing the project with Brigadier General E. H. Simmons, Director of Marine Corps History and Museums the following January, the plan was to create a biography. We would meld together input from brother Marines and others from around the globe, plus my observations gained in ten different tours with him between 1947 and 1971 with emphasis on what he had learned and how it could be best passed on to future generations.

The truth is that all incoming reports appeared to be written more about a man slated for sainthood rather than "Lessons Learned in Combat Leadership" in three major wars; wars of the caliber required to earn a Navy Cross in World War II, the Medal of Honor in Korea and the Distinguished Service Medal in Vietnam.

Consequently, the decision was made to turn to my pens, pencils, typewriter, tape recorder, telephone and VCR, in order to get this Marine's Marine to tell it as he sees it, so that those that follow him as protectors of our freedom might have understanding.

Never a shouter, never profane, never a grandstander, Ray Davis expressed his thoughts with gentlemanly precision and razor-sharp logic, never closed his mind on a topic, ever remaining willing to re-open the dialogue or reconsider a decision. His soft-spoken guidance carried more authority than the strident bellowing of some other leaders.

His leadership style was to "suggest" that his subordinates do this or that. We all soon realized that his "suggestions" were not idle chit-chat. He fully expected, unless his subordinates exercised their opportunity to discuss the matter, that action would result--quickly. I was privileged to work for Ray Davis as an immediate subordinate on three occasions: the educational environment of the Marine Corps Schools in Quantico, Virginia; the Marine Corps Headquarters environment in Washington, D.C.; and the combat environment in Vietnam.

(Major General Carl Hoffman, USMC, Retired)

The situation in Korea was so desperate that if he had failed, 1,000 other Marines as well as this writer definitely would never have had a chance to live this long. In addition another 6,000 Marines in the 7th and 5th Marine Regiments could easily have been lost. The situation involved his Marine battalion being surrounded, along with the entire First Marine Division, by over 100,000 Chinese Communist troops who were in North Korea to counter our threat to their mainland and Mongolia. In addition, more than 100,000 North Korean escaped from communist terror through the port of Hungnam with American troops.

Ray Davis saved many lives, including those of Marines in combat in Korea as well as in World War II and Vietnam. As carefully as I have researched, I have not uncovered any other Marine with his most impressive display of personal decorations for valor in combat.

In addition to his unsurpassed combat record, he filled every one of the possible staff and command assignments over three-plus decades: G-1 (Personnel), G-2 (Intelligence), G-3 (Plans, Operations & Training), G-4 (Supply & Logistics), "5" (Executive Officer & Deputy Commanding General), "6" (Commanding Officer & Commanding General).

And he was Assistant Commandant of the Marine Corps, a billet which called for excellence in all of these staff and command skills--and a Presidential appointment. Like the legendary General C. B. Cates, who commanded on all five levels in combat: platoon, company, battalion, regiment, division, Ray did the same, except on the regimental level, where he was the Executive Officer, 7th Marines (Korea).

In addition to his unparalleled career, Ray Davis appears to be proud of the fact that his wife Knox was asked to christen a ship named after the battle in which he was awarded the Medal of Honor, the guided missile cruiser, USS CHOSIN (CG 65), in late 1989 in Pascagoula, Mississippi. "Marriage to this remarkable woman is still ongoing after 50 years. She wrote every day (and got a reply) to make me a part of the family during three wars plus unaccompanied tours of duty which lasted ten years. Knox is a varsity player in my life. She has the highest standards--"Scout Code," church, family unity, social graces, WORK ETHIC--

you name it. Born the 4th of ten children on a 240 acre farm in North Carolina, she chopped and picked cotton, milked cows and carried firewood. So strong was the family bond that all ten of them finished college by hard work and supporting one another!"

Enough of introduction. Permit me now to bring out the Marine who says that one of his greatest claims to fame in our Grand and Glorious Corps is that his first Commanding Officer and tactics instructor in The Basic School at Philadelphia, was "Chesty" Puller!

And here is that student, teacher, and pragmatic practitioner, Ray Davis--of Guadalcanal, Peleliu, Chosin, and Dong Ha--and these United States of America!

General Creighton W. Abrams, Jr., a career Army officer (West Point, 1936) who commanded the U.S. Military Assistance Command in Vietnam from 1968-72 once observed to General Leonard F. Chapman, Jr., during the Marine Commandant's visit to Vietnam, "of the 50 or so division commanders I have known in Vietnam, General Davis has no peer. He's the best."

CHAPTER 1. LESSONS LEARNED IN VIETNAM

Thanks, Bill Davis, for forcing me to experience many great moments in my life again through working on this book. You know that I was not noted for my speaking and writing abilities while in the Corps, but you caused me to enjoy this challenge.

Unlike most of my talks and interviews, I am not going to begin by speaking about the Medal of Honor that my troops gained for me in Korea. I would rather leap off in the attack by offering my views on how and why Vietnam was lost, because I feel that the twelve major lessons learned there might prove to be of value in preventing more of the same in our politico-military future.

My ideas were published in the *Marine Corps Gazette* headed: POLITICS AND WAR: TWELVE FATAL DECISIONS THAT RENDERED DEFEAT IN VIETNAM. The reader and I know that politics dominates war, but for war to be waged successfully, those responsible for political decisions must comprehend not only the larger circumstances of the war but also the effect of their political decisions on the military situation. Thus, as a long-term senior Marine commander, let me assess what several political decisions really meant to all those who fought the war in Vietnam.

Through the years since the Vietnam War, I have watched expectantly for authors, historians, writers, and commentators to discover the real causes for the disastrous total defeat in Vietnam. Somehow every effort I have seen misses the main problems by a wide margin. I have been increasingly concerned that if we don't face up to the root problems that led to the Vietnam disaster we can expect no better results in the future.

My participation during the Vietnam era was from a number of crucial vantage points. Initially, as Marine Corps manpower coordinator, I worked with the buildup and deployment of forces. Then, as a Marine Division commanding general in Vietnam, I experienced the effects of our policies, goals and efforts. Finally, as commander of the Marine Corps Development and Education Command, it was necessary to study and analyze the decisions concerning the war and the results thereof.

In recent times I reviewed many ideas and joined in discussions of the causes and results of decisions made throughout the Vietnam era. My interest is not in how the decisions were arrived at nor who the participants were, but in what decisions resulted in the disastrous defeat in the Vietnam War. I have selected a dozen key decisions that in their sum total could have brought no other result than that which we experienced.

1. ROLE FOR MILITARY FORCES

While we were planning for military deployments in early 1965, it became obvious that a force of about a half-million troops would be required in Vietnam. In retrospect, the prompt application of that size force would have brought early success by enabling us to destroy enemy forces and secure the countryside. Instead, it was 1968 before sufficient military forces were available to accomplish these tasks.

The Military Assistance Command approach, which tended to downplay the requirement for a sizable troop commitment, distorted the role of our forces from the beginning. The size of the military assistance force was actually shrinking in 1964-1965. The near-unanimous resolution in Congress after the Tonkin Gulf incident was taken as support for our entry into the conflict.

From the beginning it was known that the real enemy would be those 14 North Vietnamese Army regular divisions plus the Viet Cong main force regiments and battalions. This was ignored; and limited war, graduated response, and tit-for-tat ideas, all based on some theory of human rationality and effective gamesmanship got in the way of a clear statement of purpose and role for the armed forces being deployed.

2. LIMIT ON FUNDS

The Fiscal Year (FY) 65 supplemental budget was established at $11.2 billion as being needed to deploy our forces. The so-called "Senate Kitchen Cabinet" let the President know that funding the war would conflict with fully funding his Great Society Program--a program envisioned as the cornerstone of the Johnson administration. A decision was then made to fund only $1.7 billion of the $11.2 billion needed. Although some funds were buried in nondefense appropriations, most of the money required was deferred to later years. Deployments were slowed down as necessary to remain within these limited expenditures.

3. WITHHOLDING THE READY RESERVE

Thirteen active divisions were ready for deployment (10 Army, 3 Marine). However, the backup forces necessary for these divisions to be sustained in the field were in the Ready

Reserve. This was by design. Secretary of Defense Robert McNamara required such a design on the basis that the "second trip" of available transportation would provide for the time needed to call up the Ready Reserve. It was never envisioned that the active divisions would be deployed without the essential backup units from the Ready Reserve such as heavy transport, artillery, armor, engineer, medical, communications, legal, supply, fuel farms, administration, etc.

A decision was made to withhold the Ready Reserve and replace it by multiplying the size of draft calls in order to build new units from scratch. This was to require more than three years. Members of the Ready Reserve who had been organized, equipped, trained and paid as backup for the active divisions stayed at home, while the increasingly heavy hand of the draft found replacements to organize, equip, train and send in their place.

The unduly heavy draft calls caused a near breakdown in administration with resultant injustices; national borders saw floods of evaders going to Canada, Mexico, Sweden, etc. At home, many viewed Reserve units as havens for draft dodgers.

Deployment of the essential military forces was delayed and the war prolonged. A vicious cycle developed: The inadequate forces in Vietnam, both American and South Vietnamese, could only defend themselves. A substantial, steady stream of casualty reports went back home with little to show in the way of progress in the war.

Support for the war diminished, and this led to less aggressive pursuit of our objectives--thus more casualties and less progress. Confusion resulted from the fact that operational requirements had to be geared to the availability of additional units as they were built up with trained draftees.

It became routine to ready a group of units and send the list of them to Saigon. The command in Saigon would then request them, and the units would quietly deploy. Field commanders were severely limited in their ability to adopt a forward-looking strategy. News reporters reflected this uncertainly to our citizens at home, with resultant reduction in confidence.

4. PACIFICATION IN REVERSE

Inadequate forces meant that many key areas of Vietnam could not be protected. As a result, large segments of the population were uprooted and moved from their homes and concentrated into camps where they could be protected. Their confidence in their government and in ours eroded as they saw their homes, their property and their livelihood abandoned. Again, people were being severely hurt with the appearance of negative progress in the war.

Those areas that were protected could, in many cases, be protected only during the day. The night belonged to the enemy. People were caught in the middle and forced to support and/or do the dirty work of the enemy. They were punished both by the Viet Cong (VC) cadres and by our patrols as the two sides fought back and forth in the area. The "search and destroy" operations conducted in response to this pattern were not fruitful.

No real progress in pacification could be made until all our forces finally arrived in 1968. Then the North Vietnam Army divisions were destroyed, the VC main force regiments were destroyed, and the VC cadres were removed from the villages. People returned to their homes and were protected day and night; they rebuilt their homes and schools and recovered their farms and gardens. Significant progress was apparent for the first time. But it all came too late. Pressures at home brought on another tragic decision: to withdraw U.S. support from Vietnam.

5. AREAS OF SANCTUARY PROVIDED FOR ENEMY FORCES

The enemy was given sanctuary for his forces in Cambodia, Laos, and North Vietnam itself. The result was that he had freedom of movement along a 1,400-mile border. He could concentrate his forces at the place and time of his choosing, picking our weak points, and launch an attack into South Vietnam. Then when he got hurt, he fled back into his sanctuary to get ready to come again at another site. Our "gain" was another long list of casualties with no progress to show for it.

From his sanctuary the enemy fired heavy artillery and rockets in sneak attacks. We could shoot back at these fleeting targets, but were not permitted to go and destroy the attackers. Enemy forces could never be decisively defeated and destroyed because of these sanctuaries. We could not exploit the tactical advantages of maneuver to gain deep penetration into his rear or on his flank because of the restrictions of the areas of sanctuary.

The sanctuary areas were prescribed to support ideas about the neutrality of Cambodia and Laos, on the one hand, and fear of the Chinese on the other. These faulty concepts had no validity as was proved early in the war. Cambodia and Laos were fully occupied by the North Vietnamese Army; thousands of trucks traversed the roads in Laos hauling munitions used to kill American troops. Sihanoukville Port was used to supply North Vietnamese Army divisions in Cambodia where they posed a serious threat to Saigon. The Chinese never once challenged our assault of North Vietnamese targets. The removal of these sanctuaries even as late as 1968 would have permitted the destruction of the North Vietnamese Army and guaranteed victory for South Vietnam.

The absurdity of the "sanctuary syndrome" extended beyond Cambodia and Laos. The North Vietnamese Army operated throughout the demilitarized zone and fully occupied the northern half. We could not enter it. Military leaders also argued loud and long for the blockade of Hanoi harbor to limit enemy resupply, but to no avail. The sanctuary syndrome prevailed even there.

6. THE MCNAMARA LINE--A $6 BILLION BLUNDER

Although enemy elements were entering South Vietnam throughout the 1,400-mile border, a decision was made to control infiltration along the 26-mile northern front. A series of strong points were built, each to be manned by a battalion (about 1,000 men). These heavily fortified positions were surrounded by barbed wire and minefields.

Between the strong points were continuous chains of sensors. The forward positions were supported from the rear by fortified artillery positions. The price tag was six billion dollars!

The design was to detect and prevent infiltration, a faulty role indeed created by the sanctuary syndrome. Infiltrators had a free run everywhere else along the border. Besides, we were not concerned with infiltration--our enemy was coming in division-size units. Not only was the system not needed for infiltration defense, it hindered our effort to fight the larger forces. Rules required that the fortified positions be fully manned a night. Large patrols were ordered to break contact if they were in a late afternoon fight in order to rush home before dark. Added casualties resulted.

The forces tied down in the McNamara Line would have been much more effective out in the mobile mode as was proved in 1968 when the rules were finally change

Success came and morale soared when the troop units finally escaped from those fortified position and launched out to find and destroy the enemy.

7. AIR DEFENSE BUILDUP

Intelligence reports from every source portrayed clearly that the North Vietnamese had embarked on a massive effort to build up airfield and antiaircraft installations. The serious consequence of this development was obvious to all, and deep concern generated quickly. However, a decision was made to withhold Air Force and Navy attack on these emerging defenses; such attacks might disturb the Chinese.

The ultimate result was that we were soon faced with one of the best air defense systems in the world. Later, the hills around Hanoi became a depository for downed U. S. aircraft; Hanoi prisons were filled with downed U. S. pilots.

8. CEASE-FIRE

Periodically, "cease-fires" were agreed to that permitted Viet Cong (VC) soldiers to visit their home areas. Actually these lulls permitted them to reestablish their presence over larger areas with resupply, recruiting, reorganization, etc. The massive, surprise "Tet Offensive" of early 1968 was the capstone of their deceptive use of the cease-fire.

9. ARTILLERY/ROCKET/BOMBING HALT

In 1968 the enemy wanted to talk, and we agreed to stop shooting across the demilitarized zone if they would cease firing rockets into cities. As was typical practice, the enemy was seriously hurt and was looking for some breathing room. The pattern was clear: whenever the enemy was hurt, he would then want to talk; and, of course, Washington gave him what he wanted.

In this case, two circumstances dictated the situation. We had captured his supply of rockets--3,500 of those 7-foot models--in the western mountains. And we had destroyed his ability to shoot at us across the demilitarized zone. An experimental, computerized, state-of-the-art counter battery system was brought to Quang Tri Province and set up at Con Thien base near the demilitarized zone. Our heavy artillery was moved well forward, and an all-out shoot was conducted against what was estimated to be 160 heavy cannons on the Red side of the demilitarized zone. After this, our 8-inch howitzer batteries were maintained in forward positions where they could respond to the computerized system. This weapon was the most accurate artillery piece developed to date. Multiple inputs of sensor information were fed into the computer--flash, sound, radar, and visual--from various points along the demilitarized zone. Observation aircraft operated overhead with photo capability. For 40 days whenever an enemy gun would shoot, the computer would provide data to sight the 8-inch; the 8-inch would shoot a spotting round; the computer would correct the splash; a second round from an 8-inch would hit the enemy gun.

More than 40 enemy weapons were shown in photos to have been hit--tube separated from carriage, entire piece turned over or otherwise disabled..

So, with no rockets to shoot, the North Vietnamese agreed not to shoot any. And since they could no longer shoot across the demilitarized zone, they wanted us to agree not to shoot. There was never a question in our minds, though, that if they got more rockets they would use them; and if we gave them a fat target, they would shoot at it.

Compounding the problem, various "bombing halts" ordered by Washington limited the pursuit of an effective air war against enemy forces, supplies, and installations. A worst case example: in 1972 the enemy launched an all-out offensive against the south--roads were jammed with troops and vehicles. Our tactical aircraft clobbered him--so much so that he asked for a truce. Subsequently, he signed a treaty with Mr. Kissinger that included, among other things, a promise not to use the Ho Chi Minh Trail in Laos.

In 1975 he launched a column of tanks, troops, and trucks down the trail--obviously as a test. Washington would not commit U. S. tactical aircraft--a decision that led directly to the capture of Saigon a short time later.

10. South Vietnamese Army REGIONAL CONCEPT

Our limited military resources and limited response syndrome led to a faulty concept in the organization and deployment of the Army of the Republic of Vietnam. It became regional in its outlook and application. Divisions were fixed in place with no concept or experience as a national army. A limited number of units, prominent among them the Airborne and Marines, were used as a strategic reserve throughout the country.

South Vietnamese Army leaders gained little experience in large-scale field operation; no attitude of seeking out and destroying the enemy existed. Some experience was gained in the expeditionary efforts into Cambodia, but not enough to prevent the lack of experience from becoming a factor in the disastrous defeat suffered in Laos.

11. WITHHOLDING OF SUPPORT IN LAOS

After a successful expedition into Cambodia, preparations were made to destroy the North Vietnamese Army bases in Laos. Forces were assembled at Khe Sanh. Normal U. S. support was included in the design. Unfortunately, the day before the operation was to begin the news media broke the story in Washington. The enemy was given confirmation of precise details of the forces, the time and the place of the operation. Worse, the clamor around our capital city caused some hurry-up, disastrous decisions to be made about the participation of U. S. forces.

First, there was an announcement that "no U. S. forces would participate," followed quickly by certain exceptions; our bombers and helicopters would go along. But, more importantly, the essential support for the helicopters would be withdrawn. The long-range reconnaissance patrols, which were essential for keeping the choppers on safe routes, would not be put into place. The guidance and control communications teams normal to South Vietnamese Army units were withdrawn, depriving the South Vietnamese Army units of a secure voice radio capability. This meant South Vietnamese Army communications were open to interception and disruption when the North Vietnamese Army entered nets with deceptive messages.

An extreme loss in helicopters and their crews resulted (120 craft is the number I recall), the most ever in the Vietnam War. Pilots found themselves flying over insecure routes, responding to instructions from Vietnamese controllers who had no experience, no secure communications and limited language capability. Plus the North Vietnamese Army entered these nets and caused greater confusion. A disastrous defeat for the South Vietnamese Army resulted. Their armored forces were abandoned and lost, their elite units destroyed, and some of their finest leaders were killed or captured.

This was indeed the beginning of the end. A successful expedition might have eliminated the North Vietnamese Army threat as had been done in Cambodia, but Washington's wrong decisions made that impossible. Instead, a defeated, much weakened South Vietnamese Army soon was to begin the withdrawal of forces from key areas that they could no longer hold under pressure from the North Vietnamese Army.

11

12. PREMATURE WITHDRAWAL OF U. S. FORCES

Pressures to end the war and the decision of "America's most trusted voice," Walter Cronkite, that it was "time to get out of Vietnam" brought on a program of premature withdrawals. This takes us back to the role of U. S. forces. Had it been clear from the beginning that we were to destroy the enemy forces, it would have been equally clear in 1969 that our mission had not been accomplished. Since the North Vietnamese Army had been only partially destroyed, the result of our withdrawal was predictable. Withdrawal commenced in the same year that we finally got our forces deployed in full strength--such was the result of the accumulation of bad decisions.

As soon as it became apparent that U. S. support was finally, fully withdrawn, the South Vietnamese Army found itself boxed in on every front with no hope of salvaging even a portion of its country. A final death blow was delivered to the South Vietnamese Army when it was denied essential ammunition supplies--60,000 tons of ammunition already in Saigon harbor in six ships were sent back to the United States in 1972. Fighting without ammunition was a situation the enemy never once faced because support by China and Russia never faltered.

CONCLUSIONS

These 12 decisions with their main genesis coming from Washington, which was some 10,000 miles distance from the battle area, could bring but one result--total disaster.

I join those who proclaim "No more Vietnams," but for different reasons than most. I am not ready to surrender our role as protectors of freedom. Our friends must know that we do support their quest for freedom. "No more Vietnams" means to me that when we do launch military forces in that noble cause of freedom we must do so with an absolute desire to win. To commit our military forces and then withhold support is to betray those men and women who so bravely serve our Country. When we go to war, we must go to win--that, or stay home. And if staying home becomes our policy, we will soon stand alone in a hostile world.

Some would say "Better Red than dead." But if we are to survive in freedom we must continue to follow the challenge of Patrick Henry: "Give me Liberty, or give me death!"

(Note: It appears that these Twelve Fatal Decisions might serve our Commander-In-Chief as well as a pragmatic Standard Operating Procedure (SOP)/ Checkoff List for any future undertaking, such as in the Middle East... Bill Davis)

Raymond G. Davis with The Medal of Honor

CHAPTER 2. MEDAL OF HONOR

I have given many talks since December, 1950 concerning my battalion and our historic cross-country trek which accomplished the mission of rescuing Fox Company of 7th Regiment's 2nd Battalion which was protecting Toktong Pass from a Chinese Regiment which had surrounded it. Of many questions asked during such talks, the first one is usually: just what did I do to rate the Medal of Honor (MOH)? And how can someone get the Medal and still be alive? This event is best placed in perspective with Major M. E. Roach's official written statement of 6 December 1951, when he described how he had planned to deploy his "Composite Battalion" (remnants of Dog and Easy Companies, 7th Marine Regiment, plus Baker and George Companies from the 5th Regiment, and mortar units from the 1st, 2nd and 3rd Battalions of the 7th Regiment):

Jointly Lieutenant Colonel Davis and I studied aerial photographs and maps and discussed our plans. There was no time for reconnaissance. A total of six enemy divisions was estimated to be in the Yudam-ni area. Heavy snow and ice covered the mountainous countryside and the temperature was well below zero (minus 10 to minus 25). Due to the extremely rugged terrain to be traversed and the sub-zero weather condition, only minimum equipment and arms would be carried. From my study of the impending operation I knew that it would require super-human effort to push it to a successful conclusion.

On the morning of 1 December 1950 I had a few last words with Lieutenant Colonel Davis and observed him and his battalion move off the road into the hills for the attack. This was the last time that I saw Lieutenant Colonel Davis until the regiment assembled at Hagaru. "Composite Battalion" did not execute the original plan. It was dissolved at approximately 1330 on 1 December 1950. Component elements returned to parent control with the exception of Dog-Easy Company which remained in the vicinity of the 7th Marines command post as regimental reserve. (My caps) LATER, FIRST LIEUTENANT GEORGE R. EARNEST (049337) USMC, A PLATOON LEADER IN GEORGE COMPANY OF THE THIRD BATTALION, TOLD ME THAT HIS MEN ACTUALLY SAT DOWN AND CRIED WITH JOY WHEN THEY LEARNED THAT THEY WOULD NOT BE REQUIRED TO MAKE THIS MOVE.

(Note: George Earnest, a 4th Basic School classmate of Bill Davis, was held in high regard as a Platoon Commander, both by his troops and brother officers, so the reader gets a valid picture of what a momentous, yet hazardous, night attack that we were attempting with a 1,000-Marine infantry battalion.)

The following is the citation which President Harry Truman approved, signed and presented to Lieutenant Colonel Raymond G. Davis in a White House ceremony on 24 November, 1952, for the people of the United States of America:

For conspicuous gallantry and intrepidity at the risk of his life above and beyond the call of duty as Commanding Officer of the First Battalion, Seventh Marines, First Marine Division (Reinforced), in action against enemy aggressor forces in Korea from 1 through 4 December 1950.

Although keenly aware that the operation involved breaking through a surrounding enemy and advancing eight miles along primitive icy trails in the bitter cold with every passage disputed by a savage and determined foe, Lieutenant Colonel Davis boldly led his battalion into the attack in a daring attempt to

President Harry S. Truman, in the White House Ceremony on November 24, 1952, reads the citation accompanying Marine Lieutenant Colonel Raymond G. Davis' Medal of Honor. His wife, Willa Knox and children Raymond G. Davis, Jr., Gordon, and Willa look on

relieve a beleaguered rifle company and to seize, hold and defend a vital mountain pass controlling the only route available for two Marine regiments in danger of being cut off by numerically superior hostile forces during their redeployment to the port of Hungnam.

When the battalion immediately encountered strong opposition from entrenched enemy forces commanding high ground in the path of the advance, he promptly spearheaded his unit in a fierce attack up the steep, ice-covered slopes in the face of withering fire, and, personally leading the assault groups in a hand-to-hand encounter, drove the hostile troops from their positions, rested his men and reconnoitered the area under enemy fire to determine the best route for continuing the mission.

Always in the thick of the fighting, Lieutenant Colonel Davis led his battalion over three successive ridges in the deep snow in continuous attacks against the enemy and, constantly inspiring and encouraging his men throughout the night, brought his unit to a point within 1500 yards of the surrounded rifle company by daybreak. Although knocked to the ground when a shell fragment struck his helmet and two bullets pierced his clothing, he arose and fought his way forward at the head of his men until he reached the isolated Marines.

On the following morning, he bravely led his battalion in securing the vital mountain pass from a strongly entrenched and numerically superior hostile force, carrying all his wounded with him, including 22 litter cases and numerous ambulatory patients. Despite repeated savage and heavy assaults by the enemy, he stubbornly held the vital terrain until the two regiments of the division had deployed through the pass and, on the morning of 4 December, led his battalion into Hagaru-ri intact.

By his superb leadership, outstanding courage and brilliant tactical ability, Lieutenant Colonel Davis was directly instrumental in saving the beleaguered rifle company from complete annihilation and enabled the two Marine regiments to escape possible destruction. His valiant devotion to duty and unyielding fighting spirit in the face of almost insurmountable odds enhance and sustain the highest traditions of the United States Naval Service.

/s/ HARRY S. TRUMAN

Processing of the award took almost two years between the actual deed and the physical presentation of the Medal of Honor. One basic stipulation for a Medal of Honor is that there must be a minimum of two witnesses who swear separately under oath and in writing that the event transpired as stated in the final citation signed by the President of the United States.

This requirement was met by stipulations made in writing by FOUR extremely knowledgeable combat Marines, the battalion operations officer (Major Tighe), and executive officer (Major Fridrich) , as well as two of my three rifle company commanders (Captain Hovatter and Lieutenant Shea). The third completed this Fox Company operation, but was Killed in Action (KIA) prior to the end of the Chosin Reservoir Campaign. First Lieutenant Joe Kurcaba, Commander, B Company also provided eye-witness account. Their statements were especially valuable, because all of these officers served in the Corps during World War II, thus each had a minimum of 10 years in the Marines, plus the experience of having many other noteworthy examples of combat leadership for purposes of rugged combat comparisons. Particularly qualified was Major Tom Tighe, our Battalion operations officer. It is Standing Operating Procedure in the Corps for the operations officer, when the battalion is in the attack, to spend the majority of his time close by the commander as he handles combat crises, in this case with the definite extremes of weather and numbers of enemy personnel in the immediate area. In addition, 1st Lieutenant Hovatter, Commander of Able Company, had recently operated in what turned out to be a rehearsal for this particular operation, when, only two days before, he came to help C Company of 1st Battalion, 7th Marines, which had been surrounded by Chinese Communist soldiers. And First Lieutenant Shea, Executive Officer of Charlie Company, was in that unit being rescued, so he had seen both sides of this type of operation in a 96-hour period. One could not have had more reliable witnesses to a deed of this magnitude.

We will deal later with most of my career in the United States Marine Corps (USMC) in a chronological order, so that the actual cross-country trek at Chosin will be clearly spelled out for the reader in Chapter 14, in which I will describe in detail the Marine campaign in North Korea in the winter of 1950.

For now, one thing that seems confusing for most Americans is the term "Congressional Medal of Honor." What was awarded is the Medal of Honor. Back in 1918, the U. S. Congress decided to clear away any inconsistencies of previous legislation regarding the Medal of Honor and made a set of perfectly clear rules for its award. The law passed in July 1918 stated as follows:

> ...the provisions of existing law relating to award of Medals of Honor...are amended so that the President is authorized to present in the name of Congress a medal of honor only to each person who, while an officer or enlisted man of the Army, shall hereafter, in action involving actual conflict with an enemy, distinguish himself by gallantry and intrepidity at the risk of his life above and beyond the call of duty.

At the same time, the Congress created the Distinguished Service Cross (Army)/ Navy Cross, the Distinguished Service Medal, and the Silver Star Medal (all of which General Davis also earned). Thus, if one is to have a "Congressional" Medal of Honor, he would also have a "Congressional" Navy Cross or Silver Star Medal. Yet, all living MOH recipients belong to the Congressional Medal of Honor Society which was chartered by the Congress..

> In August 1956, Congress enacted legislation to create the Air Force Medal of Honor and provide for its award to members of the Air Force. However, it was not until 1963 that regulations for the awarding of the Navy Medal of Honor were amended to prevent award of the medal for deeds done "in line of Profession," but not necessarily in actual conflict with an enemy. An act of Congress in July 1963 clarified the criteria for awarding of the medal for all of the service branches, stating that award of the medal was "for service in military operations involving conflict with an opposing foreign force or for such service with friendly forces engaged in armed conflict."

Perhaps the most incongruous point of all is that there are three different versions of the Medal of Honor: Army, Navy (to include Marine Corps and Coast Guard) and Air Force:

A recommendation for the Army or Air Force Medal of Honor must be made within two years of the date of the deed and award of the medal must be made within three years of the date of the deed.

A recommendation for the Navy (Marine and Coast Guard) Medal of Honor must be made within three years from the date of the deed upon which it depends and award of the medal must be made within five years after the date of the deed.

In addition to the great honor which receipt of the medal conveys, there are certain small benefits: on a Space Available basis, free military transportation can be obtained, also, an additional pay of $400 per month tax free from the Veterans Administration for the rest of the recipient's life, plus his children are eligible to enter any of the U. S. military academies on a nonquota basis.

> Nowadays, we think of the award of the Medal of Honor in terms of a colorful military pageant or a solemn White House ceremony. But for many years the presentation involved little or no pomp and ceremony. Often the local mail carrier presented the medal in the form of a registered parcel.
> This rather indifferent attitude regarding presentation of the medal came to a halt in 1905, when President Theodore Roosevelt signed an executive order outlining basic policy still in use. The order provided that the recipient would, when possible, be ordered to Washington, D.C., and the presentation would be made by the President as commander-in-chief, or by a representative designated by the President. If it should be impractical for the recipient to come to Washington, the order provided, the chief of staff would prescribe the time and place of the ceremony in each case.
> President Roosevelt presented the first medal at the White House on "January 10, 1906,...to one of his 'old boys'--Assistant Surgeon James Robb Church, who had served in Teddy's famous First U. S. Volunteer Cavalry."

One other point of historical interest concerns remarks made by famous Americans concerning how important the MOH was to them. At the ceremony were three members of the 7th Marine Regiment, 1st Marine Division, who received the Medal of Honor: myself and Private First Class Cafferetta, a medically retired Browning Automatic Rifle man in Fox Company that our 7th Regiment's First Battalion rescued; and a medically retired Gunnery Sergeant Kennemore, of Easy Company, 2nd Battalion, 7th Regiment. Bill Davis served as escort for the Kennemore family. (Mrs. Jane Blakeney, longtime Head of Marine Corps Decorations and Medals Section in Headquarters in the Marine Corps, was kind enough to make Bill Davis a 7th Marine Korean veteran, the family escort for that Regiment's Medal of Honor recipients).

Did President Truman say anything special at the ceremony? I really don't have a recollection of President Truman making any special remarks as he placed the MOH on me. But

Gunnery Sergeant Kennemore said immediately after the ceremony that President Truman said to him: "I would rather have earned this Medal of Honor than to be President of the United States." While observing the award of the Medal of Honor to a soldier at Casablanca in 1943, General George S. Patton (cousin of a five Navy Cross-recipient Marine named "Chesty" Puller) is reported to have said, "I'd give my immortal soul for that decoration!" Apparently the devil was not aroused by Patton's Faustial invitation, for although Patton fought well and received many military honors for his display of courage and gallantry during two of America's wars, the Medal of Honor was not one of them.

At one time it was suggested that the medal be awarded to General of the Army Dwight D. Eisenhower in recognition of his leadership during the European campaigns of World War II, but when "Ike" learned of it, he refused to consider the idea. Many years later, Eisenhower told a young war hero upon whom he had just bestowed the medal, "Son, I would rather have the right to wear this than be President of the United States."

But, General of the Army Douglas MacArthur did not turn one down when he had a like opportunity in the South Pacific campaigns of the same war. It is also noted that his father was awarded the MOH, the only father and son team in history.

General Joshua Chamberlain, who received the medal for his action at Gettysburg in July 1863, wrote as follows:

> Only the Congressional Medal of Honor had been held sacred--not to be bought or sold, or recklessly conferred. It was held to be the highest honor--recognition of some act of conspicuous personal gallantry beyond what military duty required. Knowing what has happened with the cross of the Legion of Honor in France, and how sacred the Victoria Cross is held in England, we trust that no self-seeking plea nor political pressure shall avail to belittle the estimation of this sole-remaining seal of honor whose very meaning and worth is that it notes conduct in which manhood rises above self. May this award ever be for him who has won it, at the peril of life, in storm of battle, but let us not behold the sublime spectacle of vicarious suffering travestied by the imposition of vicarious honors.

A final point in regard to the Medal of Honor: legislation and regulations currently allow no margin of doubt or error when judging whether a man is entitled to the Medal of Honor. The deed must be

> ...proved by incontestable evidence of at least two eye-witnesses; it must be so outstanding that it clearly distinguished his gallantry beyond the call of duty from lesser forms of bravery; it must involve the risk of his life; it must be the type of deed which, if he had not done it, would not subject him to any justified criticism.

I have been told that rarely in the history of the Medal of Honor has a more qualified group of eye-witnesses been able to judge the validity of a combat deed in consonance with the foregoing criteria. Majors Fridrich and Tighe, Captain Hovatter, and First

Lieutenant Shea not only accompanied me on one of the toughest military movements in the history of warfare, but all four had served in World War II, so that the combat infantry experiential level jointly among them was some 30-plus years!

President Harry S. Truman (Center) presents Medal of Honor to three Marines at the White House ceremony. He is clasping hands with Marines (L-R): Private First Class. Hector C. Cafferata (Ret); T/SGT. Robert S. Kennemore; Lieutenant Colonel Raymond G. Davis. Secretary of the Navy Dan A. Kimball is in the right background.

Ray Davis (left) and brother, Lloyd (1916)

Mother, Zelma Tribby Davis, and father, Raymond Roy Davis (1973)

CHAPTER 3.   BEFORE THE CORPS

Raymond Gilbert Davis was born on January 13, 1915 in Fitzgerald, Georgia. My father, Raymond R. Davis, was a transplanted Indianian and since he was in the grocery business, we moved around a lot in those early years. Even though I began school in Fitgerald, we moved to Atlanta after only the second grade. In Atlanta I attended Cascade Springs and Samuel Inman Elementary Schools and Bass Junior High.

In Cascade Springs School I remember as a boy being in third grade in a room with two other grades. The teacher used a large switch on an unruly boy. The next morning we were shocked to see a large country woman enter the classroom and give the teacher three lashes with a similar switch. She was the boy's mother. I won a gold ring engraved with my initial for being the only student to make all A's for that year.

I suppose my first "combat" happened while walking home after school when we passed students from another school walking in the opposite direction. A road crew had dumped a load of small rocks about halfway between the schools and one day we were shocked to find the other kids on the rock pile throwing stones at us. During the next few days it was a race to reach the rock pile first, although no one got hurt since the rocks were quite small. The combat ended suddenly when the road crew used up all the rocks.

Ours was a two room school, with six grades, and two teachers, one of whom owned an open touring Ford Automobile. It would quit on occasion, while enroute to school, so we pushed it up the hills in exchange for a ride on the running board on the downhills. It was a great way to break up a dull day at school, and the teacher seemed to go easier on us on days when we pushed her to school.

My active young days in and around Atlanta included such delights as catfish seining in the Chattahoochee River, swimming in Oglethorpe's Silver Lake, refreshing drinks from Cascade Spring which we passed daily while walking to and from school 2 miles each way and playing sandlot ball. More serious youthful ventures included homegrown produce sales, and a downtown Atlanta confectionery delivery route.

In 1933 I graduated from Atlanta Technical High School, where I was a member of the National Honor Society, and won my letter in wrestling. In addition, I was initiated into a secret society called "Horned Toads." I am not sure even today what that was about.

Tech High was a boys' school, and 'sex education' was very limited. However, at least an effort was made during my time there. The main theme was that young bulls are kept separated from heifers until they mature sexually. "Boys who keep their pants buttoned until they are twenty-one can enjoy sex until age eighty," we were told.

In wrestling I was not a star but plugged away on the team and was tied for the top with another in my weight class. We were pretty evenly matched and each of us seemed to win about an equal number of matches. In addition to wrestling, I ran cross-country; however I barely made the team. In my senior year I started "pumping iron" because my Physical Education teacher had a gym in downtown Atlanta. He was a big brute of a guy named Weaver who had enormous physical proportion including a 17.5" neck. To be honest, I think that I stuck with him more for hunting trips made during the season than for gym work, but the resultant physical power served me well years later in the combat of World War II, Korea and Vietnam.

I continued to lift weights throughout my college days at Georgia Tech. Although it was 50 years ago, in some quarters weight training was frowned upon even then as the forerunner to becoming "muscle-bound." However, today's Marine Commandants have instituted Corps-wide programs of pumping iron and running in order to give the requisite power and speed in combat to every young Marine.

During my high school and college years, there was strenuous swamp rabbit and raccoon hunting over weekends because Weaver was a real 'horse' who never tired, and he had great woods instincts which I appreciated and enjoyed.

I also served on the Tech High School Army Reserve Officers Training Corps (AROTC) drill team, which caused me to be at school 45 minutes early every morning. I believe that such punctuality and dedication to duty started me down the right path to carry me through my days in the Marines. Recently at a funeral for a cousin, I saw for the first time in years my cousin, James Bales, who competed with me in wrestling and ROTC. During a Manual of Arms competition, as many cadets were eliminated, we were told to close the interval. To our mutual surprise, Bales and I were the only two left. After a few more minutes I won the title of "Best Drill Cadet in the Corps." Bales never followed a military career; instead he became a professor of Bible.

I was motivated toward ROTC partly by the attraction, in those deep Depression days, of the free uniform and the small money allowance. I stayed with Army Infantry ROTC for three years in high school and four years in college. In those days, a few pennies went a long way: 5-cent street car rides, cokes, hamburgers, ice cream cones, movies, and Weaver's gym charged only a few cents for a workout in the gym. I had a summer job refinishing plaster walls in homes for a 10-hour day at 15 cents per hour. My boss transported me to jobs.

A very close friend in high school was C. Burton Clark, son of Mrs. Florence Smith. Burt was born in Chicago, so maybe it was my Indiana ancestry that drew us together. We were constant companions, spent nights together, trips together, knew all the lyrics of the Top Ten tunes; we just "ran together." Burt flew the gap in the Burma-China supply route in World War II and I saw him twice in the Pacific Theater. After 20 years in the Air Force, he is now deceased. I kept close tabs on Mrs. Smith until she died in her nineties. She was a fine woman in every way, a great role model in social graces.

I spent a year after graduating from high school working towards college: With a partner, I set up a restaurant/bakery in Atlanta. We leased a building, renovated it, equipped it and opened for business. The deal was that I would become a silent partner when college was in session. Unfortunately, after three months, the business failed and I went to work at Lee Baking Company to earn the money to pay for my education at Georgia Tech.

Continuing my education at Georgia Tech was a touch-and-go affair because of finances. Since this was during the Depression, I worked nights for eight hours making parker house rolls at the Lee Baking Company. To get back and forth between Tech and the company, I bought a convertible (Whippet Roadster) for 25 dollars from another bakery employee. The bill of sale was written on the back of a graham cracker box.

I did well at Tech, while gaining my Bachelor of Science with Honors in Chemical Engineering. Years later I still remember my professors: D. M. Smith, my calculus professor, was my favorite person and among my fellow students, Frank dePeterse replaced Burt as my closest friend. He and I studied together at his home on some nights, at mine on others. We often double-dated at neighborhood dances/parties at various people's homes. Frank's family was recently from Germany where they left because of Hitler. They had to leave all their family holdings with relatives, and although no money could be exported, they got "Care" packages frequently. I always looked forward to those because they contained some of the best German foods, including the greatest of German chocolates, which were my favorites. Frank acquired a Textile Engineering degree and worked in the vicinity of Atlanta. I still see him from time to time.

As time went on at Tech, I developed a number of close friends in my Chemical Engineering classes. Almost every class included James Joseph Davis—"Davis, J.J.; Davis, R.G." was a roll call ritual. Joe and I were lab partners and shared seats and rooms on field trips, etc. He was commissioned in the Navy, was captured on Guam and suffered a long imprisonment. He retired on the West Coast, and we continue to exchange Christmas cards. I last saw him five years ago. Other friends include Edward L. Patton and Manuel M. Cortes who roomed together. Both were brilliant students and their room was my campus headquarters since I lived at home.

Patton had a wife in New Jersey and was our expert on married life. He was Navy ROTC and ran track. After graduation he went to work for Exxon, for whom he built refineries in such places as Oslo and Los Angeles. His last great project was construction of the Alaska Pipeline. He was President of the Pipeline consortium and after his death, they named a major bridge after him. During our careers I saw him from time to time, since he had children in Atlanta. Early in the pipeline effort, he wrote to say that 'if you will send a battalion of Marines to clear out the protesters, I can get on with the pipe laying. The delays are costing us a million dollars per day!'

Manuel Cortes was from Mexico. At his high school in New Mexico, he took horse cavalry AROTC. His father was a mid-level railroad executive and Manuel spent holidays with me since he did not want to spend money to go home.

There was great excitement when he won a 25,000 peso lottery. We caught a trolley to town to get the money, then spent the next two weeks blowing much of it at parties, on trips, etc. He was a Civil Engineer, and stayed on to get a Master's Degree. He was the main tutor for our "Ramblin' Wrecks" football team, and for years he was always their favorite guest at reunions. He returned to Mexico, published a calculus book from his Tech notes that became a textbook at the University of Mexico. He built roads and now owns a number of silver-processing plants. I saw one order for parts from Westinghouse for $140,000,000. He bought Mexico's experimental beef stations, then trained his people in Colorado. His total beef operation included over 15,000 head of cattle. Recently he built the world's largest bearing factory.

Manuel has two families because his beautiful first wife died. He comes here; we go there. We've seen him in many places throughout the world. I reserved rooms for him for our 50th Georgia Tech Class Reunion.

The foregoing indicates my overall basic attitude towards people of all kinds. It seems that somehow my inclination toward forming close, constant friendship continued in the Marine Corps. Many turning points along the way went better for me because of good advice and support from many long-term friends with whom I have maintained excellent relationships. In the Marines, for example, I was never a "smiling cobra" -- a leader who appeared to be happy with his subordinates' work, with a big smile on his face, but later "bursting the balloon" with a bad fitness report for many of those on whom he appeared to be smiling.

My romantic relationships, however, were not so constant. Seems that I was "in love" at least once a year with a different girl until I met Knox Heafner. At Tech I took a different lass to the Spring Hops every year. One was at work; one was a neighbor; one at church; one near Tech. I justify this on the basis of "Too little time—and NO money!" This trend also continued in the Corps: Two "loves" in The Basic School. Three during sea duty. Back to an old Atlanta flame, until Knox appeared at Camp Lejeune with a choral group. Then I changed—quickly!

Despite time handicaps at Tech, I made the honor roll each year, won the President's Gold Key, worked on the student newspaper, *Technique*, was a member of Phi Kappa Phi, Tau Beta Pi, Phi Eta Sigma, Alpha Chi Sigma and The Scabbard and Blade Society.

My pay at the Lee Baking Company covered the major costs of my education at Georgia Tech, but Scabbard and Blade was my best achievement in helping my move from being an Honor Grad in Army ROTC into the Marine Corps.

I really liked all of my Army Reserve Officer Training Corps (AROTC) instructors and kept track of them throughout my long career in the Marines. Colonel Edmund Lilly and others were a great inspiration to me in everyday life. I enjoyed and appreciated them so much that they influenced my decision at the time of graduation from Georgia Tech. I was a chemical engineer and had been awarded a teaching fellowship at the University of Tennessee to do some experimental work in elemental phosphorus. It had to do with the Muscle Shoals electrolysis of elemental phosphorus and was to pay me a small fee and guarantee me a Masters Degree in 18 months.

I accepted this, but just before graduation I got word from Knoxville that the money for this project had just been cut back and they could only pay me half as much. Well, what had initially been promised would be near-starvation wages, and half that much, at the end of the Depression, led me to talk to the Army instructors about the possibility of going into the service.

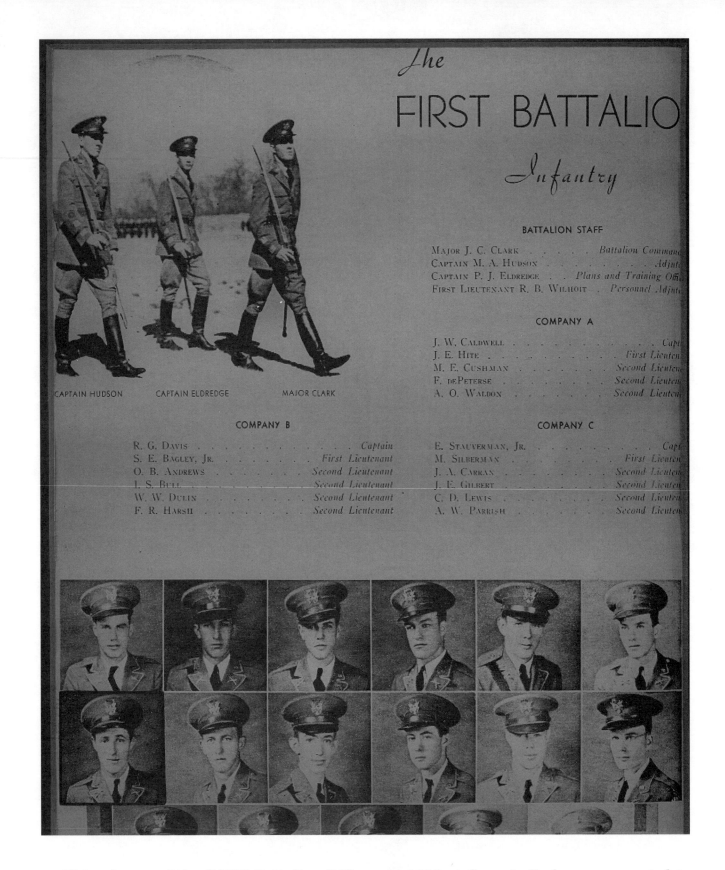

The
FIRST BATTALIO
Infantry

BATTALION STAFF

MAJOR J. C. CLARK . . . . *Battalion Command*
CAPTAIN M. A. HUDSON . . . . *Adjuta*
CAPTAIN P. J. ELDREDGE . . . *Plans and Training Off*
FIRST LIEUTENANT R. B. WILHOIT . . *Personnel Adjuta*

COMPANY A

J. W. CALDWELL . . . . *Capt*
J. E. HITE . . . . *First Lieuten*
M. F. CUSHMAN . . . . *Second Lieuten*
F. DEPETERSE . . . . *Second Lieuten*
A. O. WALDON . . . . *Second Lieuten*

COMPANY B

R. G. DAVIS . . . . *Captain*
S. E. BAGLEY, JR. . . . . . . *First Lieutenant*
O. B. ANDREWS . . . . . . *Second Lieutenant*
J. S. BULL . . . . *Second Lieutenant*
W. W. DULIN . . . . *Second Lieutenant*
F. R. HARSH . . . . *Second Lieutenant*

COMPANY C

E. STAUVERMAN, JR. . . . . . . *Capt*
M. SILBERMAN . . . . *First Lieuten*
J. A. CARRAN . . . . *Second Lieuten*
J. E. GILBERT . . . . *Second Lieuten*
C. D. LEWIS . . . . *Second Lieuten*
A. W. PARRISH . . . . *Second Lieuten*

CAPTAIN HUDSON   CAPTAIN ELDREDGE   MAJOR CLARK

This picture of the ROTC Battalion Officers in 1938 at Georgia Tech was presented to General Raymond G. Davis by the Cadre and Cadets of the Georgia Tech Army ROTC in 1985. Cadet Davis is in the left bottom corner.

I was commissioned in the Army Reserves upon graduation. However, they had what they called the Thompson Act, where reserves officers could serve on active duty for a 5-year period, but with no assurance at all that you could continue in the Army. I obviously enjoyed my ROTC time; three years in high school and four at Tech. They had a Navy ROTC Unit at Tech, but I knew nothing about the Navy and didn't think about going into it. None of my immediate family had served in the military. I did have ancient relatives on both sides in the Civil War, one in Virginia and one from Indiana, an uncle in World War I, but there were no service veterans in my immediate family.

My friendly Army lieutenant colonel, ROTC instructor, told me that the Navy had a commission in the Marine Corps that was a regular active duty commission of more permanent nature. I went to meet with Captain Falwell, officer-in-charge of Tech's Naval ROTC unit, who described the program. They reviewed my A-plus grades in Army ROTC, interviewed me and many other candidates, and then I was selected as the Marine candidate from Georgia Tech from my graduating class that year.

To be honest I wasn't really sure of what I was getting into, except that the Marines had a great reputation, and there has been a Marine or two around Georgia Tech at times. I had close friends in Navy ROTC who talked down the Corps by saying that it 'had only two star generals at the top, etc." I knew little about the Marines, but that "regular commission" on active duty sounded good, so it was into the Corps for me.

The first face-to-face encounter with a Marine was at the Main Gate, Charleston Navy Yard, when I rode the bus over to my physical examination. Like most boxers and wrestlers in college, I was underweight (both strive to put their skills to work in the lowest weight class possible). My family doctor had prescribed beer and bananas, much to the horror of my teetotaling parents. At the bus stop in Augusta, I ate a sandwich which made me ill. In Charleston, I loaded up on water and bananas. Then I asked the doctors to weigh me first thing, but they refused. They gave me the usual bottle to fill, where I certainly lost some precious ounces before being weighed. I was finally passed, after the doctors accepted my story about losing my lunch because of the bad sandwich.

The next step was the classic one of all young incoming second lieutenants in those days. On to The Basic School, for new lieutenants, which was then located at the Navy Yard, Philadelphia, Pennsylvania.

CHAPTER 4. THE BASIC SCHOOL

Second Lieutenant Ray Davis reported into The Basic School (TBS) in June of 1938. It was located in the Philadelphia Navy Yard, at the foot of Broad Street, the main thoroughfare in the City of Brotherly Love. Classroom work and drill were held in the Navy Yard, field training was at Indiantown Gap in the mountains and weapons firing was done at Cape May, New Jersey.

The official USMC Muster Roll for the Class of '38 shows that it was the biggest Basic Class up to that time. Out of a group of 75 new Second Lieutenants, many made general officer: Hugh Elwood, Lowell English, Hunter Hurst, Chick Quilter, Donn Robertson, Alvin Sanders.

In addition the class included one "Pappy" Boyington. "Pappy" was the top character of all time as far as I am concerned and I'll believe any tale anybody has about him. He was, however, a great flier even in those days. Of six aviation cadets in the class, he was among the best. A few training planes were stationed at Mustin Field in the Navy Yard in which we could fly to New York, for example. I would always get into Pappy's plane, because he was obviously a skilled flier.

Pappy and I were brother wrestlers from the days of our youth. Since we both subsequently received the Medal of Honor (mine on the ground and his in the air) perhaps there is a lesson to be learned about a little hand-to-hand and body-to-body wrestling for young Marines. Wrestling teaches control of one's body in fierce competition that is obviously pertinent to duty on land, at sea, or in the air. Fight to the end; never give up. At the Pensacola Aviation Museum there are a number of prominent displays showing the great naval "Aces" (those who shot down at least five enemy aircraft). It was interesting to see that the top Marine ace of all time was Pappy Boyinton.

The official History of The Basic School shows that Lieutenant Colonel Gilder T. Jackson was the Commanding Officer from June 1937 to May 1940. This World War I Hero, unfortunately, was not really close to the students. I guess that in those days it was tradition to keep yourself above the hue and cry of the common folk. At least he impressed me as being rather aloof—not really pompous, you understand, but he never got in there and mixed it up with any of us.

I recall his one appearance in our classroom. There had been some rumors (not known to me) which he did not like. He mounted the platform. We waited in great anticipation to hear our first words from this big boss. Very quickly he said: "Some birds were in a horse barn eating manure when discovered by the farmer. They flew to a nearby fence as he loaded his gun. The farmer did not notice where they were until they started noisy chirping. Bang! They were shot off the fence. Remember. Don't chirp when you are full of shit!" Out he walked.

I do remember TBS Executive Officer Frank Goettge as an outstanding fellow, a great footballer in the Corps and a hero in his own right. He was one who really got down and communicated with the new lieutenants on an eyeball-to-eyeball basis. Also, like the students and staff of every TBS Class, there were other types who were very interesting. At the end of the year we put on skits (perhaps the forerunners of today's TV "Roasts"?) in which we portrayed both staff and students as we saw them. For example, S. J. Cresswell, who was somewhat big and boisterous, kind of outsize and his uniforms did not fit him very well, found his initials "S. J." becoming "Sloppy Joe."

All in all, we had very competent instructors and I would not say anything against any of them. I was especially fortunate in that my company commander was Chesty Puller, one of the most magic names in Marine Corps history. His experience in the Banana wars and his tremendous leadership gave me road markers along the way that turned me in the right direction. Most of the time during my career he was a great inspiration, and among all the instructors he was the only one who was constantly asked to teach through the lunch hour.

He was just that real. He would walk in with his lesson plan—I guess a lesson plan was required—but Captain Puller would put his notes on the lectern and pick up a cue stick which he used for a pointer. He would refer to about three words out of the lesson plan, and then get down to the nitty-gritty of the wars he had been in. He would describe the kind of things that make or break people in combat and what works and what doesn't. I became convinced that as far as leading infantry organization is concerned, particularly in battalion to regimental levels, I think that Chesty Puller had no peers.

Primarily, Puller taught the tactics of small wars. Additionally, he commanded one of the two companies (in which I luckily served) and as drill instructor was the expert on uniforms for all the new lieutenants. In those days a new 2nd lieutenant had to purchase an entire set of uniforms. We were required to have complete sets of field, service and dress uniforms, summer and winter, including a sword and a boat clock. The total uniform expenditure exceeded our basic pay for the first year of service. A half dozen tailors in downtown

Philadelphia were the sole source for these uniforms.

Sartorially, you had to pass the Puller inspection for your new uniforms, and if there was "room to breathe," it was too loose! It made no difference to the captain where you had your uniform made, if it was imperfect, it was imperfect. When one lieutenant said that his uniform was made in Philadelphia by Jacob Reed (an exclusive men's shop), Puller told him, "you go down there and tell old man Jacob or old man Reed or whoever in hell is in charge that I said that that uniform is not going to pass." He got us fitted out in regulation attire, and taught us the technique of inspecting troops. We practiced close order drill to the point that we were flawless because he was a perfectionist in all things, especially in drill!

Another thing I remember, too, about Chesty was that at his quarters in the Navy Yard, he and his wife were as nice and gracious as could be. At the regular dances or parties at the Officers Club, the real gentleman and ladies' man of the whole crowd was Lewis Puller. He was a perfect host, great dancer, good conversationalist, taking care of everybody. He could display a totally different character; a true Virginia gentleman when the occasion demanded.

In a speech to the Major General John H. Russell Leadership Conference held at Marine Corps Development Education Command years later, I summed up my views on Puller and his relationship to The Basic School lieutenants:

> At The Basic School in 1938, my DI (Drill Instructor) was Lewis Burwell "Chesty" Puller. It is likely that some of you suspect that there were no drill instructors in The Basic School, and you are right—Chesty's precise position was "Leadership Instructor," but he was not unlike a DI to all of us.
>
> Even at that early date, Captain Puller was a veteran warrior. At the same time, he was a gracious gentleman from Virginia—a perfectionist on the drill field, in tactical exercises, and on the firing ranges.
>
> In retrospect, I could not imagine a more promising association for launching the career of a young Marine.

Years later, I was able to recap my early days in The Basic School both orally and in writing. In an interview, I noted that while it was a completely new environment, and a new world as far as I was concerned, I was in the middle of a great group of people. My particular class had one or two lieutenants selected from many of the top colleges or universities in the country, plus 25 men from the U.S. Naval Academy. At that time, the Naval Academy graduates going into the Marine Corps were the top ones who chose to enter. Unfortunately this is no longer the case, however, and the Corps does get a certain percentage of "slice" from the Academy.

Let me stress that these were the best—top Naval Academy graduates and top graduates throughout the country. It was just a fine group—enjoyable, smart, pleasant. One special common factor among this group of new lieutenants was that none could be married. We all knew that Pappy Boyinton was separated from a wife and two children, a few were engaged to be married, many had girl friends at home, some were playing the field. Regulations required that we all remain unmarried for the first three years of commissioned service.

As we moved from one training area to another, it was one party after another—the beer taverns in the hills of Pennsylvania, the beaches at Atlantic City were alive with lieutenants and the girls who were attracted to them. I learned one costly lesson in Atlantic City. Late one evening as one of the hotel bars was about to close, I was among the last four to depart. Problem was that two of the bar maids had bills that had not been paid. To save trouble my group agreed to pay the tabs and collect from the others later. I was the only one with an acceptable credit card. It took me four months to gradually pay off the bill—not one lieutenant would own up to owing any of the tabs.

Later in the course I had one steady relationship which developed in the Naval Hospital where I was confined briefly with CATARRH fever. Soon after I was confined, I was taking a shower when a nurse came in. She was angry because I was in the shower with my high fever and ordered me out immediately to get back into bed. This began a happy relationship—movies, dancing at the club, dates on the town. It was nice for a short time; then I was off to sea duty.

I had some advantage with my seven years of Army ROTC, because much of the curriculum had to do with the ROTC kind of things—infantry tactics, weapons, drill. Discipline was not all that tight; we were pretty much free when off duty, and the main Officers Club was available to us. It wasn't anything like today's Officers Candidate School (which is pre-Basic School), where you are under test day and night. I found it to be interesting and enjoyable, and it served its purpose.

A recent brief written update I found in my old footlocker:

TBS, Navy 'Yard, Philadelphia: Saw Director rarely—good reputation from World War I but faded in World War II. The Executive Officer, Frank Goettge (who was killed by Japs on G-2 patrol on Guadalcanal) was a big friendly, hero type, whom all students liked and respected. Favorite instructor was Lewis Puller—elsewhere I describe his teachings. Some instructors faded. Machine Gun Matheson very competent. Visit by Medal of Honor recipient Louis Cukela was remembered by all.

I do not recall much about Smedley Butler (2 Medals of Honor: Vera Cruz; 1914, Haiti, 1915). He was in a local political fight at the time, I believe. Puller was my Company Commander—and a truly great Marine! Chesty was my first USMC mentor, and our paths would cross many times in our Corps career!

Marine Basic School, 1939
Second Lieutenant Ray Davis is 2nd from left

CHAPTER 5. SEA DUTY

As a new second Lieutenant fresh from The Basic School, I reported in May, 1939, for duty aboard the USS PORTLAND, a heavy cruiser. I was delighted to learn that I had been prepared in great detail by my year in The Basic School to assume my duties as a junior officer aboard a cruiser, a new opportunity to travel at sea throughout the Pacific.

I joined her on the west coast, where she was homeported in Long Beach, California. She was a 10,000 ton, 8" gun, Heavy Cruiser, with no Flag (Admiral) aboard. My first Marine Detachment Commander was Captain Ray Crist for a short time, then Nelson Brown took over. My Battle Station (during General Quarters) was high in the mast in the fire control director whic provided data to control the 5"-25 caliber Anti-Aircraft (AA) dual purpose guns. Our 40-man Marine Detachment manned four of these guns.

Going to sea was a new experience for me. A cruiser is a far cry from the rowboat I had known as my lone waterborne conveyance prior to reporting on board. It took me awhile to get my sea legs. But, fortunately, we stayed close to Long Beach for a time where the sea was calm.

We went up the coast to Monterey for a holiday—Dress Ship with flags and pennants—and invited people on board for a visit. The boats ran full all afternoon when suddenly, while I was the deck watch officer, high seas came from a far away storm and bounced the old PORTLAND about like a rowboat. It was well after dark before we finally got all the visitors—many seasick ones—back ashore. At times it was just impossible to bring boats alongside without high risk of their being battered by the gangways as they bounced up and down with the roll of the ship. My watch was doubled, and I got a lot of guidance and support from the senior watch officers but was awarded a "Well done" from the Captain when it was over, with no casualties.

After this, I was sure I had good sealegs but found that not to be so. We soon went to sea to conduct battle drills out on the gunnery ranges, and then on out to fleet exercises. Two of our battle drills were conducted in heavy seas with my battle station high in the foremast where the gun directors were. I was cramped inside one of these directors to control the guns with assigned dials to watch and knobs to turn. The pitch and roll of the ship was greatly multiplied for those of us high up on the mast. I barely made it through the first drill. I was sick in my stateroom afterward and missed dinner. The next storm was worse

35

and so was I. I vomited in the passageway, in the toilet, in my room and could only crawl into my bunk and "wish for death." The stewards earned their pay cleaning up after me that day, but I could in no way raise a hand to help. Having survived these two bad times, however, I subsequently made a very good sailor.

Marine Detachment First Sergeant Wheeler took me in tow from the very first day that I inspected the troops with him. He knew each Marine, his qualifications, his interests, his home, his family, his problems—all about him. Afterwards, I asked him for a copy of his notes on them, but he had it all in his head! I learned an important lesson right then and there: he had perfected a traditional Non-Commissioned Officer role and that was to know all Marines in his charge and look out for them. Years later while speaking to "The Role of Non-Commissioned Officers in Leadership" at a Quantico conference, I said that Sergeant Wheeler taught me to understand the true role of a top Marine non-commissioned officer.

USS PORTLAND shortly sailed to Hawaii, then joined fleet maneuvers out in the far reaches of the Pacific, before returning to Pearl Harbor. I spent a total of 15 months aboard USS PORTLAND, and have many recollections, bad, good, and embarrassing.

As to the "bad," it was when our Detachment did poorly in fleet marksmanship competition and in whaleboat races—both were great disappointments to me. Whaleboat racing was something I knew nothing about. Although I got some good advice from an Ensign on board, we simply did not have the needed muscle power among our oarsmen.

There was no good reason why we did poorly in marksmanship. I was in the top ten percent of the shooters in Basic School and I applied all of the "Puller Techniques" in our training. The Marines seemed to be ready, but the scores just did not materialize. One of our best shooters managed to put one shot on the wrong target.

Among the "good," I had an Additional Duty as the Ship's Laundry Officer, and as a graduate engineer, I noted flaws in the entire system and completely reorganized it. For this, I received positive recognition from the Ship's Executive Officer, which was a rarity in the fleet of those days.

Most of my "embarrassing moments" were results of the fact that I was still an unmarried Marine officer. While still in California, at a ship's dance, my "blind date," brought to the party by an Ensign 'pal,' was a very dark Portuguese young lady, who was heavily made-up, not unlike a prostitute. Throughout the evening, the ship's senior officers avoided us like the plague. So I took a brace, escorted her around the club and introduced her to every officer in the ship's company so that they would know that she was a blind date.

At another dance, I had a different problem: One of the more senior officers had too much to drink and disappeared. His wife assumed that he was out with another woman so she came on to me. She sat on my lap and hung all over me on the dance floor; I was most relieved when he finally returned. My fitness report, which came soon after all these woman problems, was down a shade, but not long afterward I brought a beautiful girl from UCLA to the ship 'to set things right.'

My crazy experiences with women continued ashore. Two friends (Ensigns) and I were at the pier awaiting a boat ride back to the ship when a red convertible with three women stopped and invited us to go for a ride. Since there was no rush to return to the ship, we agreed. Once underway, we heard that they were Hollywood starlets getting away from movieland to relax. They were obviously drunk, so we encouraged them to go somewhere to eat. They took us directly to their suite at a nearby hotel (one of those California hotels with small suites around a central park/pool area). Two of them were in such bad shape that we had to help them into the rooms; the driver, who "claimed" me, made it on her own.

One of the dead drunk ones stripped out of her brief attire as she entered the room and promptly passed out on the floor. The second one locked herself in a bathroom. My red-head driver rushed for the back bedroom where I soon heard her vomiting. I went in to hold her head; found her naked except for a bra. She was so sick that I left her in the bathroom for awhile. When I returned, she was on top of the bed asleep. My friends and I looked at one another and arrived at a Navy-Marine Corps decision: "Let's catch a boat before the last one runs." One ensign somehow acquired a name and phone number and visited Hollywood later on. He brought back a report that my driver was a married woman and had been grounded after their weekend away.

In retrospect, I feel that the regulation which required us to remain unmarried for 3 years led to these kinds of temptations. Some lieutenants voiced opinions that the prime purpose of the regulation was to favor daughters of senior officers,

Upon our arrival at Pearl Harbor, I was assigned ashore as one of the Shore Patrol officers and our headquarters was in the Honolulu Police Department. It turned out that our main duty was to keep the sailors and Marines in single lines at houses in the red light district. A police lieutenant who was our point of contact maintained the file of registered prostitutes, and from this he gave us a special insight into his business. Many of his registered girls were West Coast college students who had run short of funds and were in the business temporarily to get money for the fare home. From their pictures and vital specs, some of those gals would no doubt be able to get home in a hurry!

In answer to a question on what the 15 months of sea duty did to my basic attitude towards the Navy in the situation where the Marine Detachment of two officers and 40 Marines was outnumbered 10 to 1 by Navy folks aboard, I state unequivocally: that duty did not make me anti-Navy in any way! And it really helped me to understand the Navy's role in future times of combat.

At the same time that I was serving aboard USS PORTLAND, Captain Chesty Puller was Commander of the Marine Detachment on a nearby battleship. Fortunately, I met him ashore on liberty on more than one occasion, where my mentor provided me with further professional guidance, building on The Basic School Company Commander-Officer Student relationship from the preceding year in Philadelphia.

Naturally, as you would expect, Chesty's was the best detachment afloat. When we were ashore on liberty, he always had a word of encouragement or advice. Once he said: "It's been years since we've had a war. Might be years before another, so you are being judged in your peacetime roles—perfection in drill, in dress, in bearing, in demeanor, shooting, self-improvement. But more than anything else, *by the performance of your Marines*." Those words formed another key lesson learned for me which was that whatever success I might have in the Corps would be totally dependent on how well I could motivate and lead the men who served with me. I would suggest this as a great lesson no matter what walk of life one may follow.

I might add that Puller did have a great advantage: His detachment was on a senior flag ship, and he was able to convince his admiral to give him the pick of all Marines joining the force since the senior flag ship should always have the best detachment. Chesty chose all one size--tall, trim Marines with good records, etc. Perfection was the name of the game with Chesty, and he never missed a trick.

Puller summed it up for me thusly: "Every waking hour Marines are to be schooled and trained, challenged and tested, corrected and encouraged, with perfection as the goal!" Then and there, perfection in every United States Marine Corps task became my goal!

A chapter of a Marine's life at sea would not be complete without one of my own sea stories: A big disappointment for me at sea was my failure to catch a ride in one of the scout planes. We had two float airplanes in hangars on board which were launched by catapults—one on each side amidship. Cranes would lift the aircraft onto the catapult rails which would then rotate out. The ship would turn to point the aircraft into the wind, and on an uproll of the ship, the powder-charged catapult would fire the scout plane out over the sea. The retrieval evolution consisted of a sharp turn by the ship which would create a slick on the water for the pilot to land on. After landing, the pilot would taxi to the ship and catch a hook in the net extended by a line from the ship. The net and plane were then winched up alongside the ship to the crane, to be lifted by the crane back on deck.

When I first went to sea, the Captain said that he might let me fly in the back seat, but before I got a chance he was transferred and the new skipper said 'No way!' I was unable to fulfill my determination to ride in a plane until after I left the PORTLAND at Pearl Harbor and then it nearly got me killed. My return to the States from Hawaii was on board the carrier USS LEXINGTON, and I was assigned a bunk just underneath the flight deck. Because air operations were carried on both night and day, they would rattle me out of my sleep so I was often up and around the flight crews. One day I asked for a ride in the rear seat of one the dive bombers.

They gave me a 30-second briefing on how to man the machine gun in the rear seat and I crawled in and off we went. I had to simulate firing at attacking fighters and hung onto the gun during simulated dive-bombing runs. I was doing fine until the end of the exercise when I failed to secure the gun properly. As we landed on deck and the tailhook caught the arresting wire bringing us to a sudden stop, the machine gun whipped around grazing my leather helmet as it passed over. Luckily, the sudden stop had jerked my head forward and down into the cockpit just enough to prevent a crushed skull. That was the first of many near-misses which Providence seemed to have in store for me during my career.

Every detail of my many trips in and out of Pearl Harbor came to mind later when Japanese aircraft attacked our fleet there. My ship, USS PORTLAND, escaped undamaged.

CHAPTER 6. WEAPONS SCHOOL AT QUANTICO

While still on sea duty, my interest in gunnery led me to apply for the Base Defense Weapons School at the Marine Corps Schools at Quantico, Virginia. This was the first of many tours of duty there. (Remember--The Basic School was still in Philadelphia). As the course progressed, I learned more and more about survey problems, guns and all types of ammunition, but I also discovered that all gunnery school graduates were promptly shipped to remote Pacific Islands for duty. Such out of the way coast defense positions did not appeal to me at all.

Survey was especially valuable in other endeavors. We started with national coast and geodetic survey markers near Quantico and established lines and locations throughout the area. We took sun shots on Naval Observatory time ticks for precision. Hours were spent on calculations which are done now by computers in seconds. Also, in my current civilian business in land development, I can better appreciate the problems of land lot lines, property line disputes, etc. At times it is necessary to get back to national markers as a basis for settling disputes.

Years later, when I was told that I was lucky that I wasn't ordered to one of these Defense Battalions out of that course, I always replied that it was both some luck and some design. When you go to sea and live with Marines on those 5-inch guns and the Anti-aircraft (AA) battery for 15 months, you get excited about what you are doing. Aboard ship I was asked about going back to the Base Defense School because it was touted as antiaircraft and shore guns, and that had some appeal. I really did enjoy the course. There was a lot of technical material, and I had a strong technical background from my days at Georgia Tech. I worked with early mechanical computers, shore battery guns, search lights, ammunition and so on. But as the course progressed, we started doing base defense employment problems on islands stuck way out in the Pacific. Guam and Wake were some of the bigger ones.

What probably saved me was that my friend and mentor Chesty Puller was now an instructor at this same Quantico school. I might well have shared the fate of many of my fellow classmates in base defense on remote islands had it not been for another "chance meeting" with Puller. Chesty urged me to request duty with the newly-formed 1st Marine Division because "this will assure positive offensive action against the enemy!"

Puller said to me: "Well, I'll tell you, Old Man (He always called me "Old Man" throughout our two long careers), there is a billet down in the 1st Division at Guantanamo Bay

(Cuba) where they need an antiaircraft officer. I think you would enjoy that." So I went in to see Colonel Deese, the officer-in-charge (with a long handlebar mustache), and told him forthrightly that I understood that there was a billet in the division in Cuba and that's where I wanted to go. He said, "Davis, you're the first one to ask for that, so you've got it!" And that's how I got out of the Base Defense business and into the 1st Marine Division! (Who said "God helps those who help themselves!"?).

Thus, again, it was another of those chance conversations that I had with Chesty which caused his later statement that "I had a great influence on young Ray Davis' career!"

Let me note here that my Base Defense course was not lost. As we were later packing to move out to the Pacific (secret orders to Guadalcanal), we were loaded up with new weapons: 40mm automatic Bofers and twin 20mm Orliken guns from Sweden. The Bofers came with a mechanical computer director; it worked with differential cones and disks instead of the computer in modern versions. Base Defense course had acquainted me with this equipment and gave me a leg up for the start of training crews until we got a few school-trained non-commissioned officers.

Later in Australia, (after Guadalcanal) we received gigantic search radars. Five corporals and privates first class came with them to fill the billets of senior noncommissioned officers. In those days we could promote to fill "Table of Organization" requirements so that when this crew got the radar set up, tested and working, these bright, young Marines became senior specialist non-commissioned officers. Their performance was such that I never regretted the decision to promote them. In the same vein, some of our finest officers had been young corporals and sergeants who won battlefield commissions.

As an add-on to these chance meetings that I had with Chesty over the years, permit me to offer my views on what I like to term "innovation." (I used to call it "rule-bending," but some of my tales got adverse interpretation when people thought of it as "inside traders" and "check kiters" so I have changed it to "innovation" in quotes.) This fits what I am trying to say—no rule bending for selfish purposes, but there are times when you have to fight off the system in order to make progress for those in your charge and for the good of the Corps.

So here is an example of "innovation": It was years before I got rid of the Base Defense tag. At that time our personnel records were on a heavy card with job specialty coded holes punched along the rim. After the Guadalcanal fight, I was commanding the First Special Weapons Battalion (antiaircraft and antitank artillery) when it was being disbanded. I then moved to command an infantry battalion (First Battalion, lst Marines with Chesty), where in the adjutant's office the holes in my card, which were coded for Base Defense, somehow got pasted over, and new "Infantry" holes happened to appear on the card. This helped to insure that I was never again directly involved with Base Defense.

Because of my combination of good luck and good guidance by Puller, I began a long and totally rewarding association with one of the greatest, toughest and most famous units in the History of the United States, perhaps even in the world--the 1st Marine Division.

CHAPTER 7. FIRST MARINE DIVISION

I received orders from Quantico to report to the 1st Antiaircraft Machine Gun Battery, 1st Marine Division, Guantanamo Bay, Cuba, in the summer of 1941 and I sailed with a Replacement Battalion (about 600 Marines). There was measles on board our ship, so we went into quarantine in an outlying regimental camp at Guantanamo. Since the regiment was out on maneuvers, for three weeks, all we could do to keep busy was dig deep holes for latrines. First Lieutenant "Frenchy" Lirette was the only other officer in this group, and as senior, he was in command. I found myself with this big group of non-commissioned officers and Marines in a camp with absolutely nothing to do. To keep busy, camped out on one of those coral fingers formed from dredging around Guantanamo Bay, we organized large parties of latrine-diggers. We did this because somebody had suggested that, when the regiment comes back, they'll really appreciate these latrines. This duty lasted for two full weeks.

In the process, the troops improved their tent life by "borrowing" empty boxes, shelves, etc., from a nearby camp. When Lieutenant Colonel "Bull" Frisbie returned to that camp with his battalion and discovered the "borrowing," he lined up the officers and senior non-commissioned officers in our group and ordered: "In one hour every one of our missing boxes, shelves, etc., will be returned to my troops!"

Well, we had no way of knowing what was missing, or what belonged to whom, so "Frenchy" released the non-commissioned officers to take care of the problem. The next thing I knew the men were going in all directions including the area of another battalion belonging to Lieutenant Colonel Leroy Sims. They got everything in sight, put it in Frisbie's camp and off we went. We heard no more about it because almost immediately we were ordered back aboard ship to come to Quantico, Virginia.

"Brute" Krulak was the Commanding Officer in the 1st Anti-Aircraft Battery in Cuba. It was a great lesson to watch the Brute in action with the Division staff where it was obvious that he was already a "power," even as a Captain. Brute was clearly very bright and had a great influence on me over the years, since I had many opportunities to watch him operate and observe his methods. His was another great contribution to my well-being as a Marine officer.

Captain Krulak was the CO, First AA Battery, which was equipped with .50 caliber machine guns and had just been organized. I was initially a platoon leader and then became executive officer just before we loaded out for the States on one of the old "rust bucket"

43

transports. Searching the ship I found a tiny stateroom with a porthole over the top bunk. As soon as I got my unit settled, I then crawled into my bunk right under the cool breeze from the porthole. Shortly, I was awakened by the noisy entry of two old timers—"Bull 2nd Lieutenant" (at least in their minds)—Charlie Brush and Rocky Rockmore. They growled at the top of their voices about me having the best bunk: "A new guy just arrived needed to be taught a lesson!" I played "possum" for a spell, amused at the two. Then I awoke slowly to raise up and say something like: "Welcome! You two can move into my room if you like!" Then I added something like "As Senior Officer, I'll see if we can get some cleaning up done in here." I knew something that they didn't know: I was just two months their senior. We quickly became fast friends and saw a lot of war together.

At Quantico with a battery filled with young Reserve officers just out of college and the Reserve Officers Course, we found Washington to be an attractive liberty town. "Big Red" Scott, of Pitt basketball fame, was driving a robin egg blue Chrysler convertible, which became our headquarters in D.C. It was a great attraction for college girls and kept our off duty times fully occupied. One night near disaster struck, because Red forgot to buy gas. We ran out on Constitution Avenue, pushed the car to the side and all went to sleep right there in downtown Washington. Red convinced us that all would be well because he knew of a gas station that would open at 7:00 A.M. But setting no watch, we all overslept.

Finally, we got back to Quantico where one of our number, Gene Hudgins, had to catch a flight to Norfolk with an inspection team. We hurried by our tent quarters, helped Gene into his uniform and sped to the Quantico Airfield. As Gene was about to board, already tardy, we discovered that he had no belt nor did he have 2nd lieutenant bars on his shirt collar.

In desperation I gave him my belt and bars and off he went. We then rushed by the battery to tell our CO, Donn Hart, of our difficulties and let him know that we would soon be on duty. Unfortunately we arrived in time to discover a surprise inspection was under-way by Lieutenant Colonel Collier, Executive Officer of Special Troops. We were caught.

I managed to get in my place before he got there, but the emblem on my pith (jungle) helmet was on crooked. In the process of chewing me out over my emblem, he failed to notice my missing belt and gold bars. As you might guess, Capt. Hart curtailed our liberty habits in a major way.

The new Marine base at Camp Lejeune, North Carolina had just been opened and our

44

Antiaircraft Battery was transported there before the year was out. It was expanded to a battalion with three batteries: Antiaircraft, AT (Anti-Tank) with 37mm (millimeters) and AT 75mm (half-tracks). I was Antiaircraft Battery Commander and since we were mounting out for Guadalcanal, we received all new guns: 20mm Antiaircraft, 40mm Antiaircraft, and .50 cal. Also Antiaircraft Mechanical Directors came with the 40mm. School and drill were held day and night on all the new weapons.

It was at Camp Lejeune that we responded to our first war mission. Reports of a hostile German airship over the Atlantic led to an organized AA defense around our camps. Our guns were deployed and dug in, and I performed my only engineering project in the Corps using my engineering degree from Georgia Tech: Because so much of the Camp Lejeune area was impassable swampland, I supervised the building of a low bridge so that we could move our guns wherever they were needed.

When we moved from Quantico to Camp Lejeune, Major Bob Luckey took over as we were organized into a full battalion of antitank and antiaircraft batteries called the Special Weapons Battalion. Bob Luckey was the finest gentleman I've ever been involved with. He was brilliant and competent with a great sense of humor. We were at Camp Lejeune through that winter, moving out on maneuvers frequently. During the cold winter we joined up with some Army antiaircraft units around the Solomon Island area near Norfolk where I served as an umpire. Because of this we were able to live in some warm Army barracks. They were old, but they were warm, with good chow and facilities. Writing our observer and umpire reports was about all we had to do. It was a very dull time due to little air activity. Colonel Moriarty, our head umpire, was known as one of the Old Corps tough characters but he left us pretty much on our own..

Being away from New River had one extra advantage in that it kept us out of the constant state of flux going on in Division at this time, with the formation of many new organizations with cadres from existing units. General Torrey departed, and General Vandegrift took over the Division. This didn't affect me directly, because I was an antiaircraft specialist who after three and one-half years, was just making First Lieutenant in August, 1941.

We started moving out for the Pacific the following June, but we had no idea that our destination was Guadalcanal. We were being equipped with new types of antiaircraft guns because of concern about Japanese air power. It was decided at the last minute that we would keep all of our .50 caliber heavy machine guns and take along a bunch of 20mm plus

40mm automatic guns received in crates from the factories in Sweden. Consequently we went in equipped with three complete sets of weapons for the antiaircraft. The anti-tank half-tracks were also just arriving. In the process of getting reequipped, while we were moving out, we were told to pack up everything. The word was passed that "Where you are going, you'll need every stick of lumber you can take," so we made boxes out of old scrap lumber, and filled empty boxes with more old scrap lumber, and shipped it all out.

As the Division Antiaircraft Officer, I dealt with the Operations Section of 1st Marine Division and contributed to various plans and schemes to administer AA training in the various training schedules. I ran a Division AA School, where we had airplanes pull target sleeves across Onslow Beach for all the truck drivers and others with machine guns to fire for practice. They all took a shot at the sleeves at least once so that when we went to war, they had some experience under their belts.

In our battery street in tent camp we had some undue commotion late one night. One of our Marines coming off liberty smuggled his girl friend into camp and into his tent at the far end of the street. She had so much fun in his tent that she moved to the next, and then the next. When the First Sergeant responded to all the excitement, she was halfway down the street and a line had formed outside the tent. She was escorted off the base. The First Sergeant told me that she had a pocketbook full of dollar bills, but when he accused her of prostitution, she objected, saying she only received a few "tips!"

This incident was one of many which alerted me to some of the real problems with so-called camp followers. Lejeune was at that time in a very isolated part of North Carolina, but girls came there from everywhere. They lived in attics, shanties, back rooms of roadside bars and restaurants and in nearby motels. When liberty call went at camp, they seemed to appear from everywhere.

This raised a serious question concerning the design of tent camps with the officers and non-commissioned officers separated from the troops. In future administrative training camps, we housed officers and non-commissioned officers adjacent to the troop tents, maintaining something akin to unit integrity. In hostile situations, the problem does not exist since we camped or deployed as small units.

When Pearl Harbor was attacked, I was at Camp Lejeune. Everybody was up all night listening to the news and thinking about getting ready to go. Working with the Division staff, I got to know Colonels Gerald Thomas and Merrill Twining. Colonel Leroy Hunt had

Captain Ray Davis, 1942

Willa Knox Heafner, 1942

one of the regiments, and Colonel John Selden was Chief of Staff. Captains Bill Buse, Sammy Griffith, and Wally Greene were there. Wally was the Chemical Officer. Sam was Executive Officer for Red Mike Edson in 2nd Battalion, 5th Marine Regiment. Bill Buse commanded the Scout Company with the motorcycles. They grouped Special Weapons, the Scout Company and the Engineers into a Special Troops unit with Colonel Hawthorne as commander.

Overall, it was quite a crew and among the best was a man who was to have a great influence on my life as a Marine, Jim Masters, commander of one of the battalions in the First Marines. I didn't know him then, but Jim is another one of those I really came to appreciate and admire. He had a great capacity for taking a big problem or a division or whatever and just getting his arms around it and moving it into the direction he wanted it to go. Many, many great lessons were learned just from "sitting at his knee" from time to time.

In the middle of all of the activity, Miss Knox Heafner appeared on the scene. Because of our war preparation, there was a fast, wild courtship. I've joked many times that the real reason we got married quickly was that she was teaching school 80 miles away, and it just got to the point where I could no longer survive and drive those 80 miles at two in the morning and make a five o'clock reveille.

So we eloped. After that, instead of driving 80 miles, she would meet me halfway between her school in Washington, North Carolina, and my camp in Camp Lejeune, North Carolina—at a place called New Bern. It was strange about Knox being a school teacher and going with this Marine down at Camp Lejeune—she was kind of caught in the middle. She feared that this torrid courtship would somehow affect her teaching; her friends and other teachers and her principal were concerned about her time "out of town," and her possession of my car.

We met at a small hotel in New Bern, sometimes on very short notice. Knox had my car and I rode with some of the married officers who lived in New Bern. On one of our first rendezvous we ran into a problem. I arranged our room for the night, met Knox and took her to dinner. After we returned to the hotel, a loud knock was heard. Someone was at the door. By now we were already in bed. Slipping into my shorts, I went to the door.

It was the hotel manager incensed that I had a woman in my room. He insisted that she leave and would stay right there until she did. Standing in the hall in my shorts I finally convinced him that she was my wife and would be driving back to little Washington very

Our Wedding Portrait, 1942

soon. He relented from his insistence on seeing a marriage license after I told him that we would be back frequently and that I would have the papers on our next trip. Even such a lamentable episode did not dampen the warmth of our rendezvous—we were still in honeymoon mode.

Whereas previously Knox had been involved in many civic projects, her romance now took all of her time—not good for her image as a school teacher. In the main she concealed the whole thing until school was out, then she announced that she was married and wouldn't be back the next year.

Things moved swiftly for Knox and me from then on. After spending three and one-half years as a second lieutenant, I spent only six months as a first lieutenant, and was promoted to Captain in February, 1942; married Knox, and took her on a honeymoon trip to Georgia. Soon afterward my unit, along with its new weapons and all its men were moved across the country by troop train. Mrs. Raymond G. Davis stayed on the East Coast to await our first baby. World War II was on in earnest.

I was heading out into the Pacific again, this time to an island known as Guadalcanal, The 'Canal,' where both the 1st Marine Division and I (hopefully) would go on to greater glory for the unit, for me, and for the Corps.

CHAPTER 8. GUADALCANAL

After a year of The Basic School, a year-plus of sea duty, and a year with the 1st Marine Division in Cuba, Quantico, and Camp Lejeune, I was finally going off to combat. I would get to see whether the doctrine, tactics, techniques and equipment taught in the Marine Corps Schools, by the U. S. Navy at sea, and by the Fleet Marine Force (FMF) in Cuba and Stateside were actually going to work. (Marine combat units are all assigned to the Fleet Marine Force.)

On December 7, 1941, Japan launched its Pacific offensive by attacking the U.S. Fleet at Pearl Harbor. Rapid advances against British, Dutch and U.S. possessions brought Japanese forces to a position which threatened Australia. They were building an airfield in the Solomon Islands on Guadalcanal from which they could attack shipping lanes into New Zealand. It was to become our task to block the Japanese effort.

We were aboard a converted passenger liner, the ERICSSON, for one month. We embarked at San Francisco five days before she sailed and arrived in Wellington, New Zealand on 11 July 1942. Then we remained aboard for six more days before we debarked. This ship was not prepared for the load of troops and supplies that were put on her for this long stay.

We had trouble with the food; some of it was bad. People were vomiting all over the ship and there were inadequate head (toilet) facilities. It was a mess throughout a very long voyage. There were even rumors that Marines were ready to throw the crew overboard. I do remember that there were threats against crew members who were apparently gouging the troops. The reason that we stayed aboard an extra six days before debarking was that we had to offload onto combat ships. We had left the States with all our gear in an administrative rather than a combat load, which is how civilian ships normally do it, because less stowage space is wasted. I got detailed as the Transport Quartermaster for our battalion to combat load ships, so when we got to our eventual destination, Guadalcanal, we could have the supplies and equipment in the proper order for combat unloading, as needed to fight the war.

Colonel Pate was Division Transport Quartermaster in charge of loading, and I remember that it rained constantly and all the cardboard packing boxes and all paper items on the dock got wet, melted down and trampled over--remember that the ships had to be unloaded and then reloaded. It was a rough task to get my unit spread throughout many ships, with the supplies and equipment they would need in combat, but it got done. Finally we set sail to Guadalcanal! There were many lessons learned for loading out on future operations.

As a battery commander sailing for combat with the 1st Marine Division, I was launching the building of what I hoped would be a distinguished record during operations in the Pacific. At the same time, some of my less fortunate Quantico classmates sat out the war either as prisoners of the Japanese or in the drudgery of defending various pieces of real estate on small Pacific isles.

I landed on Guadalcanal D-Day, 7 August 1942, an hour and a half after the first wave of assault troops. Essentially, it became an "administrative landing" in that the Japanese did not defend at the beaches, but chose to fight the attacking troops inland. However, as we loaded into boats and were heading for shore, a formation of Japanese torpedo bombers attacked us. This was the first engagement for these American ships, and shot and shell were flying--it seemed like everybody was shooting at everything and everybody. The sky was full--just full of bullets. I felt very uneasy out there with the Japanese aircraft strafing and bombing, and our own ships firing machine guns and AA guns--every ship seemed to be firing. Indeed, I was happy to get ashore.

By nightfall, the 1st Marine Division had captured the Japanese airstrip there, which became Henderson Field. It was to become the target of Japanese land, sea and air forces for the remainder of the campaign.

My primary mission was antiaircraft defense of Henderson Field. We farmed out some units, primarily antitank. There was a special weapons group in the regimental headquarters of each infantry regiment. Some of our headquarters Marines joined those, but our primary mission was around the airfield, where we deployed all the surplus weapons that we had been issued. My command post was alongside the upper end of the airstrip, in a coconut grove.

I had a challenging experience in that my command post was sited just 100 feet off the edge of the airstrip, which was being expanded closer and closer to me. Remember that this strip was the main target of the Japanese for the next six months. Enemy troops were trying to capture that airstrip by attacking overland, and this didn't directly involve me. They also sent airplanes over every day, and sailed warships down to shell us. As I recall, we were the first American troops in history to ever be heavily shelled by enemy battleships. During the month of October, there were 31 consecutive days during which we were bombed from overhead with the "Betty" bombers every day at noon. Also, we were shelled at night, every night, from the battleships, cruisers and destroyers offshore. It was a very busy time.

In the hurry to get the airfield in operation, one of the first things that I recall is that ordnance hauled in several airplane and ship loads of bombs and scattered them in the high grass around Henderson Field. No attempt was made to build bunkers for the ammo, just hurry the bombs in. The kunai grass grows very tall and it was a serious fire hazard. The first few times the Betty bombers flew over, they set fire to the grass after the bombs had fallen and being the local commander, I would rush my troops out in order to extinguish the fires. On one occasion I lost a boot while running towards the fire. Minutes later I found myself standing with one shoe on and one bare foot, on top of a 500-pound bomb, beating out fire around it to keep the fire off the bomb. Those were the kinds of exciting times we had in the early days of Guadalcanal.

My Marines, when enemy fire was incoming, were in small holes--no more than two men per foxhole. Some incoming did hit my installations, but there were relatively few casualties. My hole was a deep slit, covered with crisscross coconut logs to stop the instant fuze bombs. We could see the enemy bomb bays open and hear the clicks of the bomb release before we jumped into the holes. At night, we absorbed fire from ships of the Japanese Navy. They were out of range of my guns, but we watched carefully to see the ships' gun flashes because they would signal the time to go for the holes. Late one night after the first flash, I dived into my hole to come face-to-face with a large screaming bat. I told him, as I recovered from the terror and shock: "Buddy--yell all you want--I'm staying!" After the shelling was over, we got him out with some long sticks.

How did all of this look from the Marine aviator's point of view? Major John L. Smith, a fighter squadron commander and subsequently a Medal of Honor recipient, told me one day of the way his squadron operated. Every day at noon the Japanese would come over and drop bombs. The scheme of the fighter squadron was to climb to maximum altitude just before noon to wait for the "Betty" bombers, and as the bombers came by, the Marine fighters would dive through the formation. Because the Marines were few in number, they always targeted the bomber on the left wing of the formation. Every day, day after day after day, they would shoot down the guy on the left wing of the bomber formation--which would eventually cause a shortage of volunteers to fly out there, it would appear. The result was, Smith told me, it began to break up the formation. The guy on the left wing would get so nervous coming in that he'd fly erratically and maybe peel off to hide among the other bombers, causing the whole formation to be rattled.

Another thing was that as this bombardment continued, of course, we kept digging our holes deeper and deeper in the ground. When the fiasco in Beirut happened years later and we lost 250 Marines in a hotel atmosphere within a hostile environment, I remembered that after weeks of heavy bombardment on Guadalcanal, we had few losses. We had a rule that there would be two men in a foxhole. In a deep, narrow foxhole there would be two guys, so a direct hit would never get more than two Marines. This tactic really paid off.

Another lesson learned by the entire 1st Marine Division: during those first nights ashore, troops will shoot at shadows, noises or ghosts all night long. A sergeant of mine, sitting in my command post, raised up to shoot an approaching enemy in the darkness. I managed to knock his Tommy gun up just in the nick of time as I recognized our Battalion Commander, Bob Luckey (Luckey was lucky!).

When I'm asked if my guns ever shot down any Japanese aircraft, my answer is that we claimed some. The Zeros would come around every now and then and swoop down over the strip to see what was going on. Two or three were shot down, and of course, my guys claimed them. One thing is for sure. My guys enthusiastically shot any Japanese who might have been in range.

As for the attacks by Japanese infantry on Edson's Ridge, which overlooked Henderson Field, let me say that we weren't near the Ridge; we were right against the runway, on the upper end from the Lunga River. We caught the bombing and the shelling. As I said before, every day at noon those Betty bombers would come over and we got so salty that we would wait until the bomb bays opened at a certain point in the sky before we got into our holes. Colonel Cliff Cates (World War I hero who in one fight went from rifle platoon commander to rifle company commander and then infantry battalion commander, all as a second lieutenant!) located his infantry regimental headquarters nearby, just across the runway. He had a little scheme going. If people didn't get low enough in their holes during an air raid, he'd shoot towards them with his pistol. A few rounds came over my way, and as soon as that stick of bombs went by and the dust was still up, I went tearing across that runway to straighten out whoever the hell it was shooting at me with his pistol. I ran headlong into Clifton Bledsoe Cates for the first time! He told me exactly what was going on. In short, if I'd been in my hole, there would've been no chance of my getting shot. I said "Aye, aye, sir!" to the future Commandant of the Marine Corps, and moved out smartly.

Another vignette about shooting at friendlies as well as enemy with small arms--this was later termed "Intramural Firefighting" in Vietnam--shortly after coming ashore: One night the Password was something or other, and the Response (from the incoming man) was "Hallelujah!" To be sure that he is heard by the defending Marine, the man returning to the lines shouted loud and clear so as not to be fired on. The result of that, of course, was that the entire night was filled with endless shooting and shouts of Hallelujah; it sounded like a Holy Roller meeting on the 4th of July! The wild random firing at night got so intense that I parked three trucks to shine their headlights on my command post to let folks know that we were friendlies!

As a follow-up to this, one of my drivers killed three cows which he claimed was a squad of Japs moving towards his night position. After struggling to bury them--this was his punishment--he decided to burn them. Result? A major grass fire threatened a key ammo dump.

The Division Commander, Major General A. A. Vandegrift (the next Commandant), soon stopped the night firing by requiring that weapons be unloaded and bayonets fixed at night fall. This became a pattern in the subsequent landings in which I participated.

There were many problems other than that of live firing. For example, I was sent for by the Division G-4 (the Supply/Logistics Officer), a colonel named Stan Fellers. He was upset and accused my outfit of "stealing" jeeps. I wasn't aware of this, so I went back to investigate. It seems that my troops had become so hardened to the bombers' air raids that after awhile when others abandoned jeeps in the area in response to early warning and got into holes, my men would get the abandoned jeeps and haul them off to nearby woods, where they would paint out the numbers and unit symbols. Not surprisingly we did have extra jeeps, but I noted that they were always Army jeeps; Marines would not "steal" from brother Marines. The variations in paint made it easy to spot the four extras and send them back to the Army.

Then there were problems with chow and health: After the Japs drove our Navy off, we had few rations and Japanese rice with raisins (to camouflage the bugs!) became the staple diet at times. Finally some brave California fishing boats brought some supplies in to us. As a Division, our health deteriorated mostly from malaria and dysentery--our medical supply ship had been lost. Later, we found the Japanese quinine supplies which helped to keep malaria under control. Hundreds of enemy corpses multiplied the fly population, even though we soon learned to bury them quickly.

A final note from the campaign at Guadalcanal: I saw Chesty Puller several times, but we had enough problems to solve and we didn't get much talking done. However, let me point out that

Chesty, at Guadalcanal, was the commander of the 1st Battalion, Seventh Marine Regiment, the same unit that I would later command in the Inchon-Seoul and Chosin Reservoir Campaigns in Korea.

Good fortune found me fishing with a great Marine, Walter McIlhenny, who became known world-wide for his Tabasco Sauce and known to every Marine as a principal founder of the Marine Military Academy. Those of us who were fortunate enough to be Walter's guests enjoyed New Orleans Mardi Gras at its best.

When Guadalcanal was over for my men and me, we next moved to Australia to resupply and recover. While there in May, 1943, I would become Commanding Officer of the 1st Special Weapons Battalion, and prepare for further operations against the Japanese in New Guinea and Cape Gloucester.

New Guinea, 1953

Rear left to right: Jack Leonard, Dr. Cleve Hunly, Charles Koller,
Front Ray Davis

CHAPTER 9. CAPE GLOUCESTER/NEW GUINEA

Early in 1943, the First Marine Division moved to Australia to prepare for its next fight. The First Special Weapons Battalion, when Bob Luckey moved over to the artillery, came under the command of Dick Wallace. In May, I became its Commander, until old friend Joe Hankins, "an old rifle team type," took command. Although he later was to move to the First Marine (infantry) Regiment, Joe remained with us throughout the Australia phase.

It became obvious that the biggest problem for the entire force of Marines was malaria. I think everybody had it. I had both types, plus a hepatitis jaundice attack so severe that I still can't to this day give to blood banks. Fortunately, I had a friendly surgeon who kept me out of the hospital and on my feet, working out of my quarters. It all started when our medical ship was sunk in the initial invasion of Guadalcanal, so the only suppressant we had for malaria was captured Japanese quinine pills. We were overrun with malaria. With inadequate protection and an unbelievable mosquito population, the situation simply got out of hand..

In addition, we had dysentery following our first major ground battle with Japanese forces. We had killed over 700 of them in one small area and it took several days to get them buried. This delay brought a deluge of flies which was overwhelming--really awful.

Initially in Australia, it was estimated that it would take us eight weeks to get up to strength, reequipping and retrained to go back into combat. Consequently, most of the replacements from the States were diverted to the other divisions, expecting that we would soon mend ourselves and be ready.

Unfortunately the malaria reoccurrence was such that the troops would be in the hospital for two or three weeks to recover from an attack. They would get out of the hospital, spend time in the pubs and on the town in Melbourne, and in two weeks' time be back in the hospital. The "rotation" was about 5,000 troops; that is, 5,000 in the hospital and another 5,000 out. In two weeks time another 5,000 out would go back in and replace that 5,000. Result was that at the end we were there for eight months instead of eight weeks recovering from both malaria and dysentery.

I liked Australia, but the schedule was uncertain. We arrived there with an idea of retraining and reequipping, then getting back into the war. My battalion was pitched in tents in Ballarat, in a city park with 11th Marines (artillery) and 1st Tank Battalion. No one was prepared for the long, long stay that we had. Also, the training area was very limited. There was thin forest in the area where training could be done, but 1st Marine Division needed to prepare for combat in heavy jungle in anticipation of its next fight.

We really had no opportunity to get ourselves fully equipped with new weapons. Up until then we did not have the big radars that were supposed to go with the automatic antiaircraft guns (Bofors 40mm). The radars were so big that they had not been sent to Guadalcanal but were finally shipped to us in Australia. We had a serious problem of training since we had no trained personnel to serve as instructors. We did receive a few Marines just out of school who knew how to work the things, but it took an all out effort at technical and other kinds of training to get these complex weapons in hand. We wrote many Standing Operating Procedures which weren't very satisfactory as far as Army General Krueger was concerned. Lieutenant General Krueger was General MacArthur's commander of the southern axis--Admiral Halsey had the northern. General Krueger's area included the major Japanese base at Rabaul which was to be isolated, thereby enabling MacArthur to proceed by a series of envelopments up the coast of New Guinea and into the Philippines. General Krueger had come down from his Sixth Army command to conduct a readiness inspection prior to our deployment in support of his operations in Cape Gloucester.

He found us ready but did ask for better Standing Operating Procedures based on Sixth Army models. After he left, we got the troops busy on further training out in the bush. Although I don't recall having a formal rifle range, they did have a place to fire small weapons. By the time 1st Marine Division left Australia in September '43, my men were in good physical condition and well trained. We were mounted out in converted Liberty ships, which was another time that we used commercial loading, where all the space around the vehicles, and inside them, was filled; then this was leveled off, and another layer, with more vehicles and gear on top of that, up to the top of the ship. There was no interior deck space, so the vehicles were buried in the supplies. I was in charge (due to my transport quartermaster experience from New Zealand and the West Coast) of loading one of those ships, which kept me on the dock 24 hours a day for a few days.

We stopped off on Goodenough Island to reload and then on to Milne Bay, New Guinea, where we finally mounted out for Cape Gloucester. D-Day was 26 December 43. As ships were being loaded, I ran into Chesty Puller! Chesty was in charge of mounting out the Marine elements from this particular harbor. The Japanese were actually in New Britain and New Guinea, and the Australians were busy trying to keep them out of Australia!

Before I tell you about this meeting with Chesty, here's a little background: My motivation for infantry was a prolonged ongoing process. My Antiaircraft (AA) and Anti-tank (AT) units served with the infantry--I worked with the infantry through them. Then when Joe Hankins came to Special Weapons to replace Dick Wallace, Joe had a high motivation toward infantry. He moved over to the 1st Marines, then Puller became its commander. Now that I was a Battalion Commander of Special Weapons, I became more and more aware that my units were farmed out in support roles. The cohesive command enjoyed in infantry appealed to me.

After administrative loading, we sailed out from Melbourne playing around-the-clock bridge games for two weeks enroute to Goodenough Island where we offloaded and went into training camps.

Immediately after arriving we had a tremendous vehicle theft problem. Units had vehicles disappearing in staggering numbers, although, it appeared that most were taken by joy riders who would abandon them somewhere else on the island. Since my units were vehicle heavy with the many towed weapons, our problem was severe. I spent some time in innovative thinking.

I broke out all hands with shovels and entrenching tools, designed a ditch barrier, and went to work. A continuous ditch three feet deep and three feet wide soon encircled our compound, with a single controlled exit. Over the next few nights we found a few vehicles stuck in our ditch, but the problem quickly went away.

While walking the beach from which the combat-bound Marines were embarking, I spotted Lieutenant Colonel Puller, who had moved up from being the Commander of 1st Battalion, 7th Marines to serve as Regimental Executive Officer. I complained to that pugnacious officer that all of my units had been doled out and I was being left behind. Puller replied in his characteristic fashion: "It's a hell of a note when a man wants to go to war and no one will let him. Get in that ship over there!" I wasted no time asking silly questions about written orders or baggage. I complied with his oral directive and wound up commanding an infantry battalion in the Cape Gloucester operation.

Let me clarify this: I got up to New Britain and set up a command post. Of course, my headquarters went with me, my supply group and everybody, and we found a little place near a swamp from which I could keep contact with my troops. In about five or six weeks after we were there, things started to slow down.

I know that all pictures and movies taken of Gloucester show jungle right down to the waterline, but there were grassy knolls around. We had to hack out a few little places along the landing beach where there was a critical need for AA defense, but I don't think we had more than half a dozen planes come over during the operation. As soon as we moved inland, it was easy shooting from these grassy knolls, particularly from up around the airfield. I didn't have a lot to do in terms of fighting. My task was in supporting my units--which would have been very difficult from way back in Oro Bay--keeping them supplied and equipped and then inspecting them for administrative matters.

Meanwhile, Puller had moved from being Executive Officer, 7th Marines (a position I filled years later after commanding 1st Battalion, 7th Marines at Korea's Chosin Reservoir) to being Commander, 1st Marines. One of his infantry battalion commanders was Joe Hankins. I happened to bump into Joe one day and asked him how things were going. He said, "Well, fine, but, you know, the 1st battalion commander is going to become the regimental executive officer, and I don't see anybody in sight to take over that battalion. Why don't you do it?" So I "hotfooted" over to Puller and told him that I had been in this special weapons business long enough, and I'd like to get in the infantry. Puller hired me on the spot to be his first battalion commander. Thus, again Chesty was really a key in my career development through the years, without any design. He was my Basic School tactics instructor, company commander, mentor on sea duty, school director at Quantico and now he was my first regimental commander. Later on, in Korea, he was Assistant Division Commander when I was Executive Officer, 7th Marines. And when Puller was out of the Corps after his retirement, somewhat embittered because of a forced medical retirement, I got him into the swing of the Marine Corps again before he died. I enjoyed a long, good association with the "Marines' Marine" as he is known.

Thus, on 24 April 1944 I took off with the 1st Marine Regiment for Pavuvu, where I would reequip and train my infantry battalion, First Regiment's 1st Battalion, for one of the bloodiest battles in Marine Corps history: PELELIU!

CHAPTER 10. PELELIU

THE SECRETARY OF THE NAVY WASHINGTON

The President of the United States takes pleasure in presenting the NAVY CROSS to MAJOR RAYMOND G. DAVIS, UNITED STATES MARINE CORPS for service as set forth in the following

CITATION-:

"For extraordinary heroism as Commanding Officer of the First Battalion, First Marines, First Marine Division, in action against enemy Japanese forces on Peleliu, Palau Islands, from 15 to 22 September 1944. Although wounded during the first hour of landing, Major Davis refused evacuation to remain with his Battalion' s assault elements in many hazardous missions. On one occasion, when large gaps occurred in our front lines as the result of heavy casualties, and his right flank company was disorganized by point-blank enemy cannon fire following a successful nine hundred yard penetration through heavily defended lines, he rallied and personally led combined troops into these gaps to establish contact and maintain hasty defensive positions for the remainder of the night. Despite many casualties from close-range sniper fire, he remained in the vicinity of the front lines, coordinating artillery and Naval gunfire support with such effect that several determined counterattacks were repulsed. His outstanding courage, devotion to duty and leadership were in keeping with the highest traditions of the United States Naval Service."

For the President,

/s/ John L. Sullivan
Secretary of the Navy

At Peleliu, I REALLY joined the infantry! The citation for the Navy Cross, our Nation's second highest award for valor in combat, was recommended by none other than Colonel Chesty Puller, himself no stranger to this Navy blue and white ribboned medal, with a record five of them!

Perhaps the best introduction to Peleliu is contained in the foreword to Major Frank Hough's "The Assault on Peleliu," the official monograph for the Historical Division of Headquarters, U. S. Marine Corps, written in 1950. It was introduced by the Commandant of the Marine Corps, General Clifton B. Cates, who had commanded an infantry regiment in the Solomons (Guadalcanal), and an infantry division in the Marianas (Tinian), as well as a rifle platoon and company, and an infantry battalion, all in World War I in France, so he spoke with more than the usual authority:

THE ASSAULT ON PELELIU

Foreword

Many factors combined to make the assault on Peleliu one of the least understood operations of World War II. Yet it was as one of the most vicious and stubbornly contested, and nowhere was the fighting efficiency of the U. S. Marine more convincingly demonstrated. At Peleliu the enemy proved that he had profited from his bitter experiences of earlier operations. He applied intelligently the lessons we had taught him in the Solomons, Gilberts, Marshalls, and Marianas. At Peleliu the enemy made no suicidal Banzai charges to hasten the decision; he carefully concealed his plans and dispositions. He nursed from his inferior strength the last ounce of resistance and delay, to extract the maximum cost from his conquerors. In these respects Peleliu differed significantly from previous campaigns and set the pattern for things to come: Iwo Jima and Okinawa.

Because the operation protracted itself over a period of nearly two and a half months, it is easy to lose sight of the fact that the strategic objective was accomplished within the first week; neutralization of the entire Palaus group, and with this, securing of the Philippines approaches.

C. B. Cates,

General, U. S. Marine Corps,

Commandant of The Marine Corps.

Following the Commandant' s lead, Brigadier General Clayton Jerome, the Director of Marine Corps History, wrote the preface:

The assault on Peleliu is the seventh in a series of operational monographs, based on official sources and documented in detail, being prepared by the Historical Division, Headquarters, U S Marine Corps. The purpose of these monographs is to afford the military student as well as the casual readers a factually accurate study of the several Marine Corps operations in World War II. Upon completion of the series, it is planned to edit the individual piece into a complete operational history of Marine campaigns in the Pacific.

As initially conceived, seizure of Peleliu would constitute only one phase of a many-sided operation (designated STALEMATE) against the western Carolines, embracing at one time or another capture of all the Palaus group, Yap and Ulithi. Subsequent revisions of the original plan, however, raised Peleliu from a secondary target to the primary one, precipitating one of the most bitterly contested campaigns in the entire Pacific War, beside which the concurrent seizures of Angaur and Ulithi were largely incidental. Because Marine assault echelons were committed nowhere else operations on Peleliu are discussed in fine detail, whereas those elsewhere are merely summarized to round out the strategic picture as a whole.

In my experience and my studies I find many serious points about the invasion of Peleliu which need exploration. As examples, I will mention ten of the most persistent ones in brief outline.

1) Adm. Nimits overruled his subordinates (including Bull Halsey) who recommended cancellation of the operation.

2) Intelligence reports and photographs failed to uncover the rugged terrain which provided cover for Japanese defenders.

3) During planning and preparation there was no direct contact (radio or otherwise) between the lst Division and principal planners at CINPAC. Principal invasion commanders (Spruance, Kelly Turner, and Holland Smith) were away in the Marianas.

4) The Japanese completely revised their tactical plans. Lt. Gen. Sadae Inoue ordered his troops to fortify the island, no more suicide attacks; stay in their positions; kill enemy until they themselves die for the Emperor!

5) Shipping shortages caused, for example, 16 tanks to be left behind.

6) Inadequate training for infantry Marines on Pavuva -- space was limited (But every squad in my lst Battalion, lst Marine Regiment had the most realistic training in my experiences -- rifles, machine guns, mortars, rockets, flame throwers, satchel charges in live firing assaults against heavy fortifications. Visiting officers from state-side training centers could not believe that we put all this fire power in the hands of our young squad leaders in such a realistic manner.)

7) No rehearsal area was available to practice the reef crossing -- troops had to transfer from boats to amphibians.

8) Navy preparatory firing had little effect on the Japanese defenders. All hanger, buildings, etc. were flattened; foliage was cleared. But in my sector, for example, a short distance inland we came face to face with a gigantic block house -- walls of concrete several feet thick -- it had not been nicked at all, even though it was listed on the target list. We were stalled until battleship Mississippi attacked it with 14" shells. We also had to knock out pill boxes and bunkers nearby! (35 of my marines were killed or wounded in this assault)

9) Pressing infantry assaults against fortified areas after they were uncovered -- seige tactics employing heavy weapons would have reduced our casualties.

10) Delays in landing fresh reinforcements as Marine infantry units were depleted. Every problem had as a basis the near total failure of our intelligence collection efforts – an easy campaign was expected!

In my view these were the main problems wherein lessons are to be learned!

With the command and historical perspective behind us, friends have looked at the above Navy Cross citation for an immediate clue as to why I performed so well in my first infantry billet, as an infantry battalion commander, under the redoubtable (and almost omnipresent) Chesty Puller who wrote: "...Despite many casualties from close-range sniper fire, he remained in the vicinity of the front lines, coordinating artillery and Naval gunfire support with such effect that several determined counterattacks were repulsed. . . "

All those hours and days and weeks and months spent in learning and working with and firing supporting arms paid off immediately. I knew artillery and Naval gunfire capabilities and limitations from instruction in The Basic School, sea duty in USS PORTLAND, and the weapons course at Quantico. Following this there was duty in the Fleet Marine Force's 1st Marine Division under Brute Krulak, who also had similar sea duty experience after his Naval Academy and Basic School days.

I also was well-instructed and experienced in antiaircraft and antitank weapons in the same manner, plus my combat experience from Guadalcanal and Cape Gloucester. Thus, when I took over an infantry battalion and gave a mission to the artillery and Naval gunfire (and AA and AT) experts, I was already a combat experienced expert.

Then, on the infantry side of the ledger: "...when large gaps occurred in our front lines as the result of heavy casualties, and his right flank company was disorganized by point-blank enemy cannon fire following a successful nine hundred yard penetration through heavily defended lines, he rallied and personally led combined troops into these gaps to establish contact and maintain hasty defensive positions for the remainder of the night..." And where did I gain the background for moving out with the infantry in this manner? Again, in my Basic school days: Our instructor was Chesty Puller, one of the last of the Marines who had real experience in the guerrilla wars in Central America in the twenties and thirties. In our course called "Small Wars," he would come in, put his lesson plan on the lectern...then he would say, "They made me make up a lesson plan, but we are going to talk about the real things. We are going to talk about the fighting, the war." Then he would get into the details of the minute-by-minute, day-by day, week-by-week campaigning on the trail, the actual combat. I found that this was the best way to find out about the war business: to listen to the people who have experienced it. I listened well, then I applied what I had been taught!

I once made a key statement, after surviving three wars (World War II, Korea, Vietnam), that to me Peleliu was the most difficult assignment I have encountered. So, when asked specifically about this, I wrote that Peleliu was tough because we never found a way to get the enemy out of his defensive situation. The Japs were in deep caves, had small holes for fixed machine gun fire, etc. Consequently, we were being hit from all sides with no way to get at them.

Yet the 1st Marine Division was well prepared for this amphibious assault. I took the battalion over to Pavuvu, a muddy, palm-covered little island where we went on some hikes, had equipment inspections and so forth. We seemed to be in good shape because most of the key people had been through both Guadalcanal and Gloucester. We immediately started training for Peleliu in an area where we could assault four or five positions with total freedom of action. We employed mortars overhead with live ammo, plus rockets and flame throwers in assault teams. It was the best assault team training I ever witnessed and totally realistic. It was dangerous, but we were going into a very dangerous situation.

These were innovative tactics, because captured documents had given all of us an indication of the heavy fortifications we would face at Peleliu. The small unit commanders knew the lives of their men were at stake, and they really went at it with the training. We built Japanese-style bunkers, then assigned a squad of Marines, with satchel charges, flame throwers, rockets/bazookas the task of taking the bunker.

When a senior lieutenant colonel arrived from Quantico, he became Commanding Officer and I was Executive Officer. When I took him out to observe the training, he walked up on it and started yelling, "Stop it, stop it, somebody is going to get killed. You can't do that. Where is the safety flag, where is this...?" He had just come from teaching tactics in Quantico, with extensive safety rules, but he finally saw that this was the way it had to be out here. Unfortunately, he became a real hair on my chest from that day forward. Playing basketball with the battalion officers, he would trip them up, and do all kinds of dastardly things. He was a nut.

Then he got drunk one night with a friend of his and somehow got the idea that the friend had said "I understand your wife has syphilis." Well, my new commander jumped up, came over and got me, and we went back to our command post to get a pistol. He was going to kill this guy in the Tank Battalion Club! I told him to wait a minute, and I called the Tank Battalion Executive Officer, Don Robinson, told him this guy was drunk as a coot, and probably couldn't hit anyone, but he'd better get the intended target out of there. But by the time we got there, Robinson had rounded up a gang of people who wanted to see this shootout!

I got the magazine out of the pistol, but couldn't check to see if there was a round in the chamber, before he saw his "enemy." Well, "enemy" got the picture, even though he was drunk, too, and got away. My drunk commander poured a pitcher of ice water from the bar over his own head, and I was then able to get him back to his bunk. Just two days later, he took a small boat over to another island to check on our supplies--but he never came back, he just disappeared. Time went on and Puller sent for me, and asked "Where is the commander?" I said I had last seen him heading for the supply island. Turned out there was a Navy hospital over there, too, with lots of nurses, so our Commander had joined up with the Nurse Corps. Puller called me back in: "Wherever he is, he's no longer Commander of the lst Battalion, lst Marines; you are!"

Two days later, when he returns, Puller sends for him and really fixes him. Since he is a temporary lieutenant colonel for the war, but only a permanent first lieutenant, Puller reduces him to first lieutenant right on the spot! Later, aboard ship, Puller said to me: "On the way to the battle, I want you to have everybody on the ship who was associated with your ex-commander write down exactly what they recall about him." It was the worst conglomeration of tales that you could imagine. So he retired from the Corps as a first lieutenant.

We continued on to Peleliu. My battalion, lst Regiment's lst Battalion, landed in reserve, which was meaningless, because the Japanese defenses were so thick and so sturdy that when I got off the amphibian tractor on the beach, my run for cover was not quick enough, and I got a fragment from a mortar shell through my left knee. Machine gun bullets were flying from two directions.

It was on the second day ashore that I connected with Captain George Hunt. His company had become isolated and was under great pressure as he later described in *Life* magazine (he became a senior editor). My battalion moved into a large gap to ease pressure on Hunt's company.

It became the most hotly contested and brutal campaign of World War II in many respects. A figure I'm not proud of is the fact that my battalion had 71 percent casualties including me, and the whole regiment was almost as bad. The enemy had tunneled back under the coral ridge lines, sometimes 100 to 200 feet, and they would lay a machine gun to shoot out of a distant hole, with deadly crossfire from well dug-in and fight-to-the-death defensive positions. We were withdrawn within three weeks, because we had just been expended. My Charlie Company Commander, Capt. Everett Pope was to receive the Medal of Honor.

The deepest penetration the lst Marines made on the 19th was achieved by C Company, commanded by a 25-year-old Massachusetts native, Captain Everett Pope. At about noon, Pope was ordered to seize Hill 100, a steep, apparently isolated knob which dominated the East Road and the swampy low ground to the battalion's right front.

Already reduced by casualties to just 90 men, C Company was in as good a shape for this mission as any of the depleted rifle companies. The Marines approached Hill 100 - later known as Walt Ridge-through a swamp filtering forward past shell-torn tree trunks which jutted skyward like broken fingers. Reaching the road at the base of the height, they found and attacked two large pillboxes but were almost immediately pinned down by machine gun fire from the right. Firing from only 50 yards away, the Japanese machine gunner was situated on the other side of a pond where the Marines could not get to him. Unable to move forward and taking heavy casualties from the fire, Pope requested permission to pull back, pass to the left of the main swamp area and push up the road with tank support. The road here angled abruptly east, crossing the swamp over the narrow causeway. The single track crossing was located along the mouth of a wide draw, later known as "the Horseshoe." It then skirted the base of Pope's objective and angled northeast.

Pope extricated his men, but it was late afternoon before C Company was able to renew the push. The tank support did not live up to hopes. Trying to negotiate the causeway, the first tank slipped over the edge and stalled. A second tank ventured out to extricate the first and slipped over the other side, blocking the causeway to any more armored support.

Leaving the tanks behind, the Marines rushed across the causeway by squads, paused briefly at the foot of the hill, then started the steep scramble up, backed by mortars and machine guns. Here and there a blasted tree, stripped of its branches, jutted skyward, but there was little cover for the approach. Among the casualties were two Marines killed by U.S. tank fire as they tried to knock out an enemy machine gun.

Enemy fire from Hill 100 and surrounding heights took a heavy toll of the attacking Marines, but by sliding around to the right, some two dozen survivors made it to the summit. There, to their consternation, they found the maps were wrong. Hill 100 was not an isolated knob; it was merely the nose of a long ridge dominated by a higher knob only 50 yards to their front.

Pope did not need his Phi Beta Kappa key from Bowdoin College to understand he now had a major problem on his hands. Exposed to fire from the high ground to their front, as well as crossfire from a parallel ridge to the west, he was in a very precarious position.

As twilight fell, the Marines took what cover they could among the jumbled rocks. Their perimeter was very compressed-about the size of a tennis court by Pope's reckoning-perched on the edge of the cliffs. They had no real ground contact with the rear and only what ammunition they had been able to carry up in the initial assault. Noted the C Company war diary, "The line is flimsy as hell, and it is getting dark. We have no wires and need grenades badly."

At 1700, a machine-gun crew supporting C Company saw six men moving toward Japanese lines. Challenged, the strangers merely crouched down in the road. One of the machine gunners walked over to them, a belt of ammo in his hands. He was on top of the men before he realized they were Japanese. Slapping the lead Japanese in the face with the ammo belt, the Marine knocked him cold. The next Japanese fired at him but missed, his bullet striking an unlucky Marine lieutenant in the jaw and exiting through the back of the officer's head. The machine gunner shot the six Japanese, but the lieutenant was dead.

The Japanese went for Pope's men after dark, and they kept coming. At first, they tried to infiltrate the Marine perimeter; then they commenced a series of counterattacks, each made up of 20 to 25 men. How many there were and how often they came soon dissolved into a confused blur to the Marines. "The whole night was mixed up," recalled Pope.

Most of the thrusts came down the ridge. Pope had some radio contact with battalion and received some illumination. What he really needed was artillery support, but he was too closely engaged to call in fire from the big guns.

Back at a company command post, Private Russell Davis listened to the fighting over the radio. The front-line Marines were screaming for illumination or for corpsmen; men were crying and pleading for help, but there was nothing anybody could do to help them. In the CP, Davis's company commander listened to the whimpering calls from the hills, cursing monotonously and helplessly, his head down between his knees.

Up on the ridge, two Japanese suddenly materialized near the position defended by Lieutenant Francis Burke of Scranton, Pennsylvania, and Sergeant James P. McAlarnis of Kentucky. One of the Japanese ran a bayonet into Burke's leg. Burke tore into his attacker, beating him senseless with his fists. McAlarnis, meanwhile, went to work on the second Japanese with his riffle butt. They tossed the bodies over the precipice.

Pope's Marines managed to throw back the Japanese attacks, but as dawn streaked the sky, they were running perilously low on ammunition. "We used rocks," recalled Pope, "not so much to try to hit them with rocks... but you throw a rock and they wouldn't know if it was a grenade or not and they'd wait a minute to see if it was going to explode. Throw three rocks and then one of your remaining grenades and slow them down a bit."

As the fighting became hand-to-hand, the Marines pitched some of their attackers bodily over the steep cliffs. Spotting two enemy soldiers climbing the slope to his position, a sergeant heaved an empty grenade box at them, then opened up with his rifle. Private First Class Philip Collins of Gardiner, Massachusetts, picked up Japanese grenades before they exploded and tossed them back. "He did that until one exploded in his hand," reported Pope. "Then he picked up a rifle and used that until he was too weak to load the weapon."

Much of the enemy fire focused on the light machine gun, which was taken over by the assistant after the gunner was hit. The gun began jamming after a couple of hours of constant firing, and the gunner had to clear it by hand, exposing himself to enemy fire. "Every time he went up, they threw grenades," recalled a witness. The gun was finally blown off its tripod, but the gunner kept it in action until he was wounded and unable to continue.

By daylight, down to about a dozen men and out of ammunition, Pope received orders to withdraw. The order came just as the last Japanese assault began to sweep the survivors off the ridge anyway. There was little order. Those who could scrambled down the slope as fast as they could. There had been no question of sparing able-bodied men to evacuate the wounded during the night. Anyone who could not get out on his own was doomed.

Making their way through the light scrub at the base of the hill, the Marines dodged streams of enemy tracers whipping through the brush.' Pope's radioman was killed by his side as he talked on the phone. Japanese infantry could be seen against the skyline where the Marines had been only moments before. Another enemy group came around to the right, where a couple of them proceeded to set up a light machine gun, much to Pope discomfiture as he suddenly realized that they had singled him out personally for their attention. He kept moving-fast-until he and the other survivors found cover behind a stone wall near the causeway below.

Of the two dozen or so men Pope had brought up the hill, only nine made it down safely. Of these, many were wounded, including Pope himself. Sometime during the fighting, he had taken a spray of shrapnel in the legs and thighs-an injury he dismissed as "not consequential." The New Englander picked the metal fragments out with a pair of pliers at the infirmary a couple of days later. He walked off Peleliu, the only company commander in the 1st Battalion to retain his post through the entire operation.

Pope's survivors were still pulling themselves together at 1630 when the company received orders to attack up a ravine along the ridge they had just lost. Pope contacted regiment and reported that he had only 15 men and 2 officers able to attack. The order was rescinded.

It was five months before fresh units could secure that island! They did it eventually by building what they called a "moving sandbag wall." They would inch these sandbag walls forward until they could get close enough to dig the Japanese out. But the great sorrow to me of this operation was that the lessons learned were not adequately exposed to the Marines going to hit Iwo Jima some weeks later. What we had learned was somehow not communicated to them and they paid in blood for this mistake. They went into Iwo in a similar situation, but were not fully prepared for it.

When people ask me about my own personal decorations, the Navy Cross and the Purple Heart, I tell them that I never felt I fully deserved the Navy Cross because of all the hurt that my battalion endured. But in retrospect, we probably got more done for the cost than other units. To show you how bad it was, even though we came ashore "in reserve"--probably because our commander had been relieved and I was the newest Battalion Commander--the second day ashore I was assigned a mission of the central thrust up to the north of the island, in the worst of the defended territory, and we went to work on it. One historian said we expended more eleven inch battleship shells in one night than ever were expended before, trying to break up this enemy defensive system and keep them off us during the night. After three days of this deadly fighting, we had enough success to please Chesty Puller as he came forward. He then recommended me for the Navy Cross.

Puller was impressed as he was carried up there on his stretcher--he had a flare-up of a bad wound he sustained as Commander of 7th Regiment's 1st Battalion on Guadalcanal and could not walk--and he could see that this was a near untenable position with fire coming from 3 directions, but one where we held on to our gains. The situation was desperate, and we held on. While he was there Puller saw the bandage on my knee, he pulled it off, and told me that it was not bad enough to be evacuated. He was aware that they had wanted to haul me off to the hospital ship, but that I wouldn't go. He almost smiled at that.

Let me offer a little glance into the Japanese character: We had just been assigned a couple of war dogs, with their handlers, as we captured a large enemy shop area near the airfield. I used one of these heavily reinforced concrete buildings for my communications center and sick bay. My command post was outside in some holes in the ground. That night, one of the dogs yelped, a couple of shots were fired, somebody yelled, and I went to investigate. An enemy soldier, wearing nothing but a loin cloth, armed only with a bayonet, had been sent to toss a grenade into the aid station. Seems that the dog fell asleep, was frightened by the shots when his handler shot the Japanese, so he yelped. As happened more than once, the lone enemy soldier, if not shot to death, would try to stick himself with the bayonet, after he had tossed the grenade into the group of wounded Marines. He'd commit suicide after accomplishing this mission--and that was characteristic of the people we were fighting against.

In comparing actions in two separate wars, it was noted that the official monograph states that "in adjusting the lines in this area after dusk (on the evening of 17 September), a gap was created between the flanks of the 2nd and 1st Battalions. This night the prowling enemy soon discovered and commenced to infiltrate in force. To cope with this situation, it was necessary to commit Fox Company, 7th Marines, and that unit was obliged to fight its way into position before the gap could be closed." Thus, Fox Company was essential to 1st Regiment's 1st Battalion on Peleliu, and it was Fox Company of 7th Regiment's 2nd Battalion that my battalion (1st Battalion, 7th Marines) would save in the breakout from the Chosin Reservoir in Korea!!!

Later, when I was asked how I knew what to do in the crunch situations I met in my first infantry command on Peleliu, I not only gave credit to Chesty's teachings, but I also noted how in World War I, the Army's Infantry School in Georgia had gone to great pains to publish "Infantry in Battle," mostly stories of these smaller units in all kinds of situations, what happened, and how they responded. Some of it was ridiculous to the point of being laughable--how a guy gets mixed up thinking he's with his own tanks and he's actually with German tanks--you know, some things like that are just unbelievable. But that's what combat is all about. Clausewitz called it "the fog of war." There are so many things that you wouldn't believe could happen, do happen. Thus, listening to those like Puller who had experienced combat, plus the detailed study of others' experiences by reading that's all you have to go on until you get your own experience.

Thus, there would be lessons learned by and from me, Major Ray Davis, as a result of my first infantry command at Peleliu. The noted historian Fletcher Pratt, in his book "The Marines' War," titled Chapter 20: "Peleliu: The Hardest Battle," then underscored our experience with this description of the area I fought in, known with many other ridges in the Pacific War as Bloody Nose Ridge: "There was no room for maneuver, there was no story to tell but that of men climbing up vertical faces and working those cave mouths by hand with a flame-thrower and satchel charge while the Japs sniped from their rifle slits..."

Frank Hough, in his official USMC monograph, pointed out that on the tactical level Peleliu emerged as a complete vindication of the essential amphibious doctrine developed by the Marine Corps during 20 years of study and practice in peacetime and perfected on the road from Guadalcanal to the Carolinas. Harry Gailey, in his 1983 book, "Peleliu 1944" noted that "In terms of sheer heroism, every man who fought at Peleliu deserved the highest awards his country could bestow. Their courage transformed Peleliu from a questionable operation to one which should always be remembered with pride."

Orders for me arrived soon thereafter when my battalion and I returned to Pavuvu, Jim Murray took over 1st Battalion, 1st Marines, I got ordered home. Yet the real climax of my Pacific War is best described by my wife Knox: "We were married when Ray was a captain.

We weren't married but a few months; Ray went to war; I had our son Gilbert; we struggled; Ray was gone three long years!"

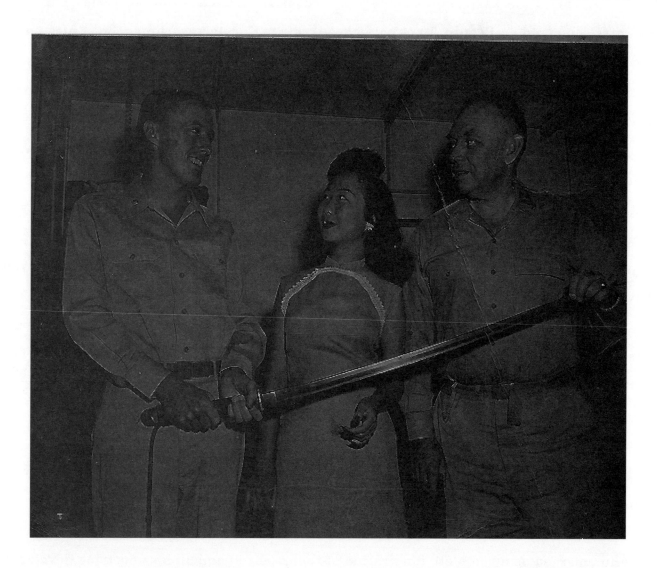

On troop transport "Billy Mitchell," Ray Davis is ready to cut a Marine Corps birthday cake. Ming Shu, a Chinese refugee student in the center, later became U.S. Marine Commissioner. Captain Coyle is on the right (November 10, 1944)

CHAPTER 11. MARINE AIR-INFANTRY SCHOOL

From Pavuvu, as a newly promoted Lieutenant Colonel, I sailed back on the BILLY MITCHELL, a converted passenger liner manned by the U. S. Coast Guard. Also along were John Chaisson, G-3 (Operations Officer) of an artillery battalion that had provided close support to my infantry battalion at Peleliu. Charley Brush, Executive Officer 2nd Battalion, 7th Marines; and others. It turned out to be an eventful trip. A day before we sailed, the division officers' mess had received an enormous ration of whiskey for everybody. Since all of the officers who were returning Stateside had put in for their share, they carried it aboard with them. The ship had one big bunkroom full of officers who spent most of their time playing cards and getting rid of their liquid rations.

I was named Commanding Officer of Troops (soldiers and Marines) for the trip, and it was an amazing collection of passengers. The ship had been by India and picked up some missionaries, students and a bunch of Army troops. It was a hodgepodge of people of every conceivable background and culture. The ship's passengers other than troops assigned to me were run by an Army transportation officer, operating under Army rules, which generated some interesting problems. Captain Coyle of the Coast Guard was skipper, and he had a Navy Reserve commander as his exec.

The Army transport fellow had set up some very strange rules. For example, for every meal in the mess, a field grade officer (Major or above) was to be in charge of each mess line. That was totally un-Marine-like, so I told him that just wouldn't happen. It would be an embarrassment to my Marines to have a field grade officer standing around watching them eat, when they were accustomed to having a sergeant in charge of the mess line. He persisted and went to this ship's executive officer and got him to agree with him. However, I was able to get Captain Coyle to instruct them that we would act like Marines on this ship. Then I got my officers together to ensure that nothing would happen down there that could disprove my premise. We put good non-commissioned officers in charge, got everyone organized, so there was never any trouble.

There was a similar situation in the living spaces. The Army officers stood watch during certain hours of the day where the troops bunked. Again, I had it out and convinced them that it would be done the Marine Corps way with non-commissioned officers in charge. It worked. Of course, the first time the ship's captain had an inspection, I assembled my officers and non-commissioned officers to make sure they understood how Marines were supposed to prepare for inspection, and that it had better be that way, and it was. All hands cleaned up the ship and put on a fine performance.

Meanwhile, my family was staying in North Carolina with Knox's people who lived near Charlotte. She had produced our first son Gilbert while I was away; he was 21 months old before I saw him. They were visiting my family in Georgia when I finally got back. Gil was a bright little boy, but he objected to my first night at home, because he had been displaced from the bedroom. I had come directly to Atlanta from the west coast via a regular train. It had troop cars with Military Police in charge, which was pretty standard in World War II.

This trip home was not my time to get along with Army rules. One of these train cars was assigned to officers with our men in two connecting cars--all combat veterans. The young Military Police men hassled the troops unnecessarily in my view and were disrespectful to the officers. After they refused to listen to reason and challenged me to do anything about it I wired ahead and had them relieved at the next stop.

Knox and I with our young son went to the beach near St. Petersburg, Florida, for some leave together, then we headed up to the Marine Corps Schools in Quantico, Virginia, for another of many tours we were to have there.

Just came back from the war (30 pounds lighter) with first-born son, Gil, 1944

Before we left for Quantico, I called a friend there to get my family a place to live, until we could get into government quarters on the base. However, this friend arranged the local motel room for the Davises for one day later than the family was to arrive. We arrived at Quantico about dark in the midst of freezing cold and deep snow. I was seriously concerned about Gilbert, our son, who had lived his first two years much further south. Fortunately we got in touch with my friend from the South Pacific and Pavuvu days, Jack Leonard. A good, friendly fellow, Jack was a bachelor living in the Bachelor Officers Quarters on the base, and he was just departing on leave. We had searched the entire area, but could find no place to sleep that night. We would have slept in the car but then Jack announced that he was going away and he offered us the key to his bachelor officer quarters room. It was at the end of the hall next to a rear door so we could move in quietly and spend the night.

I always chuckle when I think that Knox is probably the only married woman to stay in the bachelor officer quarter all night with a child. Throughout the night we continued stuffing things into Gilbert's mouth to keep him from crying and raising a ruckus. But we were in out of the cold! That was our family's introduction to military life.

My lovely wife Knox remembers that we had to go out and live on Highway One in a really old motel. Fuel rationing was such that they barely kept the room above freezing. Even with all the blankets, coats and everything we had (Knox and Gilbert stayed there during the day), it really was barely livable. Coming back from three years in the Pacific, I had suffered both malaria and hepatitis--a couple of types of malaria--and patches of hair had fallen out from malnutrition. To add to our misery, one of my wisdom teeth was giving me trouble and I had it extracted. In the process, this dentist had injected something that caused an infection deep in my throat. Repeatedly, I returned to the dentist. His response was to open it up, assuming there was some pressure or something in there. He never did diagnose it correctly, and it became worse.

One night my throat was virtually swollen shut. We were in this cold motel and as I got arranged in bed in a certain way, with my face down where I could barely breathe, I'd finally get to where I might fall off asleep. My loving wife, in her concern for me, reached over to ask me if I was comfortable. Well, I'd about bite her head off, "I just got comfortable, would you please let me be?" It got so bad that she packed me up and hauled me off to the hospital. She figured I must really be sick.

Knox says that each day when we had gone back to the dentist, even she could see a

77

pocket of infection in my throat. The dentist would put a little medication in there, but he obviously did not know what the problem was. In desperation, we went to the hospital after I read Knox off that night. As we entered, we were met by a doctor, a fine doctor. He looked in my mouth and from his expression I immediately knew something serious was wrong! He grabbed Gilbert, and they quickly took me off. Knox didn't even get to see me go. Sometime later, with the doctor still hanging on to Gilbert, he came back to tell Knox: "I think he is going to live now!" He had drained the infection.

This was Knox' introduction to military medicine!

Following this were a series of connected happenstances which moved us rapidly from a "new" service family into top echelon activity. Upon arrival at Quantico, I had as a matter of routine requested that we be quartered in a house as opposed to an apartment. However, an apartment (0-#4) became available a few weeks after we arrived, and we gladly accepted it.

It was a nice five-room, furnished, second-story abode which provided us with a substantial uplift after living in a motel out on the highway. We settled in, had friends and relatives as visitors, and entertained with small parties; it was a pleasant experience in our first family setting.

Suddenly, after 2 months an unexpected call came from the housing office asking that I meet the housing officer at Quarters 138 to inspect the house. I responded immediately, then took Knox to see it; we accepted the move without hesitation. It was a nice home, well-maintained, perfectly furnished, manicured grounds, beautiful garden out back, quarters for a maid--a dream move for us. It was sited at the foot of the Commanding General's driveway.

One problem: a senior lieutenant colonel had been told that he was on top of the house-waiting list, and he accused me of making some kind of a deal. I told him the facts as I knew them; then the Housing Officer told him that my earlier request had been misplaced.

Liz Torrey, adult daughter of the Commanding General, came down to visit and had Knox and a visiting sister, an Army nurse, Joyce, up to Quarters #1. Liz became aware of Knox' service in Girl Scouting and got her involved again at Quantico.

We attempted to limit our scouting involvement initially because we needed time to get settled in our new quarters, and our second son, Miles, was expected soon. One immediate problem was to fill out furnishings for our home. Up to this time we had few linens, crystal, silver, china, bedding, lamps, and other essentials. Knox had been an exceptional manager in my absence and had saved a nice nest egg. Off we went to Washington, D.C., to spend a full day of shopping.

A lesson learned for young husbands: Don't buy too many things on one trip! At my urging we settled patterns, colors, sizes, settings, and had a large number of deliveries the next week. I was then told that I was too hasty--shopping is better done over an extended period of time. Our initial buys were good--we still cherish them, but shopping must be long-suffering--each item savored! This was a lesson I learned from Knox and other wives.

Meanwhile Knox became "reporter" for the Girl Scouts as a beginning task. Her report was to be delivered to the *Quantico Sentry* news office early on Monday. I delivered the piece enroute to work. At times I became assistant reporter at midnight on Sunday when a memory lapse caught up with us. I would answer questions for the news clerk; this led him to request that I bring in the Boy Scout report at the same time. Soon I became the Boy Scout reporter.

Within a few weeks, Colonel Al Pollock (of Guadalcanal days), the Chief of Staff called me to his office to announce that as chairman of the Scout Committee he was concerned over the program. All his leaders were being transferred, and I was the only member left. Would I find some leaders? Suddenly, I found myself in charge!

Our kids were too young for Scouting, which meant that our efforts and other associations were with the senior officers' families. I soon became Packmaster for the Cub Scout Pack and my charges had some names that the Marine Corps was soon to honor--Hogaboom, Krulak, Butler, Schrider, among others.

As the birth of our second son, Miles, approached, we discovered that there was a shortage of nurses and doctors at Quantico. Knox' Registered Nurse (RN) sister could not arrive in time so I became assistant midwife to stay with Knox until delivery time--then be there when she came out of postop. After a successful delivery, she was placed in an outer room with a porch. Her one great desire was to see 3-year-old Gilbert. I brought him to the porch and raised the window so they could talk. In a flash, Gil was snatched through the window and into bed with his mother. Another "first things first" approach which was a mark of my friend and spouse Knox!

Thus, in a short time we became a Marine Corps family with quick and real exposure to many of the finest of families. Within a few months, we brought a young woman from near

Knox's home to live in the maid's quarters. This proved to be full of pluses and minuses--she worked hard, but was soon caught up in the heavy dating and night life enjoyed by young girls at Quantico. Of interest, this was the only live-in help we had until 23 years later at Quantico when, as a Major General, we lived in Quarters 12, which came with 3 live-in stewards.

The foregoing shows that the positive tour at Quantico--my job, in nice quarters, good friends, interesting programs--all added up to making both of us more career oriented--we had found a "home" and planned to give it our best effort.

But more on my "job." I was initially assigned as Tactical Inspector, one who checks the instruction given throughout the Marine Corps Schools. It was a fairly short tour before I was assigned as Chief of the Infantry Section at the Marine Air-Infantry School, under Colonel Pottinger. Originally, Marine Air-Infantry School had turned out Officer Candidates and Reserve Officer Candidates, but it was being changed to Junior School level, primarily for Captains and Majors. Unfortunately there were a number of unhappy young pilots in the Marine Air Infantry School. Their war experience was in flying, and they had gotten so glued to that business that they believed their lives would be in jeopardy if they got away from the controls of an airplane for more than a few hours at a time. They'd lose some of their skill and their reactions. They hammered on this idea all of the time, saying that being there in Marine Air-Infantry School was just taking them away from their primary need, and that was to fly airplanes. Of course, what they wanted was out of the school.

Fortunately, Colonel Pottinger, Director of Marine Air-Infantry School was an aviator, and he gave them no choice. My Basic School classmate, Jim Embry, was the Aviation Subjects Instructor. It was a period of transition for all of the Marine Corps Schools in Quantico. With the war still on, the Marine Air-Infantry School did very well with Jim and me overseeing the air and infantry instruction. We leaned on both our long-term combat background in our specialties. New classes were coming on board and they overlapped in such a way that we couldn't stop and revise the instruction. We had to make changes piecemeal as the courses progressed and although we had some difficulties, it all soon straightened out.

Essentially, it was this course that was to become Amphibious Warfare School, Junior Course, also known as Junior School. The Senior School became, in the early 60s, The Marine Corps Command and Staff College. Thus, the Marine Corps has had three levels of officer education and training since World War II: (1) The Basic School, where newly commissioned second lieutenants went through the basic training; (2) Amphibious Warfare School, where captains/majors received their training; and (3) Command and Staff College, where majors/lieutenant colonels (colonels when I later attended) received further high level training. The concept of assignment has varied from a "payback" tour for good work to that of those indicated by fitness reports to have the greatest growth potential for the future of the Corps.

During this time period, warriors from the Pacific War were running Marine Corps School: General C. B. Cates was Commandant, Marine Corps Schools, Edwin Pollock was Chief of Staff; Hogaboom was Director, Senior School, with Jack Colley and Brute Krulak his deputy and Number 3 man respectively. Hogaboom and Krulak had been together in the "old" China days of the 4th Marine Regiment (which was captured at Corregidor in the Philippines, after moving out of its "home" in Shanghai).

Thus, Marine Air-Infantry School was changing from an orientation course for aviators--very simple, basic tactics--to a Junior School/Amphibious Warfare School concept, with air and ground students and staff. The course was full and ongoing with overlap in classes. It took real handsprings to make major revisions in courses; it was a great challenge--but rewarding for both Jim Embry, Air, and me, Infantry. Also, it made for me some class aviator friends, such as Pete Schrider, a great flyer and fine gentleman.

Two co-workers of mine were kind enough to write the following to Bill Davis:

> My job at Marine Air-Infantry School was Student Administrator, sort of a staff secretary. Ray Davis ran the Infantry Section. He did his usual meticulous professional job. His success, wherever he served, was based on the high standards which he sets for himself and his subordinates. We were all better officers for having served with him.
>
> --Lieutenant General John R. McLaughlin, USMC, Ret (who was captured by Chinese enroute to Chosin Reservoir in North Korea; served as Rifle Company Commander his entire tour of duty in the Pacific War).

> As Section Head of the Infantry Section, Lieutenant Colonel Ray Davis ran a thoroughly efficient operation. All members of the faculty (and indeed all the students with the exception of returning World War II P.O.W.s) were combat-experienced. Ray Davis insisted that all infantry tactics used at the Marine Air-Infantry School pass the test of careful analysis by battle-seasoned officers. Only if a scheme of maneuver could meet the challenge of the Infantry Section's combined scrutiny would Ray Davis let it become a "School Solution." Leading each detailed analysis was Ray Davis, who was determined that his infantry section present the best product of which we were capable.
>
> --Major General Carl Hoffman, USMC, Ret. (another famed Pacific War fighter; later to serve as my Deputy in Vietnam).

Thus was born the "Murder Board" in the Marine Corps Schools, which continues to this day, in which all members of a given section listen to a new period of instruction given by its author(s), then proceed to "murder" it until all of the experts agree with the entire presentation of concepts.

Life was not all peaches and cream during this tour at Quantico, however. This is how Knox tells it: "When the massive releases began after World War II ended, most of our friends were Reservists who were soon to be released. Many good friends that we really liked were departing with few to be left except the Regulars. I went to a big party, four tables of bridge. One of the wives of a reservist said 'Horrors! Do you all know that Knox is the only one who is staying in?' That's one out of 16 women, you know--16 women! I went home and I told Ray the things I'd heard: 'You're living off the government, you have no initiative, you're afraid you can't get a job...' All these things so often heard in those days, I told Ray. And I said you are going to get out, you're just going to get out of this Marine Corps, that's all there is to it. I'll go back to teaching school, if necessary.

"So Ray sat me down and said: 'Well, you couldn't teach school, because we have our sons Gilbert and Miles.' Then he reviewed many reasons why the Marine Corps was his chosen profession. And I told him: 'All right, I will stay in with you, and you'll never hear that from me again.' He's heard a lot of other things, but not that. I never one time after that complained about being in the Marine Corps."

Having made a final decision to stay in the Corps, Knox and I would say good-bye to our soon-to-be civilian friends and settled into life at Quantico.

I received orders to the First Provisional Marine Brigade on Guam. Guam was one of the combat islands in the Pacific, and with the war recently over, there were no family accommodations. I would be separated from my family again.

My family arrvies in Guam via ship, 1947

CHAPTER 12. 1ST PROVISIONAL MARINE BRIGADE, GUAM

Back to the Fleet Marine Force I went after just two years Stateside. Following World War II, Marine Corps policy was "Two years overseas; three years in the States." In my case, it got a little reversed. In the Pacific War, I spent almost three years overseas, and now I was enroute to Fleet Marine Force, Western Pacific after some two years at Quantico. At that time, there was a "West Coast Headquarters, Marine Corps" at 100 Harrison Street in San Francisco, through which all Marines heading for the Pacific or China duty were ordered. I reported to this "Department of the Pacific" as it was titled, which handled all shipping and flying orders for the two primary Western Pacific posts then, Guam, Marianas Islands and Tsingtao, China.

The 1st Provisional Marine Brigade was stationed on Guam with two Marine Battalion Landing Teams, or "reinforced infantry battalions" (each with its own artillery battery, tank platoon, antitank platoon, etc.) designated the 5th and 9th Marines. Senior "bird" colonels commanded each, although normally this was the billet of a lieutenant colonel. When I arrived, Colonel E. W. Fry had the 5th Marines, and Colonel T. B. Hughes, the 9th.

Camp Witek was named after a young Marine who was awarded the Medal of Honor in the retaking of Guam from the Japanese. It housed Fleet Marine Force on GUAM and was a new Marine Corps installation. Troops were housed in Quonset huts and tents, and there were no quarters yet available for married officers and other Marines. Initially, it was an "unaccompanied tour," i.e., families could not join their sponsors.

Once quarters were available, it was designated as an accompanied tour. Knox came out about a year after I did. At that time, Brigadier General Craig commanded the brigade, and we had to build our own quarters. As soon as the quarters were ready, families could join us. They issued me a vacant lot and a knocked down Quonset hut. (Quonsets were half-moon structures built with semicircular metal frames, on to which were attached 3' by 8' pieces of tin, and the "floors" were 4' by 8' slabs of plywood.) Pieces of tarpaulin were attached to outside walls to be rolled down over the screen-covered "windows" during the heavy intermittent seasonal rains that swept Guam almost daily. No glass allowed, since strong gusts of wind would have broken it. We also had to personally order other essentials, such as commodes, stoves, and refrigerators from the States.

Because there were a number of officers awaiting families, the whole thing was a kind of do-it-yourself community. I was a pretty good plumber, so I put plumbing in four or five houses. Somebody else was an electrician. Donald J. Robinson, the old tanker (from Pavuvu days) could do fancy carpentry, cabinet-making and woodwork. He did a number of Quonsets--which we called "houses"--so it was a trade-off effort.

This was supposed to be a Fleet base. Some were convinced that construction costs had to be paid for with Fleet money. There was opposition to this, it being argued that it should come out of Marine Corps Administrative Funds. Apparently, they never finally settled that problem. It should be noted that after building these Quonsets, along with the spending of substantial amounts of personal funds, Marines who had built them had to give up their full quarters allowances or "rent" in order to live there!

General Craig's sensible reaction to all this was, "Well, we're here and we've got to live, so we'll do just what we can. We'll commit our people, and troops and resources to get ourselves out of the mud and train the best we can while the bureaucrats are hacking this thing out and deciding who's going to do what." Finally, after a year, it was determined that the Marine Corps would finance it out of Base Funds. They started building a permanent base out there after I left. "Harry the Horse" Liversedge of Iwo Jima fame was the Commanding General as a typhoon blew the whole camp down. They left the foundations and first floors of concrete buildings out there in the jungle, and the camp never did get finished.

The mission of the Brigade had been primarily to establish this base as a training camp for the Fleet Marines, and we had contingency plans for reinforcing the Marines in Tsingtao, China. The Brigade sent T. B. Hughes' 9th Marines over to reinforce the 1st and 3rd Marines, and the Marine aviation elements at the airfield at Tsingtao where Mao's forces were periodically testing them. (In addition, the 9th Marines furnished a reinforced rifle platoon, commanded by Bill Davis, to protect the U. S. Embassy, which was moved from Peking to Nanking.)

When I arrived on Guam, I was the G-3 (Plans, Operations and Training) Officer until Colonel Lew Walt arrived. Then Earl Sneeringer, who was the G-4 (Supply and Logistics) Officer, left for the States, and I took over the G-4 shop. My basic function was to get the Camp Witek facilities built. Lieutenant Colonel Morgenthau was the engineer-in-charge of the building construction program, under Colonel Louie Plain, who was the overall honcho of construction.

The next major problem became one of closing down the 5th Service Depot, which was separate from Camp Witek. Essentially, it was a massive junkyard of World War II gear. During the Pacific War, the Guam jungle was filled with supplies. No one knew precisely just what was there, and they didn't have an adequate staff to find out. Further, after an inventory of a square city block of canvas, for example, they'd start issuing canvas. It had all rotted. The same way in the lumber yard. They'd issue lumber, and in the middle of the pile it was all rotted. It was difficult separating the good from the bad. There was no easy way out of the problem. Finally it was decided to have a wall to wall or block to block inventory, utilizing troop labor to do it.

Well, General Craig wasn't about to assign his tactical troops down there willy nilly to work for the 5th Base Depot, so we organized them into task forces. I was assigned to see that this whole thing was done in a task force, orderly manner. The troops were totally responsive to General Craig in support of the 5th Base (Service) Depot. If they had an area to clean up, they'd get an operation order to clean up that area, under General Craig, and not be assigned to Colonel Thompson, who was commander of the Depot under Dave Shoup's logistic outfit in Hawaii. It was a most interesting task--treading water between General Craig and Colonel Thompson to get the work done without stepping on anybody's toes.

General Craig was great. He's another of those that, if you wanted to emulate a man in his approach to life and his aspirations, you have a perfect example to follow. I guess if any great fortune came my way, it was because of opportunity after opportunity to serve with people like that--Puller, Craig, Masters, Nickerson, Walt, Litzenberg, and others.

As for the brigade and the depot inventory, we did not find much usable stuff. We had to write it off by the ton and by the yard. So much of it was either useless or totally surplus to our needs. It might have been much better if we had turned the whole thing over to a contractor to let him take what he wanted and bury the rest. But the effort did not last long. In late '48, they brought the whole brigade back to the States.

From the beginning, the lst Provisional Marine Brigade came under Fleet Marine Force, Pacific, back in Hawaii. Lieutenant General Thomas Easy Watson was the Commanding General. He made infrequent visits to oversee airborne and airlift exercises to Saipan and Tinian, as well as amphibious landings on nearby islands. Other than these visits, we were pretty much on our own out there and we were absorbed in the problem of just living in the mud. With no financial support, nobody wanted anything to do with us, but General Craig was determined to provide quarters for his troops and to upgrade their readiness. We ran many maneuvers on Guam as well as Saipan and Tinian, where many of our rifle company commanders and Battalion Landing Team staff officers had fought as platoon commanders in World War II. This added great realism to these exercises. The maneuver area on Guam was very large with a live-firing area nearby.

Of special interest to me was the fact that, intermittently, there were Japanese soldiers giving up in various parts of Guam. I didn't see any of them, but they'd turn up, somebody would pick them up and haul them off. In addition, we had some war criminals incarcerated there, in the brig facilities of the Marine Barracks. I understand that there were some executions of Japanese war criminals conducted on Guam, although I don't remember hearing anything about that when I was in the Brigade.

The primary thing I remember about that tour of duty was serving with General Craig, who is one of the greats in my view. Not only was I close to him on Guam, I saw him last year, and I hear from him at least once a year. A great Marine!

The 9th Marine Battalion Landing Team, and the 1st and 3rd Marines (at Tsingtao) had returned Stateside from China in early '49 when Mao moved into power. The 5th Marines left Guam and became the 3rd Battalion, 5th Marines at Camp Pendleton, CA. destined to soon hit Wolmi-Do Island in the Inchon Landing. This was after the 5th Marine Regiment became the heart of Brigadier General Eddie Craig's 1st Provisional Marine Brigade in the Pusan (South Korea) Perimeter, the Battle of the Naktong, in the Korean Conflict.

This tour ended for Knox, our two sons Gil and Miles, and me in April,1949, when we departed "the sunny (and often rainy) tropic scenes" for duty with a Reserve Infantry Battalion in "The Windy City," Chicago, Illinois!

TALES OF GUAM

Before we move on, and because of this unique opportunity for a jungle-fighting Marine to live in the jungle with his family, let me pass on a few tales about the other side of this tour; tales about my family and about the time we had together.

Miles and Ants: Miles celebrated his second birthday on the ship enroute to Guam. He loved the warm climate and playing in the sandy yard in his "uniform" of shorts only. He made "roads" in the sand for his toy trucks and cars, but now and then he would sit on an ant bed. Running to the house, pulling off his ant-filled pants, yelling "Ants! Ants!!..," and he was met at the door by Knox who rushed him into the shower to wash off the ants. An all-out attack of the ants with DDT soon eased the problem.

Miles and Fungus: The ant bites probably contributed to a worse problem--fungus eruptions on Miles' face and upper torso. The treatment was to wash the raw sores with alcoholic soap, then apply a soothing, healing salve. It was torture for the young boy to be treated several times each day and night. We developed a ritual. I applied the soap, Knox the salve. We sat him in the bathroom, talked with him. He would insist that "Mommy" have salve on her finger ready to go, then taking a deep breath, he yelled at the top of his voice until we got the sores all washed and treated. Then, as it was all finished, he went out to play.

Miles and the Surf: The coral swimming beach nearby had a heavy surf; a pedestrian pier let people get out past the roughest of the coral. Miles loved to jump off the low end of the pier into my arms. By letting him go under the water, he was learning to hold his breath and cope with the salt water in his eyes. He would jump again and again until one afternoon as he was preparing to jump, I lost my footing and went under the water. He jumped without looking just as a breaker carried him under the pier. I couldn't find him--yelled for help! Someone nearby found him struggling under water and pulled him out. It was the longest moment of my life! He sputtered, blew and coughed out the water and was ready to jump again. His trust in me never waned--I saw that trust at work again during some uncertain hours in Vietnam.

Knox and Peeping Tom: Enroute to Guam my family enjoyed a cabin up in the 0-2 deck Senior Officers Area. One evening, Knox became aware of someone outside the door, the upper half of which was louvered. A sailor was there leaning against the door breathing heavily. Knox yelled: "Get away, you nasty thing!" Colonel Louis Plain, also a passenger in a nearby cabin, dashed out just in time to see a figure disappearing down a nearby ladder. A security watch was posted so Knox was able to enjoy the rest of the voyage.

Coconut Rats: The family arrived before my Quonset hut was finished, so we spent a few nights with Don and Betty Robinson--Don and I had worked together on huts. We concentrated on getting his ready as the ship approached. The first night we moved into our house we discovered after we went to bed that the place was overrun with coconut rats--big ones. Our final step in construction was to seal the house with screening and trim. In this we had entrapped about eight rats inside the house. We cured the problem by placing food near a door, waiting in the dark until we could hear them at the food. We opened the door, turned on the lights and thrashed around over the house with brooms and sticks as they ran out.

A permanent cure was to remove all the foliage well back from the house, improve the sealing and put out poison under the house where kids-and dogs could not get to it. A rat problem which stayed with us concerned a small garden. I had a good crop of cantaloupes and watermelons. I checked carefully daily for ripe ones. The first few I'd announce: "Ripe in one or two more days!" That very night rats ate a tunnel right through the heart. They were better at detecting the ripe ones than I was. I then had to pick them green at the cost of much of the flavor.

Lizards: The first few nights in the hut we discovered unwanted visitors. Small lizards lived in the upper structure of the Quonset. As Berta Hughes described them: "They slept all day and 'clicked, clicked' all night!" One especially hot night we were asleep sans pajamas when a screech shocked me awake. In the dark I couldn't find Knox--but when I flipped on the light switch, there she was, terror distorting her face. A lizard had fallen from his ceiling perch onto her bare stomach. She must have levitated over the bed at least a foot when it hit, because when I reached for her she was not there! Needless to say, we declared war on all lizards.

Bingo: Knox became an avid devotee of Bingo--frequently held in our jungle covered officers' "club." Ann Morgenthau, a neighbor, was a companion in this--those two, especially Knox, had a winning streak which probably established an all-time "record."

Bananas/local citizens: Many local residents of Guam worked in the camp and housing area, and we became friends of some. We were invited to their village festivals. In one, a young woman who worked for us was our host. She proudly took us throughout the village introducing us to the local leaders and elders, then guided us through the native holiday celebration. It was a rare, delightful experience in a very remote part of Guam. One friend who had a banana field brought us some small banana plants and helped plant them on the backside of our hut where water off the roof collected. The plants prospered, grew twelve feet high, and a bunch of bananas grew out of each plant. Luckily they matured just as we were to depart for the States. We took two large bunches aboard ship with us and enjoyed eating them enroute home. Our friend had favored us with the best bananas we have ever enjoyed.

Typhoons: Our huts had so much area covered only by screen wire that exceptional measures were necessary when storm warnings came. Canvas was normally rolled down over

89

the screen, but as storms approached it had to be nailed down using strips of wood. Much of this was done at night since security of the troops areas took priority of our time before we could go to take care of our quarters. While we lived there the storms were not severe ones and our camp received only minor damage. However, Don Robinson and I made an extra effort to secure our quarters by placing heavy anchors of concrete in the ground with cables attached. Cables were then crossed over the top of the metal hut roofs to help prevent wind damage to the sheet metal covering--keep it from blowing loose. After we departed from Guam we heard reports that our anchored huts withstood a severe storm which destroyed many others not so anchored.

Friendships: Life at Camp Witek on Guam was an important milestone in the fine tuning of Marine Corps families. The rugged existence, the day and night challenges, the adversity welded everyone together--built character in the strong, the weak fell off the sled. Our closest, most lasting friendships grew from our tour there.

Departure: We left Guam on short notice amid a lot of confusion. An early announcement stated that troop units would embark and leave dependents in the primitive camp. Since there was no known urgency, this seemed totally foolish. Threats to send emergency messages to Congressmen for help was enough to cancel that design. Then a plan was floated to abandon our huts, furnishings and belongings, while we went aboard ship immediately. 5th Service Depot would pack up our things and forward them when they could get to it. I, for one, refused to sign a certificate relieving the government of any responsibility for damage or loss. This plan was also withdrawn.

We finally got off the island in good order, after we packed our own things in containers furnished by the Depot. The trip home was pleasant: Lew Walt and the Davises were quartered in the upper staterooms and dined with the Captain. It was really first class travel! Looking back, it now seems like such a quiet and gentle time between two wars. Although my next assignment in Chicago would present a whole array of different opportunities, I still enjoy the memories of that voyage.

CHAPTER 13. WITH THE RESERVES

Early in the fall of 1949, I reported for duty as the Marine Corps Inspector-Instructor with the 9th Marine Corps Reserve Infantry Battalion in Chicago. While the weather change from the eternally hot and humid island of Guam to the brisk fall weather of Chicago was a major shock for us, the duty itself was a veritable "piece of cake" for a combat-experienced Marine infantry battalion Commander from Peleliu days. I knew the infantry battalion, its doctrine, tactics, techniques and equipment. Also keep in mind that World War II, in the main, had been fought by Reservists.

"Inspector & Instructor" (I&I) duty, as it is called, can be easy duty for some and tough duty for others, especially for those with preconceived notions about Reservists/"Weekend Warriors"/ civilians. And this thinking goes both ways. Many civilians see members of the regular military as "people who can't get a job on the outside," as the Quantico bridge partners had told Knox in very definite terms. But no matter the attitude on either side of this military equation, there are major changes in the life of the regular officer and his family moving in from duty on a relatively small island in the middle of the Pacific to a major city in the U.S. heartland.

We purchased a small house in Deerfield, just north of Chicago. Unlike on Guam, we now lived far from any military facilities. Our three-year-old, Miles, became ill with what appeared to be chicken pox, but the local community doctor kept stalling us off. His office said he would get back to us and have us in, but nothing would happen.

I came home from work to find Miles obviously in distress; he was very ill. He was on a couch where I leaned over to talk to him, putting my hands on him. I barely touched his stomach area, and he almost jumped off the couch. Immediately this alerted me that there was a chance of appendicitis, which we had not considered before. We hurried him into the car and raced over to the Great Lakes Naval Hospital. Knox adds: "That was because we could not get a local doctor there to take him. They said, well, 'you're not a patient of mine'."

But this incident built in me a great confidence in the Navy medical system once the cards are on the table. We arrived there about an hour before midnight and were met by the duty officer. He called the senior medical watch officer, who is over a series of duty officers, and they all looked at Miles. They got the surgeon--the senior surgeon got in on it--and then one other assistant, and finally, the surgeon who was going to operate on him. Remember, this was now about 11:30 at night and within one hour, all five of these doctors were involved. They operated on Miles.

Says Knox: "Besides, they had all the student doctors come in, too. It was a sight, really. It half scared me to death to see them swishing through there, putting on their uniforms and caps and jackets, caring for our little three-year old. We came back the next morning, soon after the operation and saw them cart Miles into a room with this array of people, as you see now on TV--people with the drip bottles and everything. And in this midst was our poor little kid."

We got in the room, and when we saw him we were almost in a state of shock because apparently they found perforation of the appendix, and they had to take his intestines out to clean them. And he hurt so much. We were told that this was the first time that these doctors had a child that young with peritonitis, and for that reason they called young doctors in, to see the operation and cleaning of his stomach cavity.

When we got home, the first thing Miles wanted to do was ride his tricycle. I called the doctor, and he said to let the patient do what he can do. So he rode that tricycle around the house. But maybe a year later, whenever a storm was coming up, he would go to Knox and say, "Mommy, my operation hurts real bad." I've always believed that weather had something to do with all of this.

Another little side story of our arrival in the civilian world: We actually arrived just two or three days before school started, coming from Guam where for a year sons Gilbert and Miles had lived in shorts and nothing else. There were no opportunities to go shopping. We sent Gilbert off to school in his summer clothes, in his Guam clothes. It had been as hot as Hades when we first arrived in Chicago, but the first day of school, it turned chilly, and we didn't have anything that was fitting. Well, the teacher sent a note home saying, "that his clothing is just not appropriate for this weather." So we took him shopping. End of story.

Fortunately for me, the Inspector & Instructor Unit had already been well organized by Jim Taul, my Regular predecessor. Also, John Bathum, the local battalion commanding officer had been around Chicago all of his life; and back in 1921 he had been a Private First Class in the outfit, when everybody in the outfit had to buy their own shoes, etc. I was very fond of John, and he was totally oriented towards the welfare of the outfit and the Marine Corps. He was a fine Marine himself, and we had a good unit in which we were able to upgrade the participation of the reservists. Interestingly enough, a very talented reservist, Roy Whitlock, was there on extended active duty working in the Inspector & Instructor office as my assistant. He was then a first lieutenant and ended his career in Augusta, Georgia, running an outstanding Junior ROTC at a high school. I get over to see him frequently. I commissioned his ROTC unit six or seven years ago, and in those years it has been either number one, two or three in the nation as far as Marine Corps Reserve Officers Association awards are concerned. Roy Whitlock went into an Augusta High School that was having problems, and he upgraded the whole school system. I bring this up because in those days in Chicago, I came to know Whitlock as the fellow who could do anything or get anything done.

Roy went out and recruited an entire high school football team into the Reserves. That caused a lot of anguish when the Korean War started. He mentioned one day that he needed a band. We weren't really authorized to have a band but soon got permission. He then recruited an entire high school band except for the conductor. He couldn't get the conductor to sign up, so I insisted that Roy had to really get busy now. We had a band. Somebody had to conduct them. He invited me down to practice--they practiced on Wednesday nights after we recruited them--and there was Whitlock leading the band! He could do anything! He was truly remarkable, and his style and leadership really showed up in a place like that.

Chicago always was a great Marine town. We had names like Al Thomas, Jim Donaghue, Sengewald (a company commander from Cincinnati), and another company commander named Verne Kennedy, who eventually made brigadier general in the Reserves. The Public Relations Officer was Jim Hurlbut, who became famous with a zoo program on TV. We really had a great outfit. We organized a highly successful women's unit and organized our own recruit training platoon. Anybody who wanted to join the outfit had to come down for recruit training for awhile, a few extra hours. Finally we took the battalion off to summer camp just about the time the Korean War started.

At the Camp Lejeune summer training site there occurred another one of those breaks in which I bumped into the right people. Colonel Homer Litzenberg was involved with summer training for Reserves at Lejeune. Having come from the Brigade on Guam plus my Quantico experience, I was determined to get every detail of the battalion staff work properly done before we went to Camp Lejeune. We had a lot of extra sessions with officers and had an elaborate set of operating plans and administrative orders drawn up for the movement to Lejeune. On the train enroute, we wired up the cars and ran a Command Post Exercise (CPX) with the field telephones wired throughout the train. All these plans, orders and schedules preceded us to Camp Lejeune. When we arrived, Litzenberg was relating how happy everyone was with our effort. Bathum, the Commanding Officer who knew Litzenberg from years past, gave full credit for the whole effort to me personally. Of course, it wasn't all mine. Bathum had a great part in it.

However, as we got back and were getting ready to mount out for the Korean War, Litzenberg flew with parts of his 6th Marine Regiment over to Camp Pendleton on the West Coast to get organized to go overseas. The 6th Marines was redesignated as the 7th Marines, and he needed a battalion commander. Through this relationship between Bathum and Litzenberg at Camp Lejeune, he asked that I come out and take over that infantry battalion to Korea. Without this happenstance, I might have been left out of the war somewhere.

Let me say that Litzenberg was another masterful tactician. He had a better feel for finding and hitting the enemy than most people I've been around. He really got a lot out of his regiment.

As Bathum's and my reserve infantry battalion back in Chicago prepared to leave for the West Coast, we had the expected problem of some people who wanted to stay home. We were required to set up a formal hearing process. The most serious problem I had and the most amusing in some ways: We were having an enormous number of physical failures as the reservist reported in to take their final, before-going-to-active duty physical. All of these failures somehow had a relation to the Marines' mental attitudes. I forget how the doctors were expressing it, but they were finding many members Not Physically Qualified (NPQ) to go. I looked over many of the reports; I knew the men and I couldn't believe the findings. The two doctors worked at Hines Veterans Administration (VA) Hospital full-time, and the next thing I knew, the two doctors were not qualified to go either! It turned out that they had been examined by each other, and found each other not physically qualified. With that, I took all these not physically qualified people to another doctor, had him examine them, and they were virtually all found qualified to go. We got rid of those first two doctors. The system worked much better then.

There were a few others who didn't want to go right away, or didn't want to go at all. We had several all-day sessions with these people who came in for a hearing to see what criteria they might meet. We finally put 700 on the train to go, not losing more than maybe a hundred, and most of those were authorized six-month delays to finish school. We had special trouble with a football team. I finally went along with the solution after the principal and the school superintendent came to see me, saying that there was too much at stake to let the entire team go. The school worked out some arrangements whereby published criteria would be met. The students could graduate within six months. They got the whole team deferred after I made the school officials sign papers that they would carry out the rules. Those were some interesting times, believe me!

Before I see the troops off and begin my own trip to Korea, permit me a couple of observations about this highly interesting duty with reservists in Chicago:

Transportation: The Chicago battalion was widely scattered: Headquarters on Navy Pier downtown, one company at Evanston, one in Cicero, one in Hammond, Indiana.

Our staff visited constantly utilizing a Marine pickup truck. I rode the train to the city from my faraway Deerfield home and many times would be met downtown or at a remote station to go to visit company activities. I never permitted the official vehicles to come to my home; this to further underscore my determination to restrict the use of vehicles to official visits only.

PX (Post Exchange): We established a small PX store on Navy Pier which added to the unity of the outfit and provided some profit for recreation purposes. I don't recall the details, but this innovation caused some heartburn in Washington because it was not in "regulations." But we won the day.

Band: We wanted blue uniforms for our "unauthorized" band. We were told "No" but persisted 'til we got help from the Great Lakes (Naval Training Center) Marines. Parades in downtown Chicago with a high school band in Marine blues made a very sizable splash!

Trouble: We had enough room on Navy Pier to have parties on special occasions, and this encouraged family participation. Even on drill nights, we had spaces where family members could hang out, have snacks from the PX, listen to music in the band hall, etc. We had one family member too many. The Sergeant Major's wife assumed duties as unofficial "inspector" to keep tabs on the reservists' activities. She reported her findings in a personal letter to the Commandant of the Marine Corps. Although she had pages of nitpicks and harsh adjectives, only one "major" problem concerned Washington: falsification of drill attendance records. She had names and dates, but fortunately none of the charges held water. Jim Hurlbut was one; on two occasions he came to drill but was called away for an emergency having to do with his status as a leading TV reporter. Both times he was excused and made up the time on a subsequent day. John Bathum, the Commander, was incensed even though every charge was refuted. He asked the Sergeant Major's wife not to return to Navy Pier.

Range: Another very attractive feature was added on Navy Pier--a 1,000 inch, .22 caliber rifle range. This really made a lot of people nervous, having a rifle range in the middle of the heavily populated Navy Pier. Fortunately, one of our members had access to some heavy steel plate which we used to enclose the target area. Sandbags were used to back up the targets thus reducing the danger of ricochets and spattering. Many reservists used the range throughout the week, and we were about to field a competitive team when the Korean War started.

Well, so much for duty in Chicago. I saw the 9th Marine Corps Reserve Infantry Battalion of Chicago, Illinois off on the train to the West Coast. Then I drove my family to Atlanta and flew out to join the 7th Marine Regiment in Tent Camp Two, Camp Joseph H. Pendleton, situated between San Diego to the south, and Los Angeles to the north.

Among my many lessons learned in the Corps over three decades was this: My great gain as an Inspector-Instructor was an appreciation of the spirit and dedication of Reservists. They did drill duty, extra chores away from family, summer camp. Perhaps some were a bit shy in "hands on" skill and experience, but the Esprit de Corps is there! Anyone who served in Korea knows how well they performed in combat. We had over 60 percent Reservists in the fighting battalion that I was about to join.

Things happened so fast that we were unable to assimilate what we were doing and where we were going. Who knew anything about Korea? We only knew that we had been ordered into combat in another foreign land, and we went where we were ordered. As Marines, we would deal with whatever our destinies might be when we got there.

CHAPTER 14. CHOSIN

In 1950, three factors invited North Korea to invade South Korea: (1) the small South Korean army was ill prepared, (2) U.S. forces had been downsized to skeletonized formation, (3) U.S. Secretary of State Dean Acheson announced that South Korea was no longer within our defensive area.

On June 25th, a carefully planned attack was unleashed across the 38th Parallel into South Korea. Our skeletonized forces finally stalled the attack near Pusan. In a brilliant maneuver by General MacArthur our forces landed at Inchon in September, recaptured Seoul and drove the North Korean forces back north. I was to become a part of the Inchon landing.

My second war thus began as my Reserve Infantry Battalion in Chicago was ordered out to Camp Pendleton, California for duty in the Korean War. I put it on a train, soon caught a plane to Los Angeles, then the milk train down to Pendleton. I arrived at 0500 in early August 1950. Colonel Homer L. Litzenberg, Commanding Officer of the Seventh Regiment, shook my hand, asked where the hell I had been, and told me that I had just five days to form his 1st Battalion, 7th Marines and take it to war.

What "Litz" the Blitz (as the troops affectionately termed him) failed to tell me was that personnel to man my new unit were not immediately available. Throughout Camp Pendleton, reserve units like my Chicago folks would arrive by train, be formed on the siding into 75-man platoons, just like at Marine Corps Recruit Depots, and marched off into the dark. Their equipment and records were placed in piles on local parade grounds under tarpaulins. Later administrative powers would decide what to do with them.

After two days of waiting for new personnel, I applied what I call my principle of INNOVATION. Without it, I would be leaving for Inchon, Korea, with less than half an infantry battalion. There is often a fine line between a medal and a court martial, but I did what had to be done in this, and many other situations, during my career. Fortunately there came a convoy of trucks into my Tent Camp Two, mainly hauling equipment. I told four of my senior officers to commandeer one truck each, start driving around the many acres of Camp Pendleton, and ask every group of Marines they saw, "Anybody want to go to Korea?" Soon truckloads of Marine "volunteers" came back into Tent Camp Two. All in all, we fulfilled our 800 troops requirement in this innovative manner--in just eight hours of "recruiting!"

Why would these Marines volunteer to go to war? Another of my key principles, MOTIVATION, took over. Their Reserve units were disbanded and they had just come to active duty. Many of them were in a very confusing military situation. They had "no mama, no papa," and they welcomed the chance to join a fighting military organization, 7th Regiment's 1st Battalion. My experience with that Chicago Marine Corps Reserve unit had shown me that Reserves had great spirit--the ESPRIT which drove them to be good Marines at night or weekends, after holding down their regular civilian jobs by day or all week long. We really welcomed them aboard!

We used the first two of five days just gaining the men, their equipment, and their administrative records. The third and fourth days were spent firing their rifles, praticing small unit tactics, and hiking in rough Pendleton hills. Soon they were on buses heading for San Diego and the good ship USS OKANOGAN. This was a Navy assault transport built for a 1,500 man Marine Infantry Battalion with all of its supporting units, such as artillery, plus weapons and equipment.

After 18 days at sea and a brief stop in Japan, we landed at Inchon Harbor, as the reserve battalion of the 1st Marine Division's reserve regiment, the 7th Marines. The 5th Marines of Lieutenant Colonel Ray Murray had hit Wolmi-do Island off Inchon, the Division's left flank of the amphibious assault. Chesty Puller, in command of the 1st Marines hit the right flank over the beach walls.

We had NOT relaxed for the 18 day sea voyage. We trained small units as hard as we could, day and night, during the trip. In addition to firing our rifles at every target we could find from the fantail of OKANOGAN, we fired machine guns, mortars, rocket launchers and threw hand grenades at every piece of trash, orange crates, or whatever the ship's crew would toss overboard for us. At first naturally these Navy folks were aghast to hear my operational desires, but they really entered into the innovative scheme. We had over two weeks of good, solid training for Marines who were super-MOTIVATED. This was no game; they were going to war at Inchon, the port city to Seoul, the capital of South Korea. It had been overrun by North Korean troops on 25 June 1950.

It was the same way on land. We did NOT simply go for a stroll through the country side while in the mobile rear as reserve. We hit every hill enroute to and around Seoul as if it were still covered with enemy--which the 5th and 1st Marines had mostly cleared out. Our tactics were better every day--and night--by the time we crossed the Han River and were given the mission of moving after the enemy who headed north from Seoul. We subsequently chased them for miles up to Uijongbu. Our first fire fights showed the value of our innovative, motivated training both at sea and along the trail in Korea. We were now a fighting organization.

Northwest of Seoul we had been assigned a screening mission as the Division captured the city. We had a few skirmishes with small enemy groups and were able to exercise our mortars, artillery and aircraft weapons on live fire targets. One morning I felt totally relaxed, because we had no new orders from Regiment. The phone rang. Colonel Litzenberg asked: "What's the problem? You are supposed to be moving out!" "But, sir," I responded, "I don't have any orders to move today." "You have now! Get going!" he growled and hung up.

I hurried to my operations tent in time to find an embarrassed S-3 (operation officer) scrambling to get things moving. A messenger had awakened him at 0330; he had signed a receipt for fragmentary orders from Regiment, but was not awake enough to know it had happened. Lesson learned: After that his runner slept next to him to be sure that he was awake when orders came in.

After the Inchon-Seoul-Uijongbu Campaign, we boarded Japanese LSTs (Landing Ship Tanks) in Inchon Harbor and sailed around to the east coast, where we steamed back and forth for five days while Navy ships and Underwater Demolition Team (UDT) men cleared our landing beach approaches of Russian-made mines. Meanwhile South Korean troops moved across the 38th Parallel through Wonsan and north to Hamhung, a rail center, in keeping with General MacArthur's dictum "to drive to the Yalu," the river bordering North Korea and China/Manchuria.

When we finally got ashore, landing in World War II-type assault waves in the event enemy were still in the area, we were greeted by big signs attesting to the fact that Bob Hope would soon put on one of his great shows at a nearby airfield. My troops got a big kick out of this. (I have since been at meetings with Bob Hope, who always reminds me that he was ashore when we landed). When we caught up to the Republic of Korea soldiers, in a wooded area south of Sudong, we effected a passage of lines, and Colonel Litzenberg put my battalion in the lead, since we had been in the rear in the previous campaign. The 2nd and 3rd Battalions were in our trace, followed by the 5th Marines, then Chesty's 1st Regiment. Actually, elements of his 1st Marines turned south from Wonsan to make sure that no bypassed enemy troops would come up behind the division as it headed north.

The mission assigned to my battalion initially was to secure the Changjin Power Plant above Chinhung-ni. I made a jeep recon. We took three jeeps with communications, interpreter, and riflemen riding shotgun, and visited a number of villages and the power plant. It was at that time being guarded by the Republic of Korean troops. My Korean Army lieutenant interpreter talked at length with villagers and reported repeatedly that Chinese soldiers were in the area. After his initial reports, I became concerned enough to want to move along to complete my travels before dark. I would instruct the lieutenant to ask precise questions so that we could move on.

He would agree, but then conduct what seemed to be endless discussions with the locals. Between villages, it would come out that he had discovered a mutual friend or relative who wanted to review family history. We finally skipped some villages in order to beat the dark.

At the power plant, the Republic of Korean soldiers introduced us to a wire cage full of Chinese. They claimed to be "volunteers." A team from MacArthur's Tokyo headquarters came to investigate and apparently accepted the "volunteer" notion to mean that there were only a few there to work with the North Koreans. In fact, the entire Chinese force was called the "Volunteer Army." This fact was confirmed to our great detriment later on as we were besieged by the Chinese.

As 1st Battalion, 7th Marines moved north, our intelligence folks told us that the Chinese Communist Fourth Field Army was crossing the Yalu River into North Korea with the mission of preventing our right flank force, Tenth Corps, from crossing into either China or Manchuria. The Eighth US Army was going up the west coast in what General MacArthur saw as a giant pincers movement, or double envelopment, to squeeze all North Korean forces (NK) together as we cleared out North Korea, in the same way we had done on the west coast of South Korea.

We noticed how happy the Republic of Korean soldiers seemed to be when we passed through them. My battalion had not gone over a couple of hundred yards when Able Company was hit by what turned out to be a 37mm antitank gun firing from high ground across the river some thousand yards north of them. Captain Dave Banks took his three rifle platoons into the high ground on the east of the river bed and Baker Company went into the high ground to the west. There was minor contact, mostly long-range machine gun fire, until dark, when the Chinese attacked in force. Of all things, an unescorted enemy tank (we normally send ours out in tank-infantry teams) came down the trail towards my command post, which was located just to the rear of Able Company. He turned on his big light. Instantly every rocket launcher in the Battalion was after him. I shouted to my recoilless rifle crews to knock out the tank! They fired, but sand bags on the tank saved it. It headed back north, and hurried out of the area. Our outpost on the road had been overrun before it could report the presence of the tank. The tank was found abandoned nearby the next day!

This brief maneuver had excited the troops, most of whom, except for the more senior officers and staff non-commissioned officers, had never been in a live fire night defensive position before. I called out to them, told them to dig in and prepare to repel all invaders, that we were going nowhere but forward tomorrow.

Able Company's mortar men and command group set up a defensive line across the field and road over to the river, and we waited for the enemy. When voices were heard to the direct front, Able Company's mortars fired an illuminating round straight over that position and it outlined four enemy moving towards my command post from the bend in the road. Someone yelled "Fire!" Three of them were killed on the spot, and the fourth was taken prisoner. My intelligence folks moved forward, and it turned out that Able Company mortar platoon leader, who had commanded the U.S. Embassy Guard in Nanking, China in '48-'49 said that they were Chinese Communists. My intelligence sergeant confirmed this, and we now knew that Chinese Communist Forces were all the way down here from the Yalu!

What we soon found out was that in addition to hitting Baker Company across the river, a third force was coming along the railroad tracks beside the river and below our positions and moving into a railroad tunnel from which to hit our rear. We spied them at first light. They were near where we had set up our six heavy water-cooled machine guns, and had a real turkey shoot as the Chinese Communist soldiers tried to head back north. Not one of them made it, and the final count was over 600 dead!

The Chinese Communist Forces continued to throw both fire and troops at Able and Baker Companies. They also went round our flank to hit my former executive officer, Major Webb Sawyer's 2nd Battalion. Sergeant James I. Poynter, a squad leader in Able Company, directed fire against the onrushing enemy. With his ranks critically depleted by casualties and he himself critically wounded as the onslaught gained momentum and the hostile forces surrounded his position, Sergeant Poynter seized his bayonet and engaged in bitter hand-to-hand combat as the breakthrough continued. Observing three machine guns closing in at a distance of twenty-five yards, he dashed from his position and, grasping hand grenades from fallen Marines, charged the emplacements in rapid succession, killing crews of two

101

and putting the other out of action before he fell, mortally wounded. He was awarded the Medal of Honor. Lieutenant Bobby Bradley was another hero of that critical battle!

Air and artillery continued to rack them up, and on the third day, we were moving north again, victors over the Chinese Communist Forces in our first encounter. And my battalion--OUR battalion--1st Battalion, 7th Regiment had performed admirably, not unlike its predecessor at Guadalcanal, when my old mentor, Chesty Puller, was its commander!

Litzenberg moved our battalion out in the approach march north to Chinhung-ni, where he could then pass the 3rd Battalion through us, which had seen the least action thus far, and also doing the same with 2nd Battalion. Division Commander General O. P. Smith, who had been Assistant Division Commander, 1st Marine Division, at Peleliu, ordered his Reconnaissance Company to check things out by jeep out to our front along the trail north. I hesitate to use the word "road," but since it was to become our ONLY source of supply, other than emergency air drop, thus our Main Supply Route (MSR), we would think of it as our only road north.

Suddenly the Reconnaissance Company radioed that they were in contact with enemy tanks! Initially they sighted one, but then quickly, too quickly, reported four hidden under brush just off the road in ditches. We had read gory stories in the press back in the States about how enemy tanks had broken through our brother Army troops down south, but it was exactly the opposite here. Not only did the reconnaissance company call in air to attack, but the rocket launcher Marines from my battalion and from the battalions behind us came running up looking for enemy tanks! While I personally felt a little "undressed" facing one enemy tank, never mind four, with my .45 caliber pistol, these young hard chargers roared up yelling "Where are the tanks!"

I had mounted my jeep and moved forward, alarmed that the tanks might shoot up my Charlie Company which was in an exposed position on the railroad just across the small river. After the "lone tank into my command post" episode just prior to this, I had armed my jeep with two land mines wrapped inside sand bags. At a very narrow spot in the road over a culvert, I posted my Marine runner with a bagged land mine with instructions to arm the mine and place it where the track would hit it if a tank came down the road. This was my final defense measure to ensure that we would not be overrun by the tanks.

After a quick look at the tank battle scene, I returned to the culvert to advise the Marine of his best escape route after he had placed the mine. He responded in a quavering voice:

"My God, Colonel, I thought you wanted me to hold the mine under the track of the tank!" Such is the ever present problem of communications in infantry combat!

Numerous after-action reports had air knocking out all four of them, the reconnaissance company doing the same, and every one of some dozen rocketeers claimed at least one each. But far better to have four tank kills multiplied than the opposite, where a force can be ruptured into bugouts when an enemy tank appears on the horizon. I was getting more and more proud of my Marines by the very minute!

I had personally observed enough of the tank action to arbitrate the claims. I assigned and reported the kills: One to air, one to recon, one each to two rocket teams. I also messaged to Regiment that I did not like to do hand-to-hand combat with tanks and asked "Where are our own tanks?" The response was that they were blocked by weak bridges.

My command post for the night following the tank kill was nearby in a ravine overlooking the Chinhung-ni Railroad Station. My rifle companies were in the surrounding hills, except for a platoon in reserve nearby. About midnight I was awakened in my command post tent by Major Tighe, my operations officer, who announced that an enemy patrol was inside the headquarters perimeter. I scrambled to pull on my pistol belt, then my boots as I instructed the radio operator to get Charlie Company mortars to fire star shells over our position so we could find and destroy the enemy group.

For the first time in my combat experience I felt the serious effects of fear: my left leg shook so much that I could hardly get my boot on. This soon subsided as I was able to get busy on the radio and with messengers to get units alerted. The enemy group was apparently after food--they got some canned rations and fled without firing a shot. Needless to say, we tightened up on local security.

Now Litz passed the other battalions through, and I sent Able Company to the west to protect that avenue of approach, and the rest of the battalion to hold Chinhung-ni. We were concerned that a horde of Chinese Communist soldiers might come charging in from the west, so it turned out that the company commander, Dave Banks, had a little sitdown with his platoon commanders and staff non-commissioned officers after he walked their lines to be sure that he had a tight hasty defense for the night. One of these lieutenants, Bill Davis (no relation), later told in his book "CHOSIN MARINE" how Banks mentally prepared his Marines for the most dire of emergencies, whereby the Chinese Communist soldiers might appear in such strength as to possibly overrun or outflank their position and move in on the

Division column.

Dave reassured them that if the Chinese Communist Forces appeared in such "numerical superiority," he would get all of "Stable Able" out of there "by going cross-country, where the Chinks just could not keep up with Marines who are now in good fighting shape." But realistically, he felt that with almost one billion Chinese in China, they could make a helluva lot of troops immediately available, especially if they thought we were going to attack their country and/or their industrial Manchuria.

But, Banks reminded them, "Remember that we have the most combat-experienced battalion commanding officer in the entire Division, Ray Davis, who received the Navy Cross at Peleliu as one of Chesty Puller's battalion commanders in the First Marines!"

"Hey, Skipper, why didn't you tell us that before?" asked Bill. "When Colonel Davis spoke to us back in Tent Camp Two, he talked about being with a Reserve Battalion in Chicago, and he had on a brand new set of utilities and a cap that was a size or two big. Hell, we all thought he was an untried Reservist who might have been seagoing in World War II and not known anything about combat on land. And here he already has been a battalion commander in combat, with--and Marines always pause before saying HIS name--Chesty Puller, the Marine's Marine!"

Well, I never even thought of it. I wore hastily acquired utilities because I needed some replacements, having been on Guam in my last tour in the Fleet Marine Force, before going to Chicago, and those old utilities were so faded they almost looked like whites. And as for Chesty, I knew that Marines thought the world of him--as do I--he had four Navy Crosses by now, but I'm not normally a namedropper, and besides, many of my peers had also served with Puller over the years. But as I think of it now, it is a good idea for a unit commander on any level to reassure his troops by any means available that he is qualified by experience to be their leader. If he is a brand new 2nd lieutenant, he can run them into the ground physically and knows he is well-educated and trained from his Basic School days, so he'll lead them with confidence. That Marine private/private first class needs all the reassurance he can get as he waits in his foxhole, preparing himself mentally and physically for hordes of North Koreans or Chinese Communists he has heard about, and just seen back in Sudong in our battalion's first real fight.

In the same vein, as Battalion commanding officer I appreciated the fact that my commander, "Litz the Blitz," was a well-thought-of battalion commander in World War II; and that my subordinate commanders, like Dave Banks, was a good machine gun platoon commander in the Pacific; my former executive officer, Buzz Sawyer was a hardcharging rifle company commander then, and my other senior officers and staff non-commissioned officers were World War II-experienced. And I'm lucky it was so, since the bulk of our troops were Reservists with lots of spirit, but not too much infantry background prior to boarding USS OKANOGAN. Conversely, after Captain Mutt Emils, Commanding Charlie Company, got hit in the lung back in the Inchon-Seoul Campaign, I kept a little tighter watch on the company and the Reservist I put in as his successor. So I understand what my folks meant by my first pep talk with them. In this Corps, we all keep learning, every day--and night.

Actually, things were pretty quiet for our battalion, but the 3rd battalion had a rough firefight in taking the high ground near the power station and bridge over a deep gorge on the way up to the plateau and a town named Koto-ri, which would be very important in 1st Marine Division's operations about a month from now. Before we went up the mountain on our Marine Corps Birthday, 10 November, it was quiet enough for me to go swimming/bathing in the nearby river--even though the water was a trifle cold for a guy from Atlanta!

On our second or third day up on the plateau at Koto-ri, the Siberian winds struck, lowering the temperatures suddenly to 16 below zero. Vehicles died, everything froze, troops were frostbitten. It took two days to recover (added clothing, heaters, warming tents, antifreeze) before we were prepared to move north again.

Meanwhile, a Chinese soldier surrendered to one of our hilltop outposts; he was near frozen and very hungry. My S-2 (Intelligence) section took him in tow, kept him in a warm tent, fed him, and kept him zipped up in a sleeping bag. He was so pleased that he volunteered to go out and bring in his entire unit. I thought it worth a try and approved. One of our patrols took him up and released him near where he said his unit was and watched him move away. Soon there were shots fired, and it was assumed that his comrades had killed him. He never returned!

Except for this action, after 3rd battalion had cleared out the Chinese Communists enroute to Koto, they seemed to disappear. We spent most of our time patrolling, trying to make contact, usually with a reinforced rifle platoon, and covering dangerous areas with artillery fire mixed in with a lot of air support. We were fortunate enough to have four Marine aircraft on station above us from dawn to dusk. And longer, when my Battalion Air Officer, Captain Danny Holland, Naval Aviator from the same squadron, would keep them around as long as they could make out enemy gun flashes in the dark. One time later (as we were breaking out of Yudam-ni), when a flight leader told Danny he'd see him tomorrow at first light, and we were in a heavy firefight, Danny told him: "You stick around up there till I let you go , Pardner (everyone was Pardner to Danny), or I'll tell your wife (who knew Danny well--since they were from that same squadron) what a no-good bastard you really are!" Needless to say, those four aircraft remained on station until Danny expended their loads and then told them to go home to rearm and return.

The division plan now seemed to be taking form: The 7th Marines moved up to the town of Hagaru-ri, at the southern tip of the Reservoir--our Japanese maps called it Chosin; Koreans called it Changjin--and then the 7th Marines would move out to the west of Chosin and Ray Murray's 5th Marines would check out the situation to the east of Chosin. Our Intelligence Reports were bringing in grim information of the 8th Army situation to the west, and General Smith did not want his Division to be too badly dispersed, or surprised by large elements of Chinese Communist Forces from any direction.

Litz decided to send our battalion out to seize, occupy and defend Yudam-ni, a small town at the western tip of the Chosin, and then move in the rest of the 7th Regiment to set up a perimeter defense. With that accomplished Division would move the 5th Marines on through to feel out the enemy situation to the west, where we would eventually turn up toward the Yalu River, or continue west to link up with friendly forces of the 8th Army.

My troops felt a little down in that we moved out on the last Thursday of November, our traditional Thanksgiving Day. We moved through Toktong Pass, which would later be very important in our combat lives, without incident, and seized the high ground south of the town of Yudam-ni. Then we held up for the night on both sides of the main supply route, and at my request, Litz let us hold up in place for 24 hours, and said he would send up the fixings for us to celebrate Thanksgiving Day on Friday. The troops were overjoyed, though I just could not see how the cooks could pull it off for us, as cold as it was. Winds coming down from Siberia had lowered the temperature to -18 degrees Fahrenheit. Remember that we did not talk about the wind chill factor back in 1950, but it finally got down into the low -20s, and some say -30s, to what would now be a wind chill factor of -70 degrees! The very thought of that chills my native Georgia blood even now!

The duty cook announced that the turkeys could not be cooked. After a powwow with all of the mess crew, we designed an innovative solution: Two tents were erected one over the other for double thickness; two stoves were fixed up inside and the frozen turkeys were stacked around the stoves in the sealed tents. By rotating the stacks, the birds thawed enough to cook. However, one false report flawed the turkey feast. I was told that "all units have been fed" and some turkey remained. We passed it around to nearby units; I even had an extra leg myself. Then came a report that a platoon on outpost had not eaten. I felt totally ashamed, but we were able to find some turkey and a lot of shrimp to boil for them. This was to be the last good meal for 1st Battalion, 7th Marines for the next ten days.

There was one strange happening on our first night at what became, in Marine parlance, "Turkey Hill." At about midnight, a heavy volume of enemy fire came in our direction from west of the nearby valley. It continued for a full ten minutes; then silence for the rest of the night. We scrambled to get mortars and artillery going, but suddenly discovered that the enemy projectiles were all landing in the next valley just south of us. The Chinese scouts or map readers favored us with a faulty calculation. Our blackout discipline really paid off! No one was hit!

The ironic part of our Turkey Day celebration is that we fed the troops in a deep gulley just south of "Turkey Hill," and a few days later, my Charlie Company would be trapped in this same gulley when Chinese Communist soldiers streamed down this hill in a horde.

But I'm getting ahead of my situation. When we went into the high ground to the southwest and west of Yudam-ni, and 2nd and 3rd Battalions moved in to form the perimeter, with the Reservoir as our eastern flank, I sent Able Company on a long-range patrol to the southwest, where air reported enemy troops moving from hut to hut in a small farmers' village. To give them heavier firepower, I sent along a couple of our Battalion's 81mm mortars, primarily to see if they could keep up with the infantry while carrying their heavier loads. Also, we were discovering that when it snowed hard, plus the intense cold, artillery was having difficulty in completing fire missions. I've always been a believer that a Marine rifle company of some 200-plus troops, within artillery range of that Artillery Battalion supporting its parent infantry regiment, could never be overrun. But with temporary failure of communications, due to snow and cold, the 81s might prove of great value on the trail with that company--if they could keep up.

Able Company had solved this problem somewhat with its own "Company commander's weapon of opportunity" its 60mm mortars. It had some rugged Reserves from Seattle who had been telephone linemen pre-Marine Corps. They kept the normal three-piece, 42-pound

60 mortar in one piece on the gunner's back/pack. As soon as the company received incoming mortar or artillery fire, the gunner plopped his 60 mm in place, and immediately responded to his platoon commander's fire directions towards the source of incoming rounds. Even if they could not see their target, the rapid return of fire gave the enemy the impression that they were under observation, which usually resulted in immediate cessation of the enemy fire.

Unfortunately, on this patrol, Able Company ran into a tough firefight, and its First Platoon Commander, First Lieutenant Frank Mitchell of Roaring Springs, Texas, who was to have received a Silver Star Medal from Litz the next day as a result of his fine actions at Sudong, was KIA (Killed In Action). An enemy unit advanced with a white flag to supposedly surrender, and Frank ordered a cease fire, then moved forward to take them in. When the enemy suddenly opened fire, Frank covered the withdrawal of his Marines, many of whom were wounded. He fired a Browning Automatic Rifle, an M-1 rifle, his .45 pistol, and threw hand grenades until he was shot to death by this numerically superior force. Frank was awarded the Medal of Honor for his heroic actions. Able Company reported to me by radio, then pulled back under cover of darkness, carrying several wounded in action on stretchers. It was tough going uphill in the ice and snow, but proved to be a good rehearsal for our oncoming trek to Toktong.

Meanwhile, as Dog and Easy Companies, 2nd Battalion, 7th Marines moved into position north of Yudam-ni, they came under heavy attack by waves of Chinese. Their situation turned desperate soon after dark. Regiment called and asked me to give them support, and assigned them to my operational control. Communications were difficult; I was not fully aware of their situation or their precise deployment. A shortage of small arms ammunition was their expressed prime concern.

I was able to bring more artillery and mortar fire to support them, and sent a jeep convoy with ammunition with my operations officer, Major Tom Tighe, in charge. He was able to contact the units and deliver ammunition to unit carrying parties. I wanted to send reinforcements, but my companies were deployed in defensive positions out in the hills or involved in the extraction of Able Company from its long patrol. By the time I had some units available for possible relief of Dog and Easy Companies, reports from them indicated that they were holding their position, and that regiment had sent relief..

After debriefing Gene Hovatter, Dave Banks' successor as commander of Able Company,

I sent Baker company down the next day to see how much of a threat this incoming force was to our position at Yudam-ni. Unfortunately, the enemy was still there in strength, as Captain Wilcox, Commander of Baker Company, found out when he was shot in the mouth while talking to me on the radio! I ordered Baker Company to break contact and to return to its defensive positions in the battalion line across the southwest approaches to Yudam-ni. Baker Company was obviously hurt and a long way from home. I got permission from Regiment to take Charlie Company out to meet them and help them back. We moved quickly to Turkey Hill and established closer contact with Captain Wilcox's command group. We fired mortar illumination rounds to mark the way through the mountains and used truck lights to guide them into our position. We loaded their casualties, including Commander, B Company, Captain Wilcox, onto a truck convoy going to Hagaru.

While it was relatively quiet in Yudam-ni, Litz ordered my Charlie Company to remain on Turkey Hill to protect the main supply route leading into Yudam from Hagaru. Unfortunately, they got into position just before dark. With darkness came many, many Chinese Communist soldiers. Apparently our troops climbing from the main supply route through Turkey Gulch up onto Turkey Hill in the darkness met Chinese coming down the hill. Result: Charlie Company was quickly surrounded and needed to be extricated as soon as possible.

Much the same had happened to Fox Company of 2nd Battalion, 7th Marines which was a few miles south in the Toktong Pass area, through which the main supply route from Hagaru passed. Litz wanted my First Battalion to get them both out as soon as possible. It was to extricate C Company, then move a few miles further south to save Fox Company.

My plan was to move out after first light, with Able Company going up into the high ground leading to Turkey Hill, while my command group and Baker Company moved along the main supply route ready to move up the gulch into the Charlie Company positions, when Able Company had seized the high ground overlooking it. This worked well, since Able company had moved down this same terrain when we moved into Yudam-ni originally. Thus, their machine gunners and mortar men knew the exact distances to the enemy positions on Turkey Hill, which enabled them to put highly accurate fire on the Chinese Communists with their first rounds.

We were slowed down by many, many Chinese in that position, which, coupled with the intense cold, stalled the attack and Able Company did not gain the high ground overlooking

Charlie Company until just before dark.

Charlie Company casualties were severe. Many of the wounded had been carried down to their company warming tents from the hill position. In the dark it was difficult to move the casualties over the rough terrain to the trucks we had assembled at the turnaround. We used a few truck lights in an effort to hurry the process. Prolonged delays would increase chances of a Chinese reaction.

I climbed upon a boulder to better supervise and to keep the carrying parties moving. Years later, one of the truck drivers, Lou Tragas, told my wife Knox this tale: As Lou's truck pulled into the turnaround to load casualties, he was directed to turn on his lights. A fog was coming in and his lights covered the area near the boulder upon which I was standing. Lou asked a member of my command group who was standing on the rock? "That's the old man, Colonel Davis," he was told. Lou responded: "Look there in the fog; he has a halo overhead. I know now that we will all get out of here." Lou told that to everyone nearby that night. Providence on our side?

It turned out to be several hours after dark before we got all Charlie Company survivors out and down to the trucks on the main supply route. By then it was much too late for my First Battalion to move out along the main supply route and hit the Chinese Communist soldiers surrounding Fox Company. Fox Company Commander, Captain Barber radioed that he could hold if artillery and air kept supporting him, a classic example of my contention that a Marine rifle company under our artillery fan could not be overrun. Thus, I recommended to Litz that my battalion return to Yudam-ni, and come up with another plan to extricate Fox Company from its rapidly deteriorating position at Toktong Pass.

After we returned, Litz wanted to reinforce my battalion with troops from other battalions, which sounded good initially, but my experience told me that control would be far better if I worked with my three rifle companies that I knew well by now, even if it cut down the numbers available to me.

Meanwhile, MacArthur had passed the word to pull back all U.N. forces. This was fortunate since Yudam-ni had been hit hard the very night that Ray Murray's 5th Marines had arrived by truck and moved into positions to the northwest and north. The thought of moving out in the attack the next morning seemed a little optimistic at best. That night the Chinese Communists had moved many divisions around Yudam and hit all elements along the perimeter in great strength, and in many cases seemed to break through rifle company

110

lines. It was hard to tell the precise situation: enemy and friendly fire, whistles, bugles, reports of enemy on horseback, grenades coming in and going out, plus our wonderful artillery power entering the fray whenever it appeared some company was about to be overrun.

The next day the Chinese Communist soldiers sat back and pumped in both artillery and mortars on Marines who could not dig in anything but mini-foxholes in that icy ground, while we planned how to carry out MacArthur's order. General Smith had two-thirds of his infantry power right there at Yudam-ni, with Chesty's three infantry battalions strung along behind us: 1st Regiment's 3rd Battalion defending Hagaru (and General Smith's command post); 2nd Battalion defending Koto (and Chesty's command post); and 1st Battalion below The Pass, whose bridge over the gorge and abreast the power station, had been damaged severely, and might not hold our vehicles. Plus, the Chinese Communist soldiers were believed to hold the high ground to the south. That is the same high ground which 7th Regiment's 3rd Battalion fought so tenaciously to secure weeks before on the way up from Chinhung-ni to the plateau at Koto-ri.

It was midday when Litz sent for me. He had just moved his command post south of Yudam-ni close to mine. He was most concerned about Fox Company, described the efforts from Hagaru and his own to get to them. "Nothing works," he said, referring to four prior efforts. "You have got to get to them. Come back here in twenty minutes with a plan."

I had been over the road and around the area enough to know that a road approach was hopeless. I proposed a bold dash over the ridges to high ground overlooking Fox from the north. I would streamline the battalion, leaving with the regimental train all vehicles, all wounded, and disabled, half my heavy mortars and heavy machine guns, all supplies and equipment not to be carried by the troops. Gun crews were doubled up; ammunition was strapped to litters; men carried spare mortar or rocket rounds in their big parka pockets; some carried extra belts of machine gun bullets. We carried one hand-crank ANGRC-9 radio, because our battery-powered sets were dead, with rare exception.

Litz said: "Plan approved! Go!" He had How Company launch an attack at our breakout point to get us a head start. We moved out early afternoon, with Able Company moving up to assist How Company in the breakout at Turkey Hill. Litzenberg and Murray would move their regiments toward Toktong Pass when we had broken out. It was dark before we could destroy all the defenders on Turkey Hill, with B Company joining in the fray.

As we reorganized in the dark, the cold wind struck. Artillery in the valley was report-

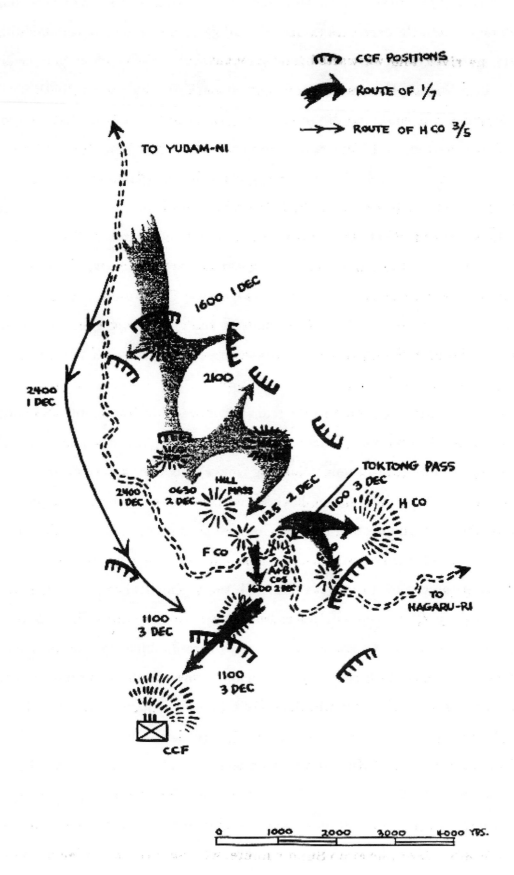

TO YUDAM-NI

1600 1 DEC

2100

2400
1 DEC

2400
1 DEC

0630
2 DEC

HILL
PASS

1135 2 DEC

TOKTONG PASS

1100 3 DEC

H CO

F CO

AMB
COS

1600 2 DEC

TO
HAGARU-RI

1100
3 DEC

1100
3 DEC

CCF

0   1000   2000   3000   4000 YDS.

Our attack from Yudam-ni to Toktong Pass to rescue Fox Company ing -24 degrees; in the wind on our mountain top it could have been 75 degrees below zero wind chill. We would freeze if we did not move. I got down into a Chinese gunpit with a map, compass, and flashlight, under a poncho, to plot our route. Getting up out of the hole, I lost my bearings and could not reconstruct what I had done while in the hole. It was that numbing cold. Another try with a staff member determined an azimuth. And the Lord God somehow brightened a star precisely in the direction we were to move towards Fox company. Providence again?

Off we went in single file through the snow without security elements out front or on the flanks. Aircraft had reported few enemy detected where we were going, and with dead radios, we could not control security units in any event. As lead elements compacted the snow, ice sheets were formed which caused units in the rear to grasp twigs and roots or to crawl on hands and knees to keep going forward.

With their bedrolls, ground cover, extra clothing, extra ammunition, three days' rations, the troops were overloaded indeed. Each chose their own rations. I chose dry crackers, reinforced chocolate bars, and small cans of fruit. Everything was frozen, including the canteens. Canned rations could be eaten only if carried inside clothing against the warm body for several hours. Small cans thawed much faster. The experts who said snow would do to drink, never tried it for three days with dry crackers and chocolate bars. The thirst was nearly unbearable.

A crisis situation soon developed. As lead elements traversed the ridges, they would lose sight of the bright star and drift down the ridge finger toward the south. They moved closer and closer to prearranged artillery barrage targets--dangerously close. I passed the word "Stop the column!" Nothing happened! I sent a runner to stop them. Still nothing!

In desperation, I took my radio operator (Roy Pearl) and a runner and we beat a parallel track toward the head of the column. I checked as we moved out; with hoods over heads and ice over their faces, it was no wonder that the word-passing failed. I found my runner a few yards up the column. A non-commissioned officer stopped him because he was making too much noise. I was cursed for the same thing, then knocked to the ground by a leader hurrying back to his unit in the opposite direction!

(Note: At a reunion some years later after Chosin, an old veteran came to me to confess: "I'm the guy you have been looking for these past years. I'm the one who called you a son-of-a-bitch for making so much noise. I'm ready for my punishment." His punishment was a warm handshake and embrace.).

When people ask me to describe just what happened on the Trek to Toktong, truthfully I am at a loss for detailed information on the step-by-step sequence. My mind was so numbed by the cold that when I did get my commanders together for a talk when the battalion literally dropped from exhaustion about halfway to Fox, I made them repeat to me what I had said to them about what we were going to do when we moved into Fox Company's perimeter. I could not remember what I had just said to them, and I wanted to make sure that we were all "on the same frequency." Perhaps if I had been a son of Minnesota rather than Georgia, years of snow and skiing and skating would have made me more adaptable to this tremendous cold weather, but friends in the Corps later told me that such is not the case: Minus 70 degrees Wind Chill is just too cold for any government work, no matter what state or town you come from.

While the Battalion rested in a circle of troops, officers and staff non-commissioned officers ran small patrols to maintain alert sentinels. We did receive much incoming rifle fire over our prostrated heads, but I ordered the men not to return the fire in the belief that the Chinese Communists in the high ground between us and the Main Supply Road did not really see us. They were keeping up their own frozen morale by firing out to their direct front, but did not really see us. However, I have never been able to understand how they could have kept from hearing us, with our assorted moans and groans, and crying out from occasional rifle rounds that hit into Marine parkas and soft Marine flesh. Possibly those Siberian winds masked our sounds at great distance?

We established our first contact with Regiment with the hand-crank radio. I asked Regiment to tell Fox Company where we were and that we would not attempt to establish contact until first light. Then I took a round through my parka hood, grazing my forehead and a piece of shrapnel bounced off my helmet that grim night, but other than that, all seemed relatively well. After two hours or so, the troops had gained newfound strength from their much-needed nap, like a short break on the bench in the middle of a tough T-Day high school football game, and they were ready to move out again towards Fox.

Now that we were about a mile from that position, my radioman motioned that he had contact with Captain Bill Barber, Commander of Fox Company, who brought tears to my eyes when he volunteered to send a patrol out to lead us into his position. Obviously, from where he was inside the perimeter, Bill could not see that there were Chinese Communist soldiers in all of the 360 degrees around him. We knew where he was, and we would fight our way in, I told him. Then I thanked him and told him that we were on our way.

His artillery officer set up fires around their perimeter except for one entry area. Barber's air officer--we had no radio contact with Marine air--guaranteed strafing fires to accompany us, and my battalion moved out on the final phase of accomplishing its hazardous, ice-bound mission! The Chinese withdrew when we approached from their rear.

Throughout this lengthy ordeal on a mission which only they thought could succeed, I heard not one complaint from my troops. What motivated them? First, Marines were in trouble and we would rescue them. Then some of the units in our formation had themselves been rescued on prior days and were enroute to return the favor. Marines know that they can rely on other Marines.

My battalion, 7th Regiment's 1st Battalion, had matured. Over several days, units had rescued and supported one another under the most severe of combat situations. They had no peers, and they felt it!

One of the first questions I am always asked about entering Fox' perimeter is what Bill Barber and I said to each other at this relatively historic meeting. I suppose I could have asked "Captain Barber, I presume?" in keeping with another meeting of note, but I honestly cannot recall exactly what we both said. While I know Bill well now, I had never seen him before Fox Hill. We met with a warm hand shake, emotional words were exchanged, and then it was on to business!

Barber was crippled by his wounds; he spent much time on a stretcher. He described his immediate situation; we agreed on my battalion strengthening his positions. One immediate problem was an errant air drop, much of which went outside the Fox perimeter. The drop aircraft were lucky to find us at all with the low clouds and blinding snow. We got busy on plans to retrieve as much as we could.

My major concern soon became the security of the main force from Yudam-ni. I wanted to ensure that no pockets of enemy would fire on them as they came near Toktong Pass. After my units were dispatched to various points in the pass, I directed that many small fires be started throughout the new perimeter. This was designed to attract any enemy forces nearby in the hope that they would expose themselves. We could then destroy them before the main force arrived.

After we extended Fox Company's original perimeter and killed any Chinese in the area,

I divided my battalion into two attack forces: Hovatter's Able Company and Kurcaba's Baker Company under my Operations Officer, Major Tom Tighe, and Morris' Charlie Company and Newton's How Company under my control to accomplish two missions: (1) To clear the finger ridges projecting towards Hagaru, and (2) To clear the hill mass on both sides of the pass. Naturally, with the separate actions going on, both of these plans plus the security of the perimeter and the approach of the main force from the north, I could not leave the command post inside the perimeter. Stories that I personally led the second force were just not accurate. I directed them from my command post.

While walking along the perimeter positions, we discovered movement of a sizable force extending southward. We could see Chinese Communist Forces crews pulling machine guns on two-wheel carts. Maybe this force was coming our way in response to all the smoke from my small fires, or possibly in response to the 5th Marine movement along the road from Yudam. In any event, those machine guns could do a lot of damage.

Since Tom Tighe had the second effort, that of clearing the hill mass on both sides of Toktong, he was ordered to attack the approaching column. He moved towards them immediately. Meanwhile, I called Litzenberg to alert him to the danger. As Tighe launched his attack, the Chinese, apparently surprised, fled. Litz was immediately told about this.

Later I heard that Hal Williamson's How Company of the 5th Marines trapped them.

Apparently there was a Litzenberg/Murray/Taplett (Commander, 5th Regiment's 3rd Battalion) conversation on this subject also. I never had direct contact with Lieutenant Colonel Taplett until later when his unit arrived at the Fox Hill position.

My battalion entered Fox perimeter on 2 December, and the parallel effort by the 5th Marines along the main supply route from Yudam-ni reached our position and tied in with us at 1300, 3 December. In late November I had walked that tortuous road on the way up to Yudam-ni. With my troops on both sides of that deep valley, it was a slow move, and at all times I felt exposed to long range fire from many positions throughout those hills, and at that time we had no defenders to overcome.

With known defenders I did not on 1 December give the road approach to Fox Company's position any serious thought; over the hills the way we went seemed to be the only way for a fast move--and it was. Even after we arrived at Fox, it took another day for the 5th Marines to break through on the road. Without our efforts in the pass area it could have taken them much longer. I am firmly convinced that the parallel effort of the 5th on the main supply route and my battalion cross country was for the best!

As 5th Regiment's 3rd Battalion approached our position, I watched the oncoming tank (D23) from a high point just outside the perimeter, about 50 yards from and above the main supply route. I moved down the road to meet the tank. Commander of 3rd Battalion, 5th Marine, Lieutenant Colonel Taplett and I reviewed our situation leaning on the back end of the tank. I don't recall that, as later reported, Taplett wanted to pass through and lead the way to Hagaru. None of us knew it was to be a "free ride."

Further, my clearing efforts had positioned lead units well beyond the pass towards Hagaru. Much valuable time would have been wasted if we had stood by for Taplett to work his deployed, tired troops through us. I can't believe that anyone gave that a thought. As it was, a short message to my companies got us moving toward Hagaru. Charlie and How Companies were to hold their positions overlooking the main supply route until the rest of my battalion passed, then join the tail of our column.

I should note here that after my battalion reached Fox Company and I launched my companies to clear the pass and nearby hills of enemy, I did participate in a three-way radio talk with Litzenberg and Murray. Murray wanted me to send a force back towards Yudam-ni "to ease the pressure on his units on the road." I objected on the basis that "my orientation was in the other direction" in efforts to clean out high fingers extending toward Hagaru. Litz commented that any move on my part towards Murray's units "would complicate the situation on the road." He did not approve.

Back to the column, which now included not only Fox and my battalion, but the remainder of the 7th Marines, plus the 5th Marines. In a brief few moments, my full attention was shifted from the complex problems of Fox Hill and the pass area to movement of the major portion of the 1st Marine Division into Hagaru! With all of those Marine units behind me, a bold rapid plunge down the road seemed to be in order. So off we went! Even when the tank had trouble traversing a bad spot on the road, we moved on without it.

Well down the road, Litz' executive officer, Fred Dowsett, on foot, caught up with me. Out of breath, he said: "You're a hard man to catch." We paused while he relayed orders from Regiment for placing two company security outposts on nearby hills. This led to a problem for Charlie Company being placed on outpost with radios not functioning. Realize that in every large fighting unit, one of its elements seems to be a "hard-luck outfit." Charlie Company had been surrounded back at Turkey Hill, suffered many casualties, was low in

Ray Davis, CPL Seifert, SGT Payne, Col. Homer Ltzenberg

With Colonel Homer Litzenberg (center) and my executive, Buzz Sawyer, 1951

Lieutenant General Shepherd, Commanding General, Fleet Marine Force, Pacific,
Major General Thomas, Commanding General, 1st Marine Division, Ray Davis,
Executive Officer, 7th Marine Regiment

Don Williams

Charcoal drawing from photograph, "At Chosin," 1950

War bond Sales Poster, 1952

Wife, Knox, with daughter, Willa Kay, born during the
Chosin battles, 1950

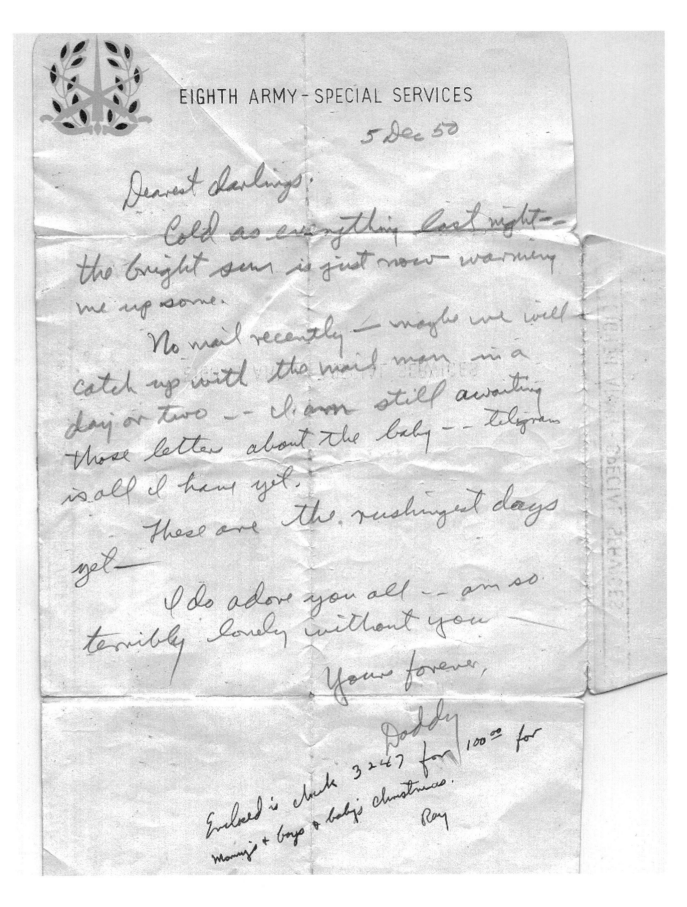

EIGHTH ARMY - SPECIAL SERVICES

5 Dec 50

Dearest darlings,

Cold as everything last night — the bright sun is just now warming me up some.

No mail recently — maybe we will catch up with the mail man in a day or two — I am still awaiting those letter about the baby — Telegram is all I have yet.

These are the rushingest days yet —

I do adore you all — am so terribly lonely without you —

Your forever,

Daddy

Enclosed is check 3247 for $100.00 for Mommy + boys + baby's christmas.

Ray

A typical letter home to Knox during Chosin Battles, 1950

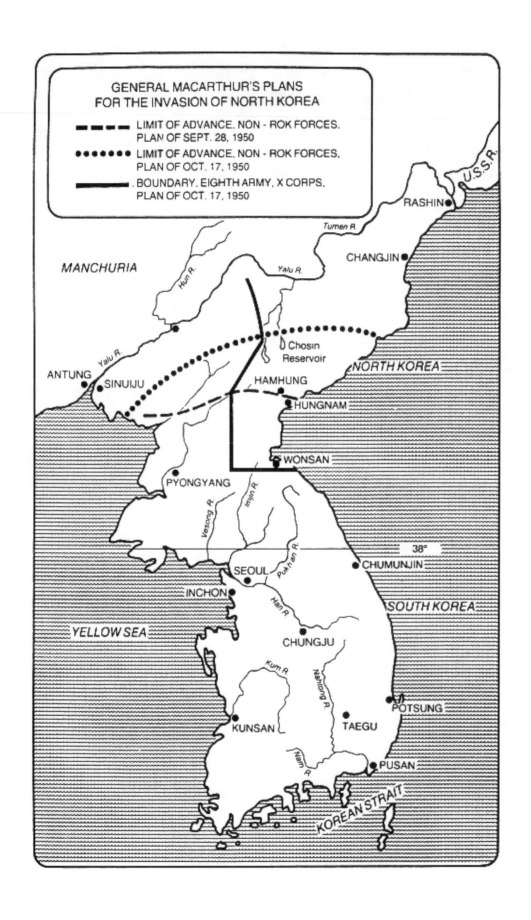

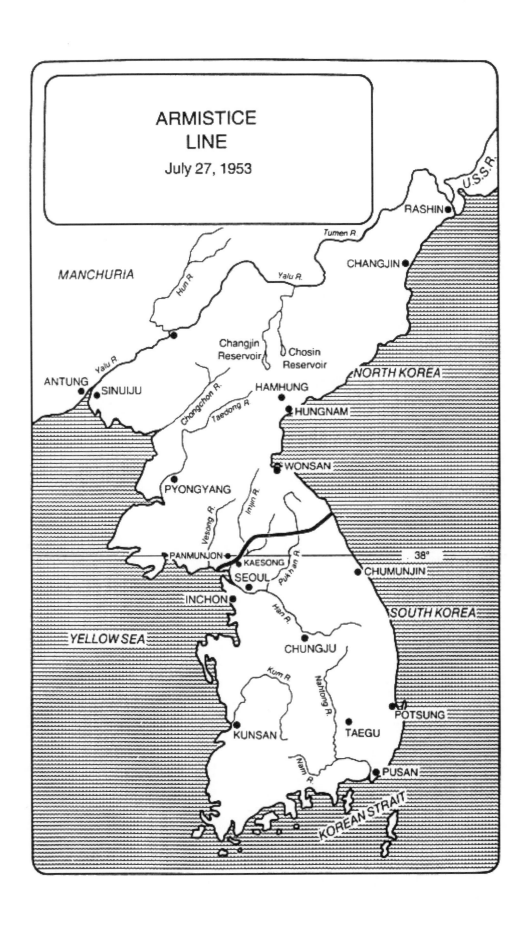

ARMISTICE
LINE
July 27, 1953

numbers when we started out to extract Fox. They lost some superior company commanders early on: "Mutt" Emils above Seoul; "Red" Shea had a severe foot problem at Turkey Hill. John Morris, who joined a company with depleted ranks, worked hard to hold things together, but once a unit is really hurt, its reduced strength makes it less effective, so it is much easier hurt.

Following its order, Charlie too soon abandoned its security mission as flank guard on its hill to join the tail of the column. Since their radios were dead, a long break in the column misled them and they erroneously concluded that the column they were protecting had passed. That is why the column was later fired on from positions Charlie had abandoned, and artillery pieces were lost needlessly.

As Dowsett and I moved along the Main Supply Road, two Marines from my Command Group discovered some enemy moving on the far side of the valley. My reaction was to "give them a few shots." Even though they were obviously out of range, and there were only a couple of them, I knew this was a chance for the Headquarters Marines to shoot at enemy.

However, I did not count on the sudden appearance of the Regimental commanding officer. He said: "Have those men cease fire--those people are too far off." I stopped the shooting and told Litz that the Headquarters Marines needed to shoot at enemy now and then. He shrugged as if in half agreement as I moved away from him on down the main supply route.

A comment on Litzenberg: He and I seemed to have developed a deep mutual respect by this time. I knew his tactics were well-considered and solid, and that he would see them through with whatever support was required. He would also listen to reasonable suggestions or ideas. On the other hand, he let me run my battalion; asked valid questions at times, but supported my position almost 100 percent. This minor event illustrated another aspect of our relationship. Whereas early on he might have yelled at my Marines to "cease fire," he now appreciated the fact that these were MY Marines so he addressed me to stop them from firing. Probably, if I had pressed the point, he might have let them get off a few more rounds.

Having said this, let me hasten to add that when I got orders from the commanding officer, 7th Marines, they were accepted without question. If the situation changed, I knew I could get a full hearing if I wanted changed instructions.

As we approached Hagaru, Dowsett and I walked briskly forward overtaking the lead rifle company. As Stonewall Jackson always did, we were in effect "marching to the sound of the guns." Closing in on Hagaru could get complicated if some defensive unit failed to get the word of our arrival. I needed to be up there if there was to be trouble. By the time we came in close contact with the Hagaru friendlies, we were with the leading rifle platoon. I addressed the lead troops deployed along the road: "Let's go in like Marines; shape up and stand tall." Others joined in. I think Dowsett said a few words. Marines, officers and non-commissioned officers, responded so that by the time we reached the friendlies, they were "parade ground."

Plans were quickly drawn for the further movement of our forces out of Hagaru down to the coast. I received orders that my battalion would provide flank security for the road to Koto-ri by traversing the mountain range which overlooked the main supply route from the west. We would depart from the outposts south of Hagaru at 0400 and seize the nearby hills before the main body departed Hagaru over the road.

A delay in the issuance of ammunition moved our departure back to 0430, but fortunately for us, our lead elements found a Chinese strong point asleep atop our first objective just at daylight. Had they been alert, we would have been badly hurt as we traversed an open area just below their strongpoint position. The quick elimination of this large enemy group left my battalion unopposed for the remainder of our mission enroute to Koto-ri.

As the skies cleared, we detected a large force of Chinese deployed in a crosscorridor depression several hundred yards ahead of our leading elements on the road below. I agreed to spot fires for 81mm mortar crews as they adjusted on this lucrative target. We bracketed the target quickly and fired five rounds for effect from three mortar tubes. Tragically, the rounds walked away from the enemy positions We repeated the process with, again, similar results! It was then discovered that the mortar baseplates were not holding in the icy ground, thereby dispersing the rounds. We returned to single round adjustment and scored enough direct hits to cause the enemy to abandon the position. With this major opposition eliminated, the leading Marine forces moved out smartly toward Koto-ri.

As the roadbound forces began to outdistance us on the icy mountain trails, our security role was canceled, and we were called down from the high ground. As we moved down a snow-covered slope toward the main supply route, we were "discovered" by a friendly tank unit which took us under fire. The cannon projectiles missed us by a wide margin, but the entire area was strafed by tank machine gun fire. I personally observed a dozen rounds in the snow within a few yards of my command group. The firing stopped suddenly as my radio operator, Roy Pearl, reported that he had managed to shift to the tanks' tactical frequency. Pearl said to the tanks: "You are shooting at friendlies!" The response was: "Oh, my God!-- CEASE FIRE! CEASE FIRE!" Pearl authenticated his call, and it was all over. Again, God was good to lst Battalion, 7th Marines; with hundreds of rounds fired at us, not one casualty resulted. Roy Pearl was a true and fearless professional who always came through in crisis situations.

Near the base of the mountain, we encountered a 15-foot vertical drop. Posting two Marines at the top helped lower troopers as far as they could reach. At the bottom of the drop, others were posted to get the dropped Marines up and out of the way. Even though heavy laden and landing in snow which was soon packed hard, no one was seriously hurt.

One more problem was encountered: As we approached the forces on the road, a number of rifles were fired by friendlies in our direction. One bullet pierced my clothing at my right hip to graze the skin, but again my luck held. No casualties as loud distress calls got the firing stopped. Once we reached the road, the walk into Koto-ri was uneventful.

While in the mountain security role, I had received word that the Regimental executive officer, Lieutenant Colonel Fred Dowsett, had been wounded. This resulted in my assignment to Regiment in his place, where I was to serve for the remainder of my tour in Korea. As we reentered Koto-ri from the north, it mentally brought me back to when we first entered it from the south back in early November, a full month earlier:

Back then as we approached from the south Colonel Litzenberg had displaced his command post out of the town because I told him I could not guarantee the security of that area. Then I found my own command post established in the railroad station! We remained there one night, although I conducted emergency displacement drills on the basis that our installation was an obvious target, and we were very vulnerable. (I had an alternate command post nearby). No doubt was left in the minds of my staff that future command post locations would not sacrifice security for comfort!

It was good to see my old friend and mentor Chesty Puller there in his command post in Koto-ri. He welcomed me as an old friend. Since I no longer had a battalion to care for, I could spend some time with Chesty. With his 1st Marines in charge of security for Koto-ri, we all relaxed and prepared for the next move toward the sea.

My immediate chore was to displace the 7th Marines' Regimental command post to a position on the outskirts of Koto in the direction in which we were to launch attacks to seize the area of the destroyed bridge at the power plant below Koto-ri. We shared a tent with an Army unit--the biggest tent I had ever seen in combat. It was from this location that the secret message went over the radio for Buzz Sawyer, who had taken over my lst Battalion command, to "take Moses down the mountains!" (Marine Engineer named Moses was at the bridge).

As the airdropped bridge spans were put into place and the truck columns started to roll down The Pass, my personal mission became one of expediter, to keep the column moving. I was aware from other operations that some truck drivers were not as aggressive nor innovative as they might be and were just content to sit back and wait. We needed to get the main portion of our forces down through the pass before dark. This meant that no delays could be tolerated.

Anytime the column would stop, I would rush to the point of trouble. One problem was a small stream which had to be forded at a precise point to avoid some deep holes. This bottleneck was fixed by posting Marines on both sides of the stream to keep vehicles on the narrow negotiable track. At another point a truck with a broken axle was pushed over a cliff by a dozen Marines. Other stalled vehicles were pushed aside. Walking back and forth using staff officers and runners, I was soon able to report that the regimental column had cleared The Pass!

At the bottom of the pass, I was greeted by Colonel Edward Snedeker, Deputy Division Chief of Staff. He explained the situation quickly and asked for my help. He had posted guides who directed all vehicles and their riders to continue down the road to the twin city of Hungnam and Hamhung. All walking troops were directed to a nearby railroad yard to entrain for the trip.

The separation of vehicles from the foot column disrupted unit organization, particularly when command vehicles were involved. The result was a milling "mob" of troops estimated at about 800 in number. They were to be loaded on to small flat cars of Korean trains which were shuttling back and forth to the coast, some 20 miles away. The loading was too slow for Colonel Snedeker whose goal was to get everyone moved out before dark. U.S. Army forces were providing security for the area, but night attacks were anticipated from any of the many Chinese forces in the immediate area. Snedeker directed me "to get the waiting train loaded and get it moving at once!"

I walked among the troops looking at ice-covered faces under the parka hoods over their heads until I found enough officers and non-commissioned officers I knew to post one on each railroad car to get it loaded. This was working well until across the way a Sergeant opened tent flaps and called out: "Candy! Anyone want candy?" He and his tent were instantly stormed by half-starved troops. Snedeker saw this and was not pleased. The main fare at the candy tent was Tootsie Rolls--the large 4-inch long ones. They were being grabbed by the handful and stuffed into parka pockets.

I quickly found a few more Marines I knew and took them to the back side of the tent. We made a hole large enough to get out several boxes of Tootsie Rolls, gave them to my carloaders who held them aloft and called out: "Anyone who wants candy get on the train!" In short order we were loaded and rolling toward Hungnam. On arrival at Hungnam, field kitchens served around-the-clock hot cakes to the arriving troops. It was said that some troopers beat the record of "Little Black Sambo, who ate 169!" Round-the-clock feeding continued aboard the ships as they sailed south to Masan.

Aboard ship I drafted a recommendation for the award of the Medal of Honor to Colonel Homer L. Litzenberg, since I felt that his was the main effort in extricating our forces from the Chosin threat. He said: "No! It was an all hands effort! But here is one that will fly!" He handed me a draft with my name on it that was my first hint that lst Battalion, 7th Marines had earned for me a recommendation for the Medal Of Honor (MOH)! I was speechless as he insisted "Don't you agree?" These original papers were lost in a Division Headquarters fire, but were reconstructed a year later, largely through the personal efforts of General V. H. "Brute" Krulak.

We left the transport ships at Masan to live in tents in what came to be known as "The Bean Patch" camp. As with other Marine units, the 7th Regiment had to be rebuilt. Our losses were beyond belief. As one example, we were short 1,300 Browning Automatic Rifles--they would not operate in the extreme cold and were abandoned by the troops in favor of M-l rifles, which would shoot. Personnel replacements and weapons and equipment arrived and retraining was quickly underway.

We were visited by historians, including S.L.A. Marshall, and subjected to endless interviews concerning "The Frozen Chosin." Units were assigned security missions in conjunction with their training. After a series of field exercises, we were ready to return to combat. Our area of operations was to become the central front east of Seoul.

But prior to this move, we went into a large, rural mountain area near Pohang, on the east coast, which was experiencing a lot of guerrilla activity. The 7th Marine were given the mission of securing the area. An all-out "guerrilla hunt" was conducted over a period of two weeks. Blocking positions were established and units were moved rapidly in response to reported activity. It was great training, but few guerrillas were caught. I learned lessons that were useful in Vietnam many years later.

After we had moved to our new operating area, in the central front of South Korea below the 38th Parallel, I experienced my first and only "disagreeable" situation with Colonel Litzenberg. Our 7th Marine Regiment was effecting a river crossing displacement near Wonju. Two infantry battalions and the Regimental Command Post Group got across on an underwater rock road. Then the river rose very quickly making it dangerous in the mind of the artillery battalion commander to move his guns across. I approved his recommendation to emplace his batteries on the south side of the river.

When Litz returned to the command post he asked about the artillery and disagreed with the artillery emplacement. In a rage, he ordered Commander of Artillery Regiment's 3rd Battalion to report to his command post immediately. The artillery commander reported, obviously shaken by the experience of crossing the now high, swift river in the dark. He was severely chastised and told that he must never again have the guns out of the immediate area of our regiment. He was then dismissed to cross the river once again.

Litz was aware that I knew that he drank two big slugs of Old Granddad bourbon whisky while waiting for his victim. He said "I wish you had not had to hear that." My response was that I was surprised not to have shared in his condemnation, since he knew that I had approved the artillery plan. He shrugged it off!

Operation "YOYO," as our central front actions came to be called, followed a pattern of attack, then withdrawal, then attack, then withdrawal again. With divisions abreast we moved north across the entire central front. Our patrols would soon find enemy defenders on high ground ahead. The patrols would then withdraw to a safe position while we applied artillery fire and air bombardment on the enemy. After several such encounters, we concluded that if the defenders were North Korean Army units, they would hold their positions; if Chinese, they would withdraw. Vigorous infantry assaults were necessary to dislodge the Koreans.

Colonel Herman Nickerson arrived during these central front operations as Litz' relief. Nick was concerned by advice he had been given at Division that he would do well to "listen to Ray Davis" in his employment of the regiment. I quickly assured him that he was the commander and the decisions would be his and his alone. We became a solid team and developed a close and lasting friendship. Nick has been one of my closest personal friends since that time--one of my most valued mentors!

On the left of our regiment was a South Korean Army division. We dispatched a liaison officer to serve with them. From his reports we came to anticipate when trouble was coming. Korean units were loosely controlled, at times outdistanced the range of their supporting artillery, and lost contact with one another. The Chinese seemed to detect this and would launch a human wave attack against them.

Caught with "both feet in the air," so to speak, the Korean units rapidly withdrew and at times fled to the rear. We quickly positioned units to protect our flanks, and almost invariably received orders to move back in order to reestablish the broken front lines. After very few miles, the Chinese units stopped. It became apparent that they had outdistanced their supporting weapons, had lost communications with higher headquarters, had run out of supplies, and found their units intermingled and disorganized. These problems were confirmed by prisoners we captured. Our application of massive artillery fire and air bombardment caused them to flee in great disorder.

Then off we went forward again while trying to regain contact seizing a few more objectives. Soon another Chinese attack came somewhere else along the front resulting in another withdrawal; hence, as this forward and backward maneuvering continued, the name "YOYO" came into being to describe our tactics.

Another somewhat strange employment of our forces was the establishment of a "protective screen of fire." Orders were received that each artillery piece would fire a minimum number of rounds each hour for 24 hours per day. All tanks would be put on to dirt inclines to increase the elevation of their guns and thereby add range; they too were assigned a minimum quota of rounds per hour. Some seventy truck loads of ammunition per day were required to support this rate of fire for the division.

On occasion we would request a cease fire in order to send out patrols to make sure no enemy was being assembled to threaten us. Our patrols brought back pleas from farmers that we stop the "shoot-out" so that they could attend to their crops.

The main result of this "screen of fire" was to drain every ammunition supply depot west of Denver, Colorado, and create a serious shortage in the national stockpile. Possibly the weakened Republic of Korea divisions were made more secure, but our infantry regiment was only hurt by it:

Gun tubes worn, crews exhausted, nearby units unable to sleep, limited ability to patrol to our front, ammunition shortages generated.

Later, as we moved forward again, we found many cross ridges with high passes through them. Enemy units would protect these passes by defending the high ground on either side of the pass. Our assault units had great difficulty in dislodging the defenders. Their only reasonable approach was along the narrow ridge top. Detecting this pattern, we designed an innovative plan which came to be called "busting through the middle." As our ridge top assault units pinned down the defenders, we launched a tank-infantry (tank heavy) force up the road toward the pass. Invariable the defenders would withdraw under this double threat and we could move quickly through the pass area.

On one occasion we displaced artillery into an area covered by gardens and orchards. Soon afterward a small aircraft landed near some of the guns. The Corps Commander, General Almond, climbed out and discovered the guns. He was most unhappy and directed us never again to displace our guns where they could endanger his aircraft. We had not known that the unimproved airstrip was there.

My time in Korea ran out during this central front campaign, and I soon returned to the States.

As mentioned at the beginning of this chapter, the brilliant strategic planning by General MacArthur resulted in the successful landing of allied forces in Inchon in the fall of 1950. The People's Army of North Korea was thus faced with a near total defeat and was retreating rapidly towards the Yalu River. At the time the unification of Korea looked like a certainty. A review of all evidences indicated that Stalin and Chou En-lai were both resigned to the total victory on the part of the UN forces in Korea.

Nevertheless, the so-called three "Musketeers," consisting of Kim Philby, Donald Maclean, and Guy Burgess, who began to work for the Russians in the early 30s, passed vital intelligence to our enemies. Philby was the liaison officer between the American CIA and British Counterpart, MI-6, in Washington, D.C. during the Korean War, where Burgess later joined him. Maclean also gave information on the Korean War to the other side. In short, Stalin and Mao Tse-tung knew in advance that the United States would not use the atomic bomb in Korea and that allied forces would not advance into Manchuria or China.

In addition to supplying such information, Philby, Maclean, and Burgess used their influence in Washington and London, thus affecting policy changes favorable to the communist side. Thanks to their works, the Chinese communist forces launched a massive attack on the UN forces in the brink of a total victory. Had it not been for the decisive information regarding the non-use of the nuclear weapons, the outcome of the Korean War would have been quite different, indeed.

133

Having obtained the latest data and information on the treacherous acts of these three secret agents, students of the Korean War are currently trying to find out answers to questions such as why and how they were recruited, what were their detailed espionage activities and roles during World War II and the Korean War, and how and why they managed to avoid detection for so long, eventually escaping to Russia. In this process they have examined many KGB documents that have been recently been made available. In the end I am convinced that their examinations will throw invaluable light upon a series of events that resulted in tragic consequences to the Korean people as well to the UN forces.

Many liberals, radical students, and left-wing intellectuals in the United States as well as in Korea, will do well to pay attention to the current research on this subject. In sum, the effort to unify Korea by the UN forces was frustrated and foiled in the last minute by the three British turn coats.

Consequently, Marines had to fight against the overwhelming Chinese units that surrounded them near the Chosin reservoir. The 1st Marine Division suffered many casualties. And in December, 1950 many North Korean refugees (numbering more than 100,000) escaped from the communist persecution by withdrawing with us from the port of Hungnam.

CHAPTER 15. HEADQUARTERS MARINE CORPS

I left the 1st Marine Division in Korea in late May, '51, took some leave, and moved on to Marine Corps Headquarters in the Navy Annex, Washington, D.C. I reported to the G-3 (Plans, Operations and Training) Division, headed by Colonel Eustace Smoak. Smoak had been General Thomas' G-2 (Intelligence) Officer in North China, and later was to serve as Professor of Naval Science at the University of Texas. He was known as a hard driving "old school" Marine.

I didn't find him that way. I had never worked for him before, but I didn't find him difficult at all. Then Tommy Wornham came in to be the G-3. One of the first questions asked of me was if I knew that I had been recommended for the Medal of Honor. My answer was in the affirmative. I knew down at the Bean Patch (home of 1st Marine Division after the Chosin Reservoir Breakout) in Masan, South Korea, that Litzenberg had written it up, but it was among things that were burned in a big fire at 1st Marine Division Headquarters. I heard nothing more about it until 1952. It was a different kind of citation in that they weren't accustomed to awarding these awards for a "command performance," so to speak. Most Medal of Honor awards were based on an individual suicidal type of act or a totally personal heroic exposure. I was told by somebody that mine took a lot of effort to convince themselves and others that a sustained heroic performance over several days was worthy.

On the other hand, there were others where this had happened before: Merritt "Red Mike" Edson's was a heroic leadership award, at Guadalcanal along with General Vandegrift; then Dave Shoup at Tarawa; so there was precedence for it. In retrospect, it doesn't seem valid now that such a concern would have come up unless it was at a time when every award was for heroic acts. In the Korean War, mine was the first recommendation for a Medal of Honor award for unit leadership over a period.

The award itself was announced when I was on a trip to Europe. We had gone over to observe maneuvers in Turkey with Brigadier General Butler plus Tex Connally, Bill Jones, Willy Enright, as a team from Headquarters Marine Corps. We were in Istanbul when the message came ordering me back. My feelings were of surprise and disbelief since I had not heard about it for more than a year. The trip back became an interesting challenge for Louie Plain who was in charge of getting me back; Louie was downstairs in Marine Corps

Headquarters in the Personnel Department. Our party was going back to Paris where I was supposed to fly out in time for the White House presentation; a very tight schedule was involved. But, as we flew over Paris, heavy snowfall covered the runway, which sent us on to London. I couldn't get a flight out of London. As usual, money was tight in the Corps and they were not going to pay commercially to get me back. Since there were no scheduled military flights, messages went back and forth between the Navy Headquarters in London and Washington about getting me back by a certain time and date to guarantee my appearance at the White House as scheduled.

Finally they sent me up on a small airplane to Prestwick, Scotland, where I arrived just in time to jump from one plane to another which had stopped in enroute from Frankfort, Germany to Washington. I made it back in time. Of course, everybody in Marine Corps Headquarters was annoyed with me and concerned that I hadn't responded more smartly to orders to get back. Apparently, for those in Washington, it was hard to visualize somebody getting lost or stranded in Europe, but that's what really happened. The naval authorities in London were exploring every possibility and discovered a flight that was stopping off from Frankfurt in Prestwick; they held a space for me and I made it! This was before jets, and with an old prop job it was a long, long trip.

When I saw Colonel Plain (I was still a lieutenant colonel), he was very much relieved that I had made it, because he had a commitment to have me at the White House the next day. He had everything arranged, my wife Knox and my children, and my family had assembled in Washington and everything was ready. The actual ceremony went off according to Louie Plain's plan.

I'm often asked how receiving the Medal of Honor affected my career with both positive and negative effects. I respond that it had some positive effects. My attitude towards it is one of great humility. I fully recognize the gallant efforts and sacrifices of those many young Marines, those young troopers who put out, who did the job, who made it all possible. It wasn't totally my doings. Contrarywise I don't know of any ill-effects that wearing the Medal of Honor might have had on my career over the next 20 years. Over the years, folks have brought up the fact that several others in the Korean War who had the award, Bill Barber, Reg Myers, Carl Sitter, did not make general officer. My answer is that the medal itself was no guarantee of any kind. I certainly never had any thought that it would be a guarantee or that I was supposed to get any special recognition. Certainly it made me work harder to live up to what it represents. If it was my fate in the Marine Corps to go ahead, it was to be based on many things. Also, I guess to some degree, on the toss of the dice. If I look back to see wherein my movement along the trail was influenced, I conclude that it was the people I worked with, plus my career assignments pattern, and that was most unusual.

You know, I never served a tour on a base in the United States other than Quantico or Washington. Never down the East Coast, Camp Lejeune, Parris Island, Cherry Point; or out west at Barstow, Twentynine Palms, Pendleton, San Diego, El Toro, Kaneohe, Hawaii. I've never served in any of these places for a tour. I've been at many of these places for a brief period, but never served a tour. My career pattern was Quantico, Washington, overseas. For the Washington experience, I've always said that every Marine should have a tour in Washington. Then I claim that if every Marine had a tour in Washington, I would not have had four. I had four tours in Quantico, and every one of those were very fruitful tours. A major advantage was that every time the alarm sounded to go to war, I was in good position to go and go quickly, at the best time to participate in the important phases. The Washington experience in the operations, the manpower and the intelligence areas, plus the experience in Europe where I performed in a key role in worldwide intelligence analysis provided me an experience which stood me in good stead in Vietnam.

I knew all the sources of intelligence, and I knew the reliability of them in such a way that I could be completely bold and confident in what I was doing, what I was responding to, and what credence I could give to things. A lot in my outlook and performance in Vietnam was because of those four years in the inner sanctums of the intelligence business. Also, from the schools in Quantico, I moved from a long study and exercise in the theories and ideas, and the staff functioning right into a field unit headed for combat. It gave me a great opportunity to exploit what had been learned and I think that this pattern of Quantico-Washington-troops units overseas contributed greatly to my ability to perform effectively.

My appreciation for those who serve in the Marine Corps Reserve continued to increase as I became involved with such greats as Walter Churchill. Walter, more than any other American, has promoted physical fitness among youth in schools. Our friendship of more than forty years was made even closer by the service of his son, Walter, Jr., with me in Korea.

When asked if being a Medal of Honor recipient caused more to be expected of me as a Marine officer, I really can't answer since I have no way of putting my finger on such indicators. I never felt that I got any different or better assignments because of the medal. Even with all my work in the personnel business, I was never aware that this was a specific criterion for any kind of assignment. When my career is compared with, for example, Medal of Honor holder, Reg Myers, who certainly had a great career, and I was aware of his outstanding performance of duty throughout; he was a leading candidate for promotion, but it did not happen. It must be remembered that, to select a brigadier general, you have about 100 to 110 names, and five or six of these can make it. The percentage selected is normally less than 9%. I've been on boards when the process of getting down from 20 to 9 is just a question of briefing, rebriefing, voting, and arguing and voting over and over to get the six votes needed for selection. It's kind of a bounce of the ball to get 20 down to 9.

I initially went into G-3's Training Section. There I set up all the training directives to Quantico and other schools throughout the Corps, as well as budgeting, money, training aids, management of the whole Marine Corps training effort. Later I moved up to the Operations and Training Branch under Bill Jones (aka "Willie K. Jones") who received the Navy Cross as the youngest battalion commander in the bloody battle of Tarawa. Jones would one day in 1969 relieve me as Commanding General, 3rd Marine Division in Vietnam. When he moved up to become the Deputy G-3, I, having just been promoted to colonel, took over the Operations and Training Branch, and was there for the rest of my tour at Headquarters, Marine Corps.

In the Operations and Training Branch, we prepared the tables of organization (T/Os) and the training directives for the Corps, as well as plans for deployment. In addition we promoted operations and training support necessary from the Washington level for the Fleet Marine Force, plus bases, barracks and detachments, known as the non-Fleet Marine Force. The Korean experience affected the orientation of Marine training. World War II was a shoulder-to-shoulder movement forward. You didn't dare let the Japanese find a space between units, because they were masters at exploiting it to wind up in your backyard. Heavily defended positions were common place. In Korea, it was more a war of maneuver on foot, a major problem in small unit communications. There were no shoulder-to-shoulder operations as we went after the key terrain all the time. Control of the high ground had to be maintained to include the passes through the mountains. Korea was a war of maneuver, application of fire support, and concentrating fire support. Let me offer a concrete example: At the time there was a big hue and cry about running out of ammunition, but the shortage was almost by design.

As mentioned earlier, there was a feeling in the high command (Army General Van Fleet was there) at the time, if you shot enough artillery, you could keep the Chinese from collecting themselves for their big offensives. We even put our tanks up on ramps so their guns could elevate enough to become long-range artillery. Our artillery expenditure was controlled by saying that each artillery tube had to expend a minimum number of rounds every 24 hours, some large number, where they were shooting all the time. We ran short of ammunition, because of the misconception that the way to screen yourself was to pop away with artillery all the time.

This was a big difference between Korea and World War II. In World War II, they developed the concentration of artillery to a fine science with dozens of batteries firing TOTs (Time On Target), a total massing of everything. In Korea, we had less of that because units were farther apart and it was more difficult to mass artillery. Also there were refinements in close air support. In Korea we had better close air support, better communications, more a war of maneuver and flexible fire power.

As a result, we changed the training syllabi in our Marine Corps Schools and Forces during the Korean War. Of course, we returned to World War II techniques late in the war when peace negotiations began and we got into fixed positions. Both the Chinese and U.S. troops dug in and fought back and forth over a heavily defended area. These were World War II type actions which resulted in very high casualty rates. The last year of that war was very bloody.

Another Marine Corps concern in my office was the fact that during the latter phases of the Korean War, a large segment of the Corps had little or no experience in amphibious warfare. Our training directives later reflected the need for landing exercises and follow-on maneuvers ashore. Between wars, we quickly moved to reestablish our capability as the nation's most ready force, leaning on our ability to work with the Navy as the worldwide ready force from the sea. Also, we trained in the area of airlift in conjunction with that.

One great gain for me was the discovery of a special talent in one of my chief subordinates in the Operations and Training Branch. Bob Elder was a master of the written word. I brought him to my office with a desk and assigned him the task of upgrading our written products--plans, orders, correspondence.

It took a while for my section chiefs to get used to the idea, but every document prepared for my approval got the Elder treatment. I even invited them to submit a finished draft before going to a final product. The Elder style was simple, direct, clear, positive and was a key to getting a lot of ideas through our bosses. Even now I can call on Bob to clean up ideas for me.

Realize that life was not all Plans, Operations and Training for the Davises during that Headquarters Marine Corps tour of duty. Says Knox: "Washington had many high society ways and I detected a bit of a cast system based somewhat on rank. Ray's decoration moved us up a bit at times which gave me a better feel for the social status concerns. Many wives who had long broad experience had much to offer less experienced wives, but seemed loath to do so. This was a lesson learned for me. Thereafter I made sure that I maintained good communication with more junior wives."

Let me jump in here and offer a description of who these senior wives were. They had been in the Marine Corps, say, for 12, 15, 20 years, and had come up through the ranks, as a lieutenant's wife, then as a captain's wife, a major's or lieutenant colonel's wife and were now married to a colonel or general. They had the experience and the military language and everything that goes with it. And here was a newcomer, Knox, who was entering the scene as a new wife of a lieutenant colonel. It was totally disadvantageous for Knox and other new wives to cope with these old timers who normally would be considered near equals. That was the root cause of the problem.

Let me note that Quantico was to prove to be a total contrast. Also, great good was to come of Knox' experience with some of the older, veteran wives. The adversity she felt generated a deep-seated determination to better the status of younger wives. She developed an acute sensitivity for the needs, concerns and aspirations of younger officers and their families. It became a persistent pattern that opportunities would present themselves to do special things for young families. An aide or junior staff member's wife would be given a baby shower in our quarters with two or three dozen of her friends in attendance. Knox also played a key role in our free-wheeling meetings with junior officers and their wives.

From a mixed environment of Marine Corps Headquarters and Washington society, we were transferred and headed down the road to Quantico, and The Senior Course, Marine Corps Schools.

Homecoming with Knox's family, Lincolnton, N.C., following Chosin Battle, 1951

CHAPTER 16. SENIOR COURSE, M.C.S.

Because my relief in Marine Corps Headquarters reported in early, I was able to experience "an interesting side trip" enroute to the Marine Corps Schools in Quantico, Virginia. I was ordered to a six week course in Norfolk, Virginia in Atomic Weapons Employment, where I received a deep exposure in the nuclear weapons business. I had been to three brief atomic courses at Sandia Base in Nevada, but this was the in-depth course. The essential reason was that atomic weapons instruction in Quantico was going to be upgraded. After a year as student in the Senior Course which was subsequently renamed Marine Corps Command and Staff College, I would become Assistant Director for one year, and then Director.

At that time, the emphasis in the Senior Course curriculum was staff and command in general, and very broad in scope, since the students were lieutenant colonels and colonels, Division staff and regimental command were the focal points. The Corps was not reliving World War II at this point, since the development of the helicopter concept and tactical use of nuclear weapons "with a Marine Corps flavor" were at hand in the Schools. All of this had begun when I was serving on staff of the Junior School, known as Marine Air-Infantry School back in 1946.

Remember that during this decade, from 1946 to '56, which I began and ended in the Marine Corps Schools system, the Corps had changed drastically in size, and therefore scope. In World War II it was a maximized Corps of 580,000 plus with six Marine Divisions, yet shortly after the war's end, "Only 100,000 Can Serve!" became its realistic motto. And the United Nations War/Conflict in Korea had not exactly been in anyone's plans for the Corps' future.

In discussing this period, let me say that during the period of the late '40s when I was on Guam, they cut our strength way back and made our brigade a part of the 1st Marine Division at Camp Pendleton, California. It was a very difficult time because you can't split off a brigade out of a division and not add some pieces; some pieces in a division won't split into two parts. All of this had a bearing on our instruction in the school. Also, we in the Senior School had people on the Amphibious Warfare Presentation Team which traveled throughout the Corps and to Allied countries with the Navy-Marine Corps version of how we saw the near future of the amphibious business. We were involved in developing a new presentation while the old one was being presented. The concept and scenario including tactics, and weapons employment were reflected in our teaching in the Schools.

The outstanding thing to happen when Herman Nickerson was Director and I was his assistant was the development of conference type of instruction. In the basement of Breckenridge Hall we built about a dozen small rooms and special oval tables. Gerry Thomas commanded Marine Corps School where he and Nickerson developed the idea and pressed us ahead. Initially called, 'Seminar' but it was more conference type in strict definition. We were initially under pressure to develop as near a course of total conference instruction as we could, and this took some doing because there was some resistance to it. It is much easier for them to give a lecture than to develop a dozen instructors who can take a carefully prepared piece and involve all of the students in discussing it. But it was, I thought, a most effective and fine effort. It was highly structured in that each student group--and we'd change these groups every month or so--would have two or three infantry officers; a couple of artillery officers, air, tank, supply, logistic, and so forth across the board; plus a foreign allied officer, and an Army or Navy officer. It was a total mix of colonels and lieutenant colonels with long experience, each with 16 to 20 years in the Corps. They would discuss each piece of instruction with an instructor as each student contributing from the standpoint of his individual experience and expertise. Instructors were sometimes a weak point since we had too few with the experience and knowledge needed.

There was in the group as much expertise as you could gather together in the Marine Corps, and it was a great opportunity for the real experts in whatever was being taught to help sell and convince the whole group on the ideas that we were promoting. It was very carefully structured in the preparation of material. The overall package was well-researched and documented in a form where experienced instructors--even where it was not their specialty--could sit down and lead the group through the instruction.

In the main, the reactions to it by the students was most outstanding. They were totally sold on it. The thing that hurt it most in the form that we developed it was that in our first year we overdid it. The next year we backed off from an 1100-hour syllabus to a total of 700 or 800 hours in these rooms. There were obviously some courses that were better done through lecture or illustration problems or exercises. The next year we cut it back to 500 hours, which was about right, I believe. This system did have such a fine reputation that we were getting visits from the army schools at Forts Leavenworth and Benning, plus a few civilian colleges. People were coming to see it work. In fact, the Army followed suit in some of their instruction. But that first year when we overdid it led to its demise, because those same few courses that didn't produce very much got to be the ones that people talked about.

When General Krulak came back to take over the Education Center, a staff member told me that he came with instructions from General Twining "to get back there and straighten out that mess in the basement of Breckenridge Hall." Thus, when he arrived we were faced with: "Get rid of that mess." Without even understanding precisely what the mess was, he obviously had his orders to carry out. There really wasn't much need to change because, as I said, we had recognized immediately that we had 300 to 400 more hours transformed into this type of instruction than we should have, and we had corrected it. Unfortunately even though the correction had already been made, the concept was disapproved and pretty much killed. My resistance to those who destroyed the conference instruction got me an "early move" out of Quantico.

Inevitably, any discussion of the Schools at Quantico leads into who should attend as students? I would answer that I think a prerequisite to going to any schools should be a good performance elsewhere. I don't think we should use Quantico to try to pick up someone who has not performed nor do l think we should let passed-over officers attend. This caused concern at times--when we had a class at Quantico with a lot of passed-over students in it. However, you can't avoid some of that because the selection board sometimes met when the class was in session. In any event, the high performers should be the ones to go to school. It was to accommodate these high performers that we went to the conference instruction. And one of my bitter disappointments was that it didn't take. When you get people with 16 to 20 years experience in the Marine Corps and two wars under their belts, I believe that they can sit down and help solve problems and contribute to a discussion in a meaningful way, and educate one another as opposed to having an instructor stand up on the platform and talk to them. I'm sure there was a great loss to our total development as Marine officers in tearing down that system. It was very unfortunate.   (In recent times, conference instruction has been reinstated.)

Conversely, I don't agree with the advanced civilian degree programs at some service schools. You only have so much time there, and the course should be designed so that it is a maximum effort. There should not be any loose time in the schedule so that a military student can get a Master's degree on the side.

Advanced degree programs should be for those not assigned as full time students. Ideally, through the school system we should present all officers with an opportunity for an adequate education. It should be either through attendance at the resident schools or through correspondence, or a combination of both. The military business is so complex that you cannot find out how to do it all in a unit or in a barracks or working in a job. You cannot train yourself on the job to be the kind of officer it takes to run the military. You need the schools. So I think such schooling should be available to all. But the primary assignment to the resident schools should be to those best qualified, because that is where we develop our concepts, where we examine our application.

Also, the instructors have to be top quality and totally experienced in their specialty. They have to have continuity, to stay there long enough to get through two or three classes. And their relief has to come on board and try to gain from the experience of the one being relieved. It needs to be a special assignment program at Quantico schools if they are going to do what they are supposed to do: to give that extra effort and capability to senior Marine officers so we can excel and show the way for all the armed forces in the world!

Especially in the Senior School there should be available instructors who have done their broad duties and are totally experienced in what they are going to teach. A great part of our effort there was the Instructors' Orientation Course, known as "The Charm School," where John Chaisson could take a very experienced officer and work with him, and make a skilled instructor out of him. We had a great advantage in our military schools which some of our civilian counterparts are envious of but also afraid of: that is, an ability to monitor the instructor and his instruction, a command and control of it that you just do not have in an educational institution outside the Corps. Many of the college professors who visited Quantico were amused, astonished, and alarmed about how we were managing the instruction and the instructor, as opposed to--as they say--'when I walk in that door with my class and close that door, no dean or anybody else had better stick his head in to see what I'm doing, because that is an invasion of academic freedom.' I am convinced that as a result, college students many times suffer from poor instruction. I think our educational institutions could gain from some monitoring of the instruction and the abilities of the instructors to teach. Our students grade the instructors. A poor instructor is not going to hack it in our schools. The students are going to be after them; the faculty is going to be after them; the administrators are going to be after them. They are going to hack it or get knifed out of there.

Life at Senior School and Quantico was more than merely filling the billets of student or staff member for Ray Davis. There is much and varied family life at Stateside bases in the corps, and Quantico is far from being an exception to this rule. As time went on and Knox wondered about those days when some senior wives seemed to fail their juniors, we agreed that all of that was behind us. They fell by the wayside, as we outstayed them. Our survival illustrates to me one of the reasons that Knox has been a very successful military wife, and that is that she's real, her approach is realistic. She says what she thinks, not to hurt anybody, but tells it the way it is; she always has. She works hard and she obviously contributes a lot, as opposed to some wives who just tried to look around to see precisely what had to be done to get their husbands ahead. Efforts like picking out little things such as having parties as a way to get ahead, or working for the right generals, or getting the right jobs. Be on the right team, take the right courses in school or other things were worked at, oftentimes to the detriment of doing the job at hand. Whereas, Knox and I tried to take what job we had and put our minds and energy to doing the very best we could. And that, plus a lot of luck, paid off.

Here's another minor incident that made life in the military so interesting. When I was Director of Senior School, the General in charge was noted for his memory of names. He just somehow could fix on a person with one introduction and he never lost a name. So he was introduced to Knox, and as he told it later, he related her to Fort Knox. As we were going through the receiving line a week or two later and Knox greeted him, he called her "Goldie." His system had failed, as he had related Fort Knox to our gold vault there. And certainly Knox Davis is one of a kind, and her name is one of a kind, except that in the history books we find that the first wife of the President of the Confederacy was named Knox Davis.

At the same party, the shoe was on the other foot as we were telling people goodbye. The Commanding General was there, as was the Chief of Staff, and they were coming down the line. I had reminded Knox of who they were, by name and station, so she'd be alert when they came by. Well, about three yards from us, they switched positions. I didn't clue Knox, and she was so fixed on what I had said that when they came by, she grasped the hand of the first guy and called him by the totally wrong name. She went right through the floor, because he corrected her right away!

One more story of Quantico days to illustrate life in those times: Many bases like Quantico had equitation, horses, where the whole family could ride... Knox breaks in: "Sure, we'd ride around, but of course, I fell off my horse, after which I decided that somebody in the family had to stay alive. We were all the way up to getting ribbons. My son Miles had some nice riding ribbons. He got first prize because he really sat well on a horse. And we had a few for Ray and Gilbert. Ray was a colonel on this tour when we were all riding; Willa Kay was an infant. It was right after we came down from Headquarters that I fell off, and I hurt myself, too, and I decided that I'll stop this. Just to keep on riding and bouncing--see, when I grew up, we rode the old western saddle, and I'd go as fast as I could go. I'd be clutching leather, as they say. Boy, I'd clutch leather and go, and I just adored it. So it was pretty hard for me to learn to sit like a lady on a horse English-style. There's a big difference!"

Let me add my view of why Knox wanted to stop riding. She had a big old horse named Ruby. Ruby had what they called a rubber neck. You could pull her red head right around in your lap, with that big, long neck. We were riding around the ring just practicing various things you do in riding class, and this horse for some reason stumbled, stopped dead, and put her head right down to the ground. Knox slid the full length of that neck, right up behind the horse's ears. She finally got the head back up, but she said that "this is nothing for a mother to do, I've got kids to take care of, this horse is going to kill me..."

Knox returns: "Mama would put me on a horse and I looked like the wind going past. However, Willa Kay was a tiny infant, so I left riding up to Ray and the boys. Ray, did you tell about Miles riding in the parade?"

It was an annual "Freedom" parade at Quantico, with fire engines and floats, and the horses of the stable were all in it. Miles was dressed in colonial uniform and my military boots and my sword on his side, and was on the last horse, just in front of the fire engine. As they came through the town, everything went well until they approached the final parade ground where they were to assemble.

As they turned off the road to go into the field, the fire engine turned on its siren and its horn, right behind Miles and his horse. That horse took off across the parade ground. I could see him coming, and Miles was hanging on. Of course, with the sword on his side, at every bounce of the horse, the sword would hit the horse and make him go faster! Luckily we finally got the horse stopped. Normally, when these things happen, the horse wouldn't stop until it got back to the stables. This time we led him back into line, but then something else happened and he took off again! Here comes Miles across the parade ground, the sword beating the horse...

Miles breaks in: "I was George Washington. I had on a wig and a George Washington uniform, all this stuff. As I went galloping by, somebody yelled out 'Tell them you're Paul Revere!' My recollection of it is that Dad grabbed somebody off a horse and chased off behind me. We ran the length of the parade ground, which was maybe a quarter of a mile. As we were approaching the far end, I realized that if the horse kept running, he was going to run onto the concrete road. And I'd always been taught that horses with steel shoes running on concrete invariably fall down and kill themselves, and their rider, too. So I was concerned! Luckily, the horse had sense enough to know that, and he stopped when he got to the road. Dad came over; I got off. And the horse was really skittish, because in this parade with all of the fire trucks and sirens, all of the horses were excited. As Dad got me off the horse after he'd run away the second time, Dad was going to get on the horse and take him back to the stables. But the horse kept being skittish and jumping around until Dad grabbed him by the reins right up near the bridle, and kneed him in the ribs just as hard as he could. The horse stopped moving, Dad got back on, and they very calmly went back to the stables."

Let me add another lesson learned from this tour at Senior School. There were 65 senior colonels and Navy captains at Quantico, but General Twining, as Commandant, Marine Corps Schools, had the junior five as his principal staff officers. He used them to ramrod many controversial ideas and efforts. (These juniors even moved into the better quarters, and rode in the best staff cars.) The resultant turmoil spilled over onto the Washington staff so much that special emissaries came down from Marine Corps Headquarters to try to smooth things over. This was in high gear when Commandant of the Marine Corps Pate moved to get Twining to be his relief as Marine Corps Commandant. There was a ground swell of opposition led by many that his ramrod young inexperienced staff officers had abused. I am not sure that Twining ever knew what happened to him! Although one of the most brilliant officers in the Corps--in this, he was not wise.

A few other timely tidbits from those Quantico days:

Party time: being a school director brought on obligations which tested our stamina. Every school and other subordinate command had an annual party--some more than one--to welcome new students or say goodbye to graduates. As Director of Senior School, I was on every party invitation list. It got so bad in what some dubbed "the silly season," that our kids would follow us to the door and plead with us not to go out. We were obliged to attend in deference to those being feted, but we did learn to go a bit late and leave early.

Historic tours: Quantico was ideally located for getting acquainted with the battle fields of "The War Between the States." I took a number of foreign students who were interested in history out to walk over the battle areas nearby. On one all day trip (10 hours) we drove to Manassas, Harpers Ferry, Antietam and Gettysburg eating and drinking from picnic baskets as we traveled. One British historian, in particular, was so impressed with some of the signs and markers that he took dozens of photos to be used as a guide to upgrade some sites in Great Britain.

Hunting/Fishing: The training areas provided excellent hunting (deer and turkey) and fishing (stocked trout and bass). On one first day of trout season, Miles who was age 11 at the time broke all records. General Al Pollock told how Miles did it. He had a long line which he tied to a tree, and on a medium size hook he threaded an active worm. He then played about in the woods for a few minutes, returned to drag the big trout out on the bank, adding another prize to his near full stringer. The fish had swallowed the hook so that a new hook was required each time. This primitive method caught twice as many fish in about two hours as General Pollock did all morning with his top quality spinning gear. The fact that Miles had staked out a hole where a number of the stocked trout were entrapped helped his cause a bit. Many of the old-timers in the forestry and grounds crew were truly experts at hunting. On early morning hunts, they could cup an ear, listen quietly in various directions, and identify the location of several turkey gobblers. I was never lucky with turkey, but these pros made excellent hunters out of a lot of Marines. We did have venison every season because of my luck on the deer hunts. Lew Walt and I went on a guided hunt up in the mountains with a group of 18 good hunters; two deer were bagged--one by Lew, one by me. Lew and I were lucky every year we hunted together.

Golf: Golf was fun, even though I never mastered the game. My scores bounced about--I had one good day to win a silver tray--one GOOD day. Golf on a military base like Quantico is so much simpler than in civilian communities. At Quantico we could get tee times, some on very short notice, which would hold. My experience around Atlanta, for example, has not been good. In fact, I've given up--gave my clubs to a nephew. Since I've become involved in a prospective golf community effort nearby, I'll probably give it another try.

Youth Programs: My involvement with youth continued as the boys grew up. Scouting, then Little League--I joined a team which Miles was playing with, as a coach--ended up as manager. It was a fine group of boys, some great parents. Soon I became aware of the "parent problem." Some wanted to dictate how, when and where their sons would play. Some chose to torment the umpires. Part of the solution was to insist that those with strong views come to participate in the practice sessions--their opportunity to work with the boys in practice opened some eyes to the strengths and weaknesses of the young players. I myself was guilty of some parental "prejudice" at "All Star" time. Miles had one of the best batting averages in the league, but had chipped a bone in his right hand near the end of the season--he wore a partial steel brace on the outside of his hand. He had played successfully in the final game. I urged the "All Star" coaches to give Miles a shot, and they did. He hit well in the practice session and handled a few plays flawlessly, but the coaches just would not take a player with a hand in a cast. They lost by one run in the All Star tourney--parental pride convinced me that Miles' bat might have made a difference.

Concussion: Two seasons earlier, Miles got his first baseball glove and was chasing fly balls--Gil was doing the hitting. Great fun until Miles lost a ball in the sun and caught it on the side of his head just forward of his left ear. He was obviously in great pain as we rushed him to the Quantico hospital. In a few minutes we were following an ambulance to US Naval Hospital in Bethesda. The emergency treatment was no medication, no fluids, which left Miles in terrible pain for two days until the clot started to heal itself. It was a long torturous time for us. (Miles broke an arm in D.C. in 1953--he had many physical hurts throughout his young years. His older brother Gil never had the slightest injury even though during his high school and college career he "lettered" in seven different sports. We never really identified Gil as a serious" professional-bound" athlete, but he was certainly a strong, tough and determined lad.)

Following this, I prepared to move back into the staff at Headquarters Marine Corps, this time into the G-2 (Intelligence) Division.

Student, Senior Course, Marine Corps School, Quantico, Virginia, 1954

General Lem Shepherd (Marine Corps Commandant) presents Bronze Star to Ray Davis

151

With South Korean President, Syngman Rhee (to my right) and Vice President Nixon,
to whose left is Colonel Reginald Myers, Medal of Honor, Korea

CHAPTER 17. ASSISTANT G-2 (INTEL), HQMC

After describing duty with me in the educational environment of Marine Air-Infantry School, Carl Hoffman returns with further scrutiny of our duty together in G-2 (Intelligence):

> Colonel Ray Davis served as Assistant G-2 (Intelligence), Marine Corps Headquarters, under Brigadier General James M. Masters (the first general officer to serve exclusively as G-2 at Marine Corps Headquarters). General Masters hand-picked Ray Davis to carry out his mission, which I believe was to revitalize the G-2 effort throughout the Marine Corps, gain prestige for the Marine Corps' intelligence effort at the national level, select the best intelligence-gathering tools available, and place them in the hands of the Fleet Marine Force as soon as possible.
>
> Colonel Ray Davis conceived "Project Cards," 3 by 5 cards on which he assigned a subordinate a specific intelligence project to research and exert appropriate follow-up effort. For example, the project might be: "Battlefield Surveillance Radar." The officer charged with this project would be required to report at least monthly on the status of the radar, scheduled field tests, promising related development, and opportunities to introduce the equipment into the Fleet Marine Force.
>
> Ray Davis assigned projects as they came into his mind--and his mind was active. Thus, at any one time, each officer might be working on several dozen projects, some complex and long-term, others simpler and short-term. But whatever the project, Ray Davis fully expected that effort would be unflagging in the completion of it. He retained a copy of each project card and required each project officer to report periodically on progress. Through this technique, goals became achievable and progress became predictable. It fit Ray Davis' style of leadership: Assign (or "suggest") a task, grant the assignee considerable leeway to carry it out, extend support and confidence, expect results.

I reported into G-2, Marine Corps Headquarters in October 1957 for my tour directly under Jim Master. While the Commandant is not an operational commander of Marine forces which are assigned to the fleets, he is responsible for the total readiness of the Marine Corps including the organization, equipment, and training. It's only in the operational areas where the fleets command. Jim saw our function in G-2 in those things for which the commandant is responsible: organization, equipment, training of people in the intelligence business throughout the Marine Corps. One of my early jobs was to chair a very broad based committee of experts on the development of a Marine Corps doctrine for Communications Intelligence (COMINT) and Electronic Intelligence (ELINT), to guide Marine Corps units in working in these areas in our field forces. Also, we concentrated on air and ground reconnaissance, including their training and equipment.

Secondarily, we surveyed the collection of all intelligence that flowed through by the carload, extracting those things which should be reflected in the Marine Corps. Plus we kept the Commandant briefed in general terms on the situation around the world, particularly as it effected Marine Corps missions and requirements. We had a fairly large staff and a busy time, much of it buried under the tight security requirements of going through three locked doors and knowing the password to get into the "inner sanctum" to see what was going on.

It was related to me that up until the World War II period, and even into the war itself, many "odds and sods" would be assigned to G-2/Intelligence billets throughout the Corps, many folks who couldn't hack it anywhere else. A result was that commanders had limited confidence in what they produced. After the beginning of the war when reserve officers, lawyers, and academicians came in and demonstrated the validity of good intelligence work, commanders became more willing to accept what was developed. My response to this was: there was a period after World War II when we did go back to what it had been before, a lack of professionalism in the intelligence ranks. But that changed with the assignment of Jim Masters to the job, one of the real fair-haired brigadiers at the time, who was very close to the people in the Commandant's office called "the Head House," and very well respected by all.

When I arrived, I recognized that this was a good place to be, because Jim Masters was in the main stream. The longer I was there, the more I was immersed in the total effort of the intelligence game. I became convinced that at any time we downgrade that effort, we're suffering and hurting because with an adequate intelligence effort you can save many tactical troop formations and many casualties. Much success is paved on the road of good intelligence, as I found later in Vietnam. I would have been much more reluctant to deliberately launch some widespread, very bold operations if I had not previously been immersed deeply in the intelligence business.

There was a reorientation with an influx of innovative thinking which encouraged both officers and enlisted Marines to become professional intelligence people. We had to have this in some of the inner sanctum areas. We had to have some specialists, but Jimmy Masters was also able to collect people like Carl Hoffman and others, including Conroy, "The Great Santini," who had broad experience, great expertise, and exceptional capabilities that could translate this intelligence effort into a broader base, into an attractive effort where commanders came to appreciate it more.

It's one thing for an expert who is totally immersed in intelligence, but who knows little else, to present proposals, but it is quite another for a broad-gauged guy like Jim Masters to come in and appraise things and go to his peers and superiors and tell them what it all means. The broad-gauged guy's views are much more acceptable than those of one who is totally immersed in it. But you need a combination of both. You have to have the technicians who can operate an effective intelligence program, but they are often flooded with so much information that it takes a high-powered fellow to put it all together. If you don't have a broad-based officer who knows what he's doing, he can get completely off the track. He can go into intelligence briefings with a view that one source of information is better than another or that everything is out of one source. It might well be invalid and inaccurate and can lead commanders astray. Somebody must take the total from all sources and put it together, structured and organized to show trends as opposed to just shooting at everything that pops up. You must detect developments of weaknesses, main efforts or main threats. The intelligence office can then become invaluable to the commander.

When it is pointed out to me that the G-2 intelligence function didn't have at one time, and perhaps still doesn't have as much weight as the G-3 (operations), G-4 (logistics), or G-1 manpower), either in Marine Corps Headquarters or the field forces, I say that certainly that is true. But overdoing that can be very detrimental. The operations officer's problems are multiplied if he kills off the golden goose that he had available in the intelligence shop. Some of them are prone to do so. As I say, you can save resources, lives, and everything else if you are attentive to your intelligence business. Everything else hinges on that. You cannot have an economy of force operation (which is the only kind of operation you can afford to have) without good intelligence.

Another view on this Marine Corps Headquarters/Washington D.C. tour comes from Knox: "There was one time that I really did something that I should not have done as far as the Marine Corps is concerned--and that was when Ray was shipped from Quantico and we moved back to Washington, D.C. They had a big luncheon, our regular Marine Wives' luncheon, shortly after we arrived. We had bought a house and were working to get settled, and I made up my mind not to go to the luncheon. I feared that they would misinterpret my reasons and assume that I was hurting because Ray was moved out of Quantico. And it happened exactly like that. One of my friends told me of concerns about my absence, and turned to me to say: 'Knox, you should have come.'" It was not a happy way to start a new tour in Washington.

Let me sum up this tour with a brief note I jotted down one time: G-2, Jim Masters, was great--well-connected in Head House, could get space, dollars, and people. We moved out in a number of directions. One was in back room intelligence. I headed a task force with Al

Gray (who later became Commandant of the Marine Corps) as a main cog. We nailed down concepts, requirements, plans, organizations, guidance to put Marine Corps into the business at Fleet Marine Force and Marine Corps Headquarters level--Radio Companies, Navy security jobs, etc., all tied into a good workable package with MOS (Military Occupational Specialty), rank structure, training, assignments all spelled out. We got a better tie-in with satellite photo and electronic collection, streamlined Fleet Marine Force air and ground capabilities--upgraded personnel to make service in S-2 (battalion/regimental level intelligence), G-2, J-2 (Joint Intelligence) recognized for its great value. Sales pitch: G-2 can make application of forces more effective for the main effort and economy of force (I believed this very strongly in Vietnam).

Duty at G-2, Marine Corps Headquarters, then the National War College, made me very current when I hit J-2, EUCOM (Intelligence-European Command Hq in Paris). This added experience was invaluable in my tour as Assistant Division Commander of 3rd Marine Division in 1963-'64; Brigade Commanding General for SEATO (South East Asia Treaty Organization) exercises; then as Commanding General of 3rd Marine Division in Vietnam. I knew the capabilities, shortcomings, reliability of sources; and could choose bold courses accordingly.

A few more lessons learned in my G-2, Marine Corps Headquarters duty come to mind: An additional major "battle" was in response to efforts in the Defense Department and Congress to downgrade the Marine Corps. An informal group was formed to prepare a counterattack and solicit support from the entire Marine Corps "family." Position Papers were prepared, key Marine staff and liaison officers everywhere throughout the top echelons of government were briefed, and "defense witnesses" such as retired General Clifton B. Cates were briefed. (Cates was the Commandant of the Marine Corps during Korean War who gained an apology from then-President Harry Truman after he called Marines "the Navy's police force"!).

The current Commandant was muzzled by Department of Defense so that our effort had to be kept from him. Inactive Marines were utilized as messengers to friendly Congressmen, particularly those on the Armed Services committees. Papers were prepared and distributed to generate support. One chore of mine was to maintain a file with a friend in a remote office of the Headquarters; he was not privy to their contents. In this way not any hard evidence of our activities would be surfaced if we were "caught." Active duty Marines were not permitted in the hearing rooms of Congress, so Nancy Walt and Knox Davis became our "spies." They were spoken to and greeted from time to time by Congressmen at the hearings, but were never challenged.

Our efforts won the day! Most prominent members of our winning team: Walt, Buse Nickerson, Masters!

Back to College: A result of being "moved" from Quantico was that for the first time I thought of retirement. I even went so far as to enter postgraduate courses in education in--the George Washington University night classes. The overload this caused resulted in me suffering "battle fatigue" to such a degree that Jim Masters made me take a few days off to "rest." This made me realize that I was pushing too hard, working day and night; my resolution to pace myself better solved the problem. There is no doubt in my mind but that the "defeat" at Quantico caused more stress than I at that time realized. While I was a George Washington University student, I found myself at odds with the psychology professor in the post graduate course. His theories of leadership violated the principles I had learned in the Corps. Among other things, he was "soft" on the absolute need for ethics and morality. We discussed and argued, but I learned to "parrot" his views on tests, with some mild footnotes in order to pass the course. I related this experience to one of my sons once when he was having a similar problem.

My advice: Thoroughly explore your beliefs and opinions, argue your points, but write what the teacher requires in order to pass the tests. You learn more by discussion, but don't destroy your grades trying to win the argument at test time!

Lew Walt & Family: We lived in the Brookville Community very close to the Walts who became close family friends. Knox to this day considers Nancy one of her dearest friends. Our kids were close. We all attended their various weddings later on. Lew was another of those bright stars who helped to light my way. We "car-pooled" to Marine Corps Headquarters and later to the National War College. I visited with him in Vietnam when he was Commanding General Third Marine Amphibious Force) where I headed up a "personnel" management team from Marine Corps Headquarters.

Later, when I became Commanding General of 3rd Marine Division, he came out as Assistant Commandant to visit me. Also, after my two terms as President of the 3rd Marine Division Association, I prevailed on Lew to serve as President. The purpose for both of us was to encourage participation by Vietnam Veterans. Lew never said so, but I heard from

other sources that he was a strong "sponsor" for me to relieve him as Assistant Commandant.

Hunting and Fishing: My sons were old enough to really enjoy some great hunting and
fishing trips. We hunted all over northern Virginia. A favorite was a canoe float trip down
the Rappahannock River above Fredericksburg, Virginia. With two cars we would park one
down river and with the other haul the canoe many miles up the river. We would then float
in the 17-foot flat bottom fiberglass canoe down the river, fishing the best places, stopping
for picnic lunch, portering around the worst shoals. We always caught limits of smallmouth
bass, throwing back smaller ones as we pulled in bigger ones. On one float trip we found a
large water turtle stuck between some rocks--big, measured 15 inches across his underside.
I barely reached one back leg and snatched him into the canoe. He was so big and determined to escape that it took a real effort to tie him down. At home we put him in water in a
basement laundry tub. He seemed peaceful enough, and the boys wanted to show him to
friends the next day. At 0200 we were awakened by a loud crash, raced downstairs to find
that "Mr. Turtle" had managed to crawl out and fall about three feet on to a metal wash
pan. We tied him to a post for the night and next day we released him into Holmes Run, a
creek near our house. He vanished that night and the boys wondered about how people
down stream would react to finding such a giant turtle in their small creek.

Perhaps the summation of my tour in G-2, Marine Corps Headquarters of which I am
most proud is my fitness report of 15 March, 1959, in which Brigadier General J. M. Masters, Sr., Assistant Chief of Staff, G-2, Marine Corps Headquarters, wrote the following:

> "As the principal assistant to the coordinator for all intelligence matters concerning the United
> States Marine Corps, Ray Davis is endowed with those qualities of mind and person which fit a
> Marine officer for command and which attract and stimulate the respect and enthusiasm of both his
> seniors and juniors (to me, "the troops"). He is highly active, moves quickly and with confidence to
> the jugular of any problem, yet at the same time, he is deferential, courteous and extremely modest.
> He is equal to any occasion as it arises and, in my opinion, is preeminently qualified for, and should
> rise to, the top ranks of his profession. His duties have involved joint effort with officers of other
> Services and high echelons of our own government."

In retrospect my "early move" from Quantico paid high dividends with the development
of close friends such as Jim Masters, Bill Buse, Lew Walt and Herman Nickerson. My next
move was from Marine Corps Headquarters, in the Arlington "North" Annex near the Pentagon to Washington, D. C., across the Potomac River, where I enter the academia of The
National War College.

General Young Nam Choi and his musical family in Seoul, Korea. (I trained many Korean Marine officers and still maintain close friendship with them, including General Jung Shik Kong, a former Korean Marine Corps Commandant.)

National War College, 1961, Ray Davis is standing in the rear, 4th from left.

CHAPTER 18. NATIONAL WAR COLLEGE

In August of 1959 I headed back into the educational environment. It was my good fortune to attend all four levels of officers' professional education: The Basic School (basic level); Marine Air-Infantry School (intermediate level); The Senior Course (high level). And I was now entering a top level school, The National War College.

It had long been my desire to attend The National War College and I had requested it in fitness reports (a Marine officer can put three choices for his next duty, either type or station, on each fitness report). Jim Masters sponsored my assignment, even though my tour, normally three years in Headquarters, Marine Corps, was shortened to two years. In a very short time I had come to recognize the sterling qualities of "Gentleman Jim," "Tiger Jim," -- his favorite title for officers he respected was "Tiger."

In addition to being immediately available in Washington, D.C. many instructors who taught at the National War College were the most knowledgeable people in and out of government. Each student writes a term paper (known as an IRP, Individual Research Project) and makes a long trip to study a selected area of the world. Thus, attendance at the National War College is much sought after by senior officers of all Services, as well as of most government agencies.

I wrote about abuses in the centralization of authority. My study of the organizational structure of General Motors versus the U.S. Government led to the conclusion that the concentration of authority was counter-productive. At a time when Pentagon leaders were attempting to centralize authority in the Joint Chiefs, my report was an attack on the centralization of authority. As you would imagine, it was not a very popular paper, but I am convinced that my conclusions were correct.

My selected study trip was to Africa, and that, to me, was a great, great gain! The choices we had were Asia, Europe, the Middle East, South America, or Africa. I made a special effort to gain my first choice, because I could foresee no other opportunity to ever go that route again.

We flew into Dakar on the West Coast, down to Luanda in Angola, to South Africa, and back up to Salisbury in Kenya, to Ethiopia and to Morocco. It was a once in a lifetime opportunity for me to become exposed to that part of the world. For that reason I was anxious to go.

I would define this particular class at the National War College as one of those "high point" classes. As I mentioned before, there were years when the Personnel Department in Marine Corps Headquarters would send people over there who had not been fitted in anywhere else. But fortunately ours was one of those classes when they decided to upgrade the students, and as a result, out of the seven Marines ordered there that year, six of them became general officers.

Not only that, but Lew Metzger received three-stars, and Lou Walt, Keith McCutcheon, and I received four-stars. It was the same thing with the other Services: Dave Jones became not only Chief of Staff of the Air Force, but Chairman of the Joint Chiefs of Staff. The Army's Kerwin became a four-star Vice Chief of Staff of the Army, and... Bill Rosson later became my boss when I was his Deputy of Provisional Corps, prior to my taking over 3rd Marine Division, in Vietnam. There were also a number of topflight Navy classmates, many of whom received three and four stars. With so many top flight people it was a really fine exposure for all of us. I've bumped into many of them all along the trail ever since.

Meeting all of these officers was one of the dividends for attending the National War College. And of course we didn't just "meet" them, but we sat around the conference tables and had in depth discussions with all of them. Not only those in the class, but those who came to lecture were outstanding. For example, Henry Kissinger came to lecture and then to participate in the conferences with us. I've been asked if I was impressed with this particular guest? Yes, very much, very much. His latest book had just been published so we could discuss his very current theories on nuclear strategy.

We also had at the podium in the National War College the voices of many outsiders, other people like Kissinger who were outside the main stream, but were about to come on line in a few years. They came from all walks of life, from the colleges, from business, the government, politics. Leaders from throughout the whole structure of our society came to lecture and discuss national policy ideas with us.

They exposed their ideas by participating in our student discussion groups. It was a splendid high-powered school, and fortunately, in my case, it lead to a higher assignment in Paris on the staff of CINCEUR (Commander-in-Chief, European Command), something I never expected in my Marine Corps career.

Permit me to expand on the trip portion of the curriculum, partly because it was such rarefied duty for a Marine, and partly because Africa is today constantly in our news:

Capetown Cable: As a part of our relaxation schedule in Capetown many of us rode the cable car into the mountains which overlook the city. Beautiful views of the entire area, but sudden windstorms closed the cable operation--cable cars were blown out to near horizontal positions. The cable operators on the mountain with us suggested that a trail was available if anyone wanted to walk down. We were told nothing about the trail, but were given strong warning that the cable might be closed well into the night, and there were no overnight accommodations on the mountain. Further, we were due at an official reception in two hours.

About five of our student group started the hike down the "trail." We soon found it was unmarked and very tortuous; it was obviously little used. Fortunately, a few people had gone ahead of us, and we determined that our only hope was to track them. Many times the tracks were very faint, but a favorable factor appeared. As darkness approached, lights went on in the city. We were able to identify a star-shaped light we had seen on previous nights. We guided on it. The trail got steeper as we went down--I thought about some of those mountains in Korea. At places an almost vertical drop for 10 to 12 feet greeted us, and backing down a steep slope using small trees like a ladder became our solution.

By following our "star" we finally made it down, clothes snagged and dirty. We were totally lost, but as we exited the woods near a busy street, a cab appeared. We were very, very late for the reception, but had a tale to tell! Reports at the party indicated that this was a rare happening indeed. In fact, none of our hosts had ever heard of a "trail" down the face of the mountain. The trek was made more difficult because of our weakened physical condition following our stay in Angola.

Angola: Of greatest interest were trips out into the countryside. We were special guests at two celebrations. A Zulu tribal celebration featured an evening of native dancing on a small village parade ground. To my surprise, we were invited to join the dancers by our hosts--some of the American and Portuguese women insisted on leading us out onto the field. It was easy to pick up the beat as we joined the stomping throng, but the unwashed sweating bodies soon took our breath away.

The next day we were to have a picnic. We were traveling by big interstate type bus, which was to prove troublesome. A river ferry was to move us across to the picnic area, but the bus got hung up on the end of the ferry. Two hours later we left the bus and shuttled over in small vans. It was a tasty spread of native foods and we were very hungry. It was not until early the next morning as we were packing to fly to Capetown that we were struck with the idea that the food we ate had been prepared and standing in the African heat for hours during our bus delay. Every member of our group, including the doctor, was ill--deathly ill--vomiting, dysentery, headaches. Our flight was delayed for hours while we recovered enough to board. It was a dead group enroute to Capetown and for two more days after that.

South Africa: While in Capetown, we were briefed and had meetings with a number of political leaders--some of British background who were against the hard racial policies of the government. We talked to taxi drivers and shop keepers--not blacks, but some coloreds (mixed races). I came away convinced that South Africa would explode within five years-- that was 30 years ago.

Sudan: On our shopping list for Sudan was "gold jewelry." Embassy staff members recommended a bazaar outside the city. To insure that I got the genuine items, an officer of the Sudanese Armed Forces volunteered to be my guide. Result was great! Knox has three beautiful 24K gold bracelets which exceed anything we see in fine jewelry stores. They have been tested by our local jewelers and test at 24K plus. The price in Sudan was less than the cost of the gold contained in the bracelets--one third the cost in the United States.

Ethiopia: My attention to map reading paid off in Addis Ababa following an evening function at the American Embassy. An embassy staff member delayed my departure to give me some papers in response to my questions, causing me to miss the bus. I was sent to a nearby busy street corner to catch a cab. None was available. I returned to the embassy gate and asked that they call a cab. None came! It appears that the sidewalks are "rolled up" soon after dark. The gate guards were pessimistic about a cab and the embassy was closed tight.

I recalled from the map that the boulevard led directly from the Embassy to the center of the city where our hotel was located. I would walk. It was a long walk--very few lights-- not a person on the streets. Hyenas crying throughout the route--we had been told that they were the scavengers for garbage throughout the city. After an hour I found the hotel, just missing a party for us by some of the local military. For the remainder of the trip--lesson learned--I was most careful not to get separated from the group.

Later, on a trip through the countryside we had a few minutes to walk along back roads at various stops. At one point three young boys came to the edge of the woods about 20 feet off the road. Communication between the boys and our small group was through smiles and waves. Suddenly they broke into a lively dance routine--really surprisingly good. We coaxed one of the boys to come close enough to give him a handful of coins.

But horror came to his face as he turned to see a giant of a man running toward the boys with a long whip in hand. Obviously a father out to punish the boys for being in the wrong place, associating with strangers. We saw them disappear deep into the woods.

Red cars: An impression I gained from the Africa trip was that native rulers were hooked on long red cars. Every chief of state seemed to have a long, long open fire-engine-red car as his official conveyance.

Female porters: An amazing sight was seen around the market areas--women carrying huge loads on their heads. Large pots of liquid, large bundles, big boxes or baskets. We took some pictures and lifted some of the loads. I'm totally amazed at the loads they could carry on heads with only a small pad cover. Often it took two to get the load up; they maintained a perfect balance with a level shuffle-walk so that no jarring occurred as they traveled along.

Gold Coast: One of the richest of African countries, its economy was based primarily on a free enterprise system of cocoa farmers, with good transportation systems--railroads, roads, sea ports. Countryside transport was via fleets of small trucks called "Mammy Lorries," because women owned and drove most of them. In the port large man-powered barges carried cargo to and from the ships. They had rounded gunwales which men straddled to paddle the barge. They moved cargo, in rough surf or calm seas. Twenty-five years later it is now among the poorest nations in Africa as a direct result of socialism. The government took over the economy, controlling imports and exports, raised government fees, much of which lined the pockets of leading bureaucrats. Railroads are closed down; cocoa plantations abandoned. This pattern of socialism (plus tribalism) had brought many African nations to near ruin.

Camera: I found an opportunity to borrow a Marine Corps fast Polaroid camera. We had been briefed that African natives did not look favorably on having their pictures taken. This proved to be false. I took a picture of a man holding a beautiful ivory carving. After the picture appeared, I took it to him. Upon seeing himself he let out a loud yell for his friends and neighbors to come and see it. As a result I was so pressed by the crowd for pictures that I was forced to get on our bus, lean out a window and take pictures as other members of our group kept the people in single file. I soon ran out of film, but that was one happy crowd. The taboo on picture-taking was because the natives had never seen a picture of themselves. Statements that they believed that cameras took away part of their spirit proved totally false. Another lesson learned from experience! Soon it was back to D.C. to finish out the course at the National War College, then on to Paris for rare Marine Corps duty with EUCOM (European Command) in truly international intelligence duty.

Ray Davis becomes President, the 1st Marine Division Association, while Lieutenant Generall Al Pollock (middle) and Colonel Lew Walt (right) looks on.

CHAPTER 19. J-2 INTEL. ANALYSIS CHIEF, PARIS

In July of 1960 I became Chief, Intelligence Analysis Branch, J-2, Staff of the Commander-in-Chief, European Command in Paris, France. I hadn't really considered it, but it came to be one of those things that I liked to do. Very few Marines get to Europe with their families for a tour, relatively few. They are very attractive assignments and I guess that the only way I would ever have been able to go would be in the intelligence business, and I suspect that Jim Masters had much to do with that.

Needless to say, my family was overjoyed with the news. They are great supporters of the Corps and tremendous tourists and travelers. We had a fine tour over there, particularly in travels as a family and at times kids traveled alone. Just one example: There was an opportunity to get on the local train outside of Paris with a bicycle, a pack on their backs, go downtown and get on a train to Rotterdam with their bicycles, ride around Holland on trails for a week, living out of the pack on their bicycles. They'd always get in a hotel for one night so they could take a bath before they came home at the end of the week. That round trip cost $11 on the train with bicycle, and lots of kids did it.

Another example was that Knox traveled with other wives to Berlin. Then, when I could get off, we all traveled together, by car, airplane, train to Oslo, Vienna, Naples, Madrid. It was just a great three years for the family to travel, and I enjoyed the duty thoroughly. As Chief of Intel Analysis, I had some highly talented specialists from all the Services, plus some brilliant civilians who had been over there for 15 or 20 years.

We were right in the middle of the Berlin Crisis, the Middle East Crisis, and tracked the Cuban Missile Crisis as we maintained a high state of readiness. Every crisis, you know, started at 5 o'clock Sunday morning in the intelligence shop, like dairyman's hours. One crisis came when we were completely duped by the Russians during a period of no test agreement. Those rascals saved up a massive effort, then suddenly violated the agreement. Starting one night for a very short period they fired over one hundred massive tests, many of which were 100 megatons in size. It completely shocked us and demonstrated the futility of any kind of agreement with those people. They deliberately cheated and duped us on this-whole effort. We were dumbfounded to observe those explosions--gigantic size, broad-based, the result of a deliberate, prolonged secret preparatory effort on the part of the Russians and a total breach of our agreement with them. It was difficult to believe that they would really do such a thing.

My entire tour there was an exciting one. Air Force General Norstad was wearing two hats: Supreme Allied Commander, Europe and Commander, U.S. Forces, Europe. His deputy on the US Forces side was Army General Palmer. On the US staff we had other Marines: "Tex" Connolly succeeded John Condon, an aviator, as J-3 (operations). Condon was to become my predecessor in my next billet on exercises in the Philippines. In the J-3 shop we had people like Jess Ferrill, a Basic School classmate of mine. Bruce Cheever, another classmate who left the Corps, was the CIA chief in Europe. This was another relationship which I enjoyed because we were in "bed" with the CIA in my business. Having Bruce as a close friend and classmate made entries into his system easy and very profitable.

I appreciated the fact that I had served in the Senior School, G-2 Headquarters, Marine Corps, and The National War College before reporting for duty in Europe. I was well prepared for my responsibilities and duties which were greater than I would have had in a Marine Division or even on the Fleet Marine Force level. The job was very broad in scope. Our commander had responsibilities from Europe to Pakistan. He commanded all the Army-Navy-Air Force in Europe,--a massive command with great responsibility. Beyond Europe he was responsible for military assistance program. The whole nuclear program, the satellite program, everything was involved, and intelligence played a key role.

We were closely related to SACLANT (Supreme Allied Commander, Atlantic) and were in constant communications and contact with the Pentagon. In a sense, we were out of the Marine Corps stream, but with Marine forces in the contingency plans. Tasking them was part of our effort. We were to ensure that the plans were upgraded, where needed, including provision for support. Overall, it was a most enjoyable tour; I wouldn't have missed it for anything.

Then, at the tail-end of my tour, I was selected to be a general officer. What was a very happy moment, getting that phone call from the States, turned sour: Jess Ferrill, a Basic School classmate, (who died recently) was my opposite number in J-3. On the phone on the day I learned of my selection, he asked what I had heard. I said "We made it, Jess" meaning Knox and I (Marines always think of their spouses as being selected and promoted with them). Jess took it to mean "Ferrill and Davis" and hung up before I realized it. I ran down the corridor to clear this up before he could tell anyone else, but it was too late!

I was actually promoted on the ship coming home. At times the Marine Corps gives a special promotion prior to moving officers into a new billet calling for that rank; this is called being "frocked" with a temporary promotion, but no increase in pay. We sailed home on the SS United States, and celebrated the new stars with friends, near the end of the voyage. Earlier we had gone over to Europe in 1960 on one of the World War II transports of the MSTS (Military Sea Transport Service), which was a long, slow voyage. It was a good relaxed time for the family and we really enjoyed it. We got off in England, had three days running around the country, then we went to Bremerhaven and rode a train to Paris. Coming back on the United States had a different flavor. You got on board this fast liner and almost before you could unpack, were home.

When asked my anticipation regarding selection as a general officer, I responded that this was never one of those things that I really concentrated on, and worked at. I was never one to measure my chances or ask "Do I need to do this or that?" Those kinds of things just never occurred to me. My effort was to perform. To me, the task at hand was always a challenge. To upgrade it, to take care of it on the basis that my reward in everything was a sense of accomplishment. In fact, if I couldn't accomplish anything, then I was frustrated. So I worked hard and concentrated on my effort at what I could do to accomplish most in the job at hand in the time available. I knew that promotion chances were minimal and with such chances, you just wait for the ball to bounce.

In other words, I had enjoyed a good career up to this point, and this was frosting on the cake. Now, before leaving this, I couldn't look back anywhere and say to myself: Well, I wished I had done this or that so my chances would have been better. I left few stones unturned as I went along that I was regretful of. I had both a good career and especially great associations. I was certainly exposed to the best people around and if you can't make it after that, after the exposure I'd had, that's just the way the ball bounces. Also, I had never received a black mark on my efficiency record. I'd had some confrontations, but I'd had many champions on my side during those periods.

Let me offer a few more thoughts on this particular tour of duty in Europe. As Chief of Intelligence Analysis, I was in a deep, sensitive, closely held business. There were two branches in my shop: One published a summary for wide distribution every day; the other a closely held Eyes Only, back channel effort. We got many salutes from the Pentagon for analysis. My secret was an Army civilian named Jamie Taylor (now deceased) who had a prodigious memory. He knew names and numbers of every political player from Pakistan to London. In the middle of the night when things looked unsettled, Taylor could spell out who was up to what and who was on which side. He never missed! Naturally, with my clearances, I couldn't visit Marxist lands, but otherwise I went everywhere in Europe, North Africa, Middle East, onto Pakistan, often with our commanders.

Wife Knox offers the following on duty in Paris: "I would like to say one thing as far as a Marine wife's life is concerned--you learn a lot, if you want to. You joined the clubs, you see, and you could learn many things. For example, flower arrangement--there were many things like that which I had not thought about back in my days as a school teacher. But I picked up many new skills by joining the clubs and going and doing. And I enjoyed it. That's where I really learned how to play bridge. I went to the classes at the Bridge Club. Ray said you should go, so off I went. You could even go to sewing clubs, decorating clubs. I loved their decorating classes. And language clubs--like in French, I took French-history--and many other things over there. And I was also busy helping to make American girls enjoy their tour as best they could. I participated as leader in the very active scouting program."

Let me offer a few more remarks before moving along from this great tour.

Language: Son Miles had one year of high school French before we went to Paris. Naturally I tested him as our train entered into France. At the first station, our train windows were open, and at my insistence, he greeted a railroad worker on the platform. This was the first of many, many situations where I pushed Miles into a conversation. He was reluctant, but I'm convinced that these conversations sparked his interest in language--he then studied Arabic from French textbooks--later on, Russian and Vietnamese.

His greatest early challenge: We took Willa Kay's cat Fluff to Paris, but ended up in a hotel because of a mix-up in our prearranged house. We had to have "cat litter" in a hurry. Miles and I entered every French store in the entire area seeking it; the French had never heard of it. But it was again good experience for Miles to mix it up with a lot of different people. It finally took a long distance phone call to Sears in New York to get "litter" air freighted to Paris.

Knox had a little French years back in college and went to classes in downtown Paris. But it was her on-the-job training that made her an expert in local conversational French. We had a femme-de-menage (housekeeper), Lucienne Guillemette, who refused to speak a word of English (She would finally say to Willa Kay: "Momma mad!"). We had a French-English dictionary which included full sentences. Knox carried the book around the house, pointed to sentences or words in the book, played "charades" to get housework done. But in a short time she mastered "kitchen" or "shopkeeper" French. Many of our friends from the Embassy would ask Knox to go shopping because of her special language talent. However, she was quiet at the Embassy receptions where Parisian French was spoken--where her kitchen French would be ridiculed.

I was personally exposed often to enough of the language to be able to shop for essentials and to get my car serviced. Enroute to work one morning a truck ran a stop sign and hit the side of my little Simca car. The driver spoke no English and in the excitement I could understand none of his French. Fortunately we were one-half block from the home of a friend, Jim Jones. Jim, a brother of our Marine comrade, General Wm. K. Jones, had been with International Harvester in Paris for years. The family was great to know--our kids played ball together, etc. (Young Jim, now Major General, was recently military secretary to Marine Corps Commandant; was rifle company commander, and later my aide in Vietnam). Both Jones brothers married girls named Charlotte, and it was Jim's Charlotte who answered the door when I knocked, with the truck driver in tow. She was helpful in getting the driver to sign a statement that his foot slipped off the brake pedal, which caused the accident. This fortunate circumstance saved much trouble and avoided police investigation.

Electricity: A few miles from Camp des Loges, where Headquarters of our command was located, we found a house in the village of Chatou. It was on the rapid rail system about halfway to Paris from my office. It was a nice old home owned by an elderly widow who was moving downtown to live with a daughter. We were very happy to get the house--moved in immediately--but we had not examined the electricity available. The first time our freezer and refrigerator started up at the same time, the fuses blew.

Subsequently friends in an apartment across the narrow street told us that they saw us with candles moving about in the house that first night and guessed that we had fuse problems. It turned out that the house had only five amps of 110-volt power. Exploration through the French Liaison Office at our headquarters revealed that the street we lived on was at maximum usage and no more power was available--unless we went to 220 voltage. This we had to do.

The electrician came and rewired the entire house. At every 220 volt outlet he was required to place a "danger" sticker. As each circuit was finished I would immediately plug in a light to test it while the worker was up on the ladder at the fuse box. Knox told me later that the man was amused that he had learned his first American word as he called out to me to "test." The addition of a transformer to each of our 110 volt appliances made it a most pleasant house with an abundance of electricity.

Almost immediately we went away for a week, not knowing that a woman next door had long been the caretaker for the house. We came home to disaster. The neighbor saw a light on in the house, used her key to get in and turned off the main power switch. We had recently filled the freezer and refrigerator--all the food had rotted. It took a week to clean up the mess and get the odor out of the house. Needless to say, we got the key away from the neighbor--no hard feelings, though, and she became a friend.

Close Friends: Even now after more than 25 years we maintain a close friendship with one of our neighbors in the village of Chatou. We also exchange letters with the woman who worked in our house. One of the neighbors who welcomed us to Chatou was a young executive at the Simca auto plant. Unfortunately he was killed in an automobile accident shortly after we arrived. I conferred with the French liaison officer concerning the appropriate response for us. They wrote a proper note and selected flowers for us which proved to be a key in developing a close friendship with his family. Over the next few months we spent many, many hours with the distraught young widow and her two children. We took her to the Marine Corps Birthday Ball in downtown Paris; she took Miles to the Riviera for six weeks to be with her son. We have been back to France to see her; she has visited us many times. Lucille de Dominices, a countess, has remained our close friend. Her mother-in-law told Knox that our closeness had saved Lucille's sanity following her husband's sudden death.

Berlin: My security clearances did not prevent me from flying into Berlin on command aircraft, but I could not travel into Marxist areas. Knox and three other wives went to Berlin by train. At the East German border the train parked on a siding while immigration clerks collected passports and train crews were changed. It was amusing to see the Communist guards sneak over to the train cars and trade insignia, etc., with the American passengers for buttons, costume jewelry, etc., all the while keeping a lookout to escape detection from their Communist seniors. After a prolonged wait, all passports were returned except one--that one belonged to Knox. She went through many anxious hours before they finally returned hers. She was sure that my position in Paris was known and they were about to turn her back or something.

The wives toured Berlin and had a side trip into East Berlin in a taxi. While deep into

Communist Berlin, the cab broke down--again causing alarm among the four American women. The driver assured them that things were OK and that they would soon be going again. It was a great trip which they would not have missed, but it was a great relief to get back to the safety of Paris.

All in all, it was an unforgettable tour for the entire Davis family. Then it was back to the States, where, as a newly-promoted Brigadier General, I spent July, August and September of 1963 in Headquarters, Marine Corps primarily on selection boards, plus briefings for my upcoming assignment to the 3rd Marine Division on Okinawa. I had been alerted before I left Europe, so I was prepared for this short stay at Marine Corps Headquarters, then back into the field, because once again, Jim Masters was reentering my career as my Commanding General in the 3rd Marine Division.

With President Kennedy at a White House reception, 1962

173

With President Johnson in the White House, 1964

CHAPTER 20. ADC, 3RD MARINE DIVISION

I returned to the Far East again in June, 1964 and became Assistant Division Commander of 3rd Marine Division stationed on Okinawa. I had additional duties as Commanding General, SEATO Expeditionary Brigade, Philippines and Commanding General, 9th MEB (Marine Expeditionary Brigade), China Sea Contingency Operations.

I relieved Jim Masters' brother, Brigadier General Bud Masters as Assistant Division Commander, 3rd Marine Division, a Marine Division of over 17,000 troops stationed on Okinawa. Bud's primary concern had been to get the supply and maintenance situation squared away throughout the division. This was a follow-on to an uncomplimentary GAO (General Accounting Office) report. My main efforts were as training inspector, infantry inspector, and readiness coordinator. The division which had recently returned from operations in Thailand under then-Commanding General, Major General Ormond Simpson was in overall good shape throughout. This was the hey-day of the unit rotation, the Trans-Pacific System: full strength infantry battalions of Marines were shipped out to 3rd Marine Division on rotation basis to stay together for their entire tour overseas.

Each infantry battalion, reinforced with supporting units, went through the routine of jungle training in the Northern Training Area of Okinawa, then live fire field training at the base of Mt. Fuji in Japan (where at least one Marine infantry regiment had been stationed fulltime until 1957, when President Eisenhower ordered all Marine and Army infantry units out of Japan), following this they went aboard ship, in the Afloat Phase, and moved down to the Philippines for more amphibious training.

We were training professional, ready units, and when the war came in Vietnam, these were the top quality units we would apply. Of course, the system was difficult in that it had to be broken down after we went to war, to permit individual rotation back to the States. Initially highly tuned team effort units with the experience of training together were invaluable. We have moved back in that direction, although there were a lot of misgivings during the early days of Vietnam because of individual rotation problems. Some of the finest units anywhere in our history were those that went through that progression with all of their troops together for the full period. There's just no substitute for that kind of readiness.

For the Okinawa unit rotation system we were using ship transport because, again, we

175

were trying to keep shipping viable by making good use of it. Less delay results with air transport, leaving all heavy gear in place in Okinawa while flying troop units out.

In the past there has been a lot of discussion of the choice between unit replacement in combat and individual replacement. In all my experience, individual replacement seems to make the most sense because your greatest cause of casualties is lack of experience. An outfit that has been bloodied a couple of times has many, many people in key positions who've been through it. It is not going to happen to them again in the same way that it happened the first time. So when individual replacements are fed in, they are exposed to the combat experience of people who are already there. This is less costly in casualties involved with the learning process than if you train a fresh rifle company, for example, and throw it in. New units go through a "learning" process and experience casualties before they can reach the expertise that it takes to save lives. On this basis alone after units enter combat, I would always opt for an individual replacement system as opposed to the unit replacement system.

Let me move on with high points and lessons learned in this tour. Duty again with Major General J. M. Masters was another of those fortunate experiences which punctuated my career. Jim had a great natural talent for getting his arms around a problem--in this case the 3rd Marine Division--and moving it carefully but quickly in a positive direction. Every subordinate knew of Jim's goals and the part they were to play in them. He anticipated problems and was there to cope with them in a direct, skillful manner. His standards were high and they were met. His fine sense of ethical and moral behavior was felt at every level of command--Marines taking care of Marines in the finest sense. The Division soon bore his stamp of excellence.

Readiness: My favorite challenge had to do with readiness. My time was spent in two primary areas: Advanced combat training and effective emergency response time. I accompanied units to remote training areas and went through the training with them: Firing exercises, movement, bivouac, rappeling, cable slide--the works. I was chagrined to find, very infrequently, a company grade officer or non-commissioned officer who would not participate fully in the training, sending their Marines through the rough events, but not going themselves. This situation was quickly remedied when the word got out that the Assistant Division Commander was going all out with the troops, and that he was ferreting out leaders who were doing less.

176

Of course we were on duty 24 hours per day since no families were present. This point was brought home to all hands through a spot check inspection routine, particularly on the highways. My driver was a motor transport (MT) specialist. In selecting him I conducted a survey of all MT specialists in the rank of corporal to find the best qualified one in the division to be my driver--upon selection he was promoted to Sergeant. He developed a rapid-fire inspection routine for vehicles including a checkoff form. We would randomly stop Marine trucks, jeeps and cars on the road, day or night, make a five-minute inspection and forward a report to the commanding officer concerned. Initially we found some unbelievably unsafe vehicles, but in a very short time the reports turned to excellent--some outstanding. My driver never got any flak, because I looked over his shoulder at every inspection, and signed the report. This illustrates but one small effort to upgrade readiness.

Rapid deployment: A major effort was concerned with the rapid deployment of units. We were in effect competing with an Army airborne brigade (173rd) which was stationed near Kadena Airfield (United States Air Force Base) and which had some priority over Marines in terms of air transportation. After exploring their routine in some detail, it became obvious that we could develop a more responsive system. One key was in getting in on the alert as it developed--sometimes the transport aircraft were enroute to Okinawa to lift troops before we knew of an alert--drill or real. Working with our Pacific Command in Hawaii, we streamlined communications so we got the signal at the same time the air transports did. This improved our response time.

Another faulty procedure soon became apparent. As our small units got ready, they were required to check in to our operations office to be logged out before heading for the airfield. A major gain in response time came when we modified the system. As units were ready, they could move to the airfield--staff officers along the route checked them through and made the necessary reports. Assembly areas at the airfield were broadened to accommodate units arriving in random order of march, again with staff officers keeping track and reporting.

This "go when you can" scheme gave us such an edge in response time that we were always ready when the transport arrived; our times were always better than the airborne brigade units.

Our response time was put to a real test when a major communist threat appeared in Vietnam. The 9th Marine Expeditionary Brigade was placed in an alert status--a local decision by us, not from higher command. By happenstance Secretary of the Navy Paul Nitze was passing through Okinawa as the Vietnam situation worsened. Even though he was not in the chain of operational command he "approved a training deployment" to Danang for the brigade headquarters. We flew off quickly before he could change his mind. Fortunately we could move in and lean on the Marine helicopter units (called "Shu Fly") near Danang. They took me on a number of orientation flights as we designed plans for a brigade landing. Our Navy with brigade Marines units were steaming our way as orders were formulated to deploy the brigade by sea and air if needed.

The airfield at Danang was obviously not ready for the deployment of our Marine Aircraft Squadron; our report of this led to plans for upgrading the air base at Danang in the coming months. Our beach studies and landing site selections were used a year later when the 3rd Marine Division landed in 1965.

Initially upon my arrival by air at Danang, I reported by phone to Saigon and was welcomed because at that time the threat from North Vietnam seemed very real with reports of forces moving south. In a few days, however, as the threat subsided, the Saigon staff wanted to know more about my presence and who sent me there. We sidestepped the issue by arranging to go aboard the flagship of the amphibious force as it arrived off Danang. Then we "bored holes" in the South China Sea by steaming in circles for the next few months before sailing to the Philippines as the situation in Vietnam seemed to ease.

My aide, Lieutenant Clay Atkins, loved to fly as much as any non-aviator I've known. While at Naval Air Station at Cubi Point in the Philippines, he got rides in some two-seater trainers. He was offered a ride to Okinawa and back and asked permission to go. Happenstance caused me to approve. We were alerted to a formal Navy reception for some foreign dignitaries, and I had no dress uniforms. Clay got his ride and my white uniform came back in a bomb bay. Clay Atkins was an outstanding Marine in every way, and remains to this day a close valued friend. (A son of his is named for me: my Godson!)

Chinese tailors and artisans: On Okinawa we kept a number of Chinese tailors busy-- their headquarters was Hong Kong--buying clothing, civilian and military, for ourselves and our family: shirts, suits, jackets, coats, dresses. We also collected artifacts of all varieties. Two happenings are noteworthy: We discovered that one of the shirt makers was giving a special price for seniors while charging the younger Marines more. We invited the owner out to our Headquarters and confronted him with our findings. He was "directed" to charge one price to all Marines or be "blackballed." He complied readily and the word spread throughout the businesses on Okinawa. We found no further such practices.

One Chinese merchant with whom I had dealt extensively came to my office in great distress saying that his license had been canceled by senior U.S. authorities and he could not find out why. My inquiries brought no information other than that customs problems were involved. I asked our security/counter intelligence units to explore the problem through their special channels. It turned out that the merchant allegedly had been caught up in a "sting" operation. There were photos of him purchasing items in Hong Kong, flying these items to Okinawa, hauling them to his shop without customs declarations or duties. His license was canceled but he was not told why so as to protect the ongoing sting. But the merchant was innocent. The items photographed were actually some which had been purchased in Hong Kong by a senior U.S. official on Guam who had flown them to Okinawa and had asked the merchant to pick them up at the airport for modification and refinishing. I obtained a letter confirming this; the license was cleared. The Chinese merchant was very relieved, most grateful, but greatly mystified. He felt that I had "saved his life" and made many efforts to favor me with gifts. When I returned home I discovered that some artifacts which I had refused to accept had been surreptitiously packed in my personal effects shipments at the time of my departure from Okinawa.

Five years later, my son Miles, a Marine lieutenant, saw my photo on the walls of this merchant's store, and made himself known. The old man became very emotional and wanted to reward Miles with a gift. Instead Miles ordered a set of fine furniture made by the merchant, which he paid for, but feels to this day that a lot of extra care went into its construction.

A Masters-full Tale: This was told by the staff (and confirmed by the Commanding General)--when the two Masters brothers were serving on Okinawa before my arrival, a problem arose which resulted in Brigadier General Bud Masters reporting to his brother Major General Jim Masters. The meeting did not go well and the Senior Master spoke disapprovingly to his younger brother and dismissed him summarily. Bud retreated to the door, but paused briefly before departing to say to Jim: "Blood does not mean a damn thing to you, does it?"

Aussies: I have often said that Australians come as close to being Yanks as any people I have known around the world. This was illustrated when an Aussie special mission company reported to Okinawa to participate in our SEATO Brigade exercise. Before the first night passed, there were reports from all over the island that they had arrived--every club, every bar, every hot bath parlor knew of them.

Wood and Glass: Aside from the tailoring, there were two other enterprises of note. Giant mahogany logs were shipped from the Philippines and unloaded offshore to be floated into inlets near Naha City. These were soon cut up for furniture, screens and other artifacts. All glass bottles were collected up, melted and blown into decorative glass grapes. Cola bottles were used primarily, with brown beer bottles next in popularity. Treasured were gin bottles for crystal clear grapes and blue medicine bottles. Glass blowers were found throughout the island each with a small electric furnace in his home. Through frequent shopping visits, I selected dozens of the very best grapes and kept them in my quarters for off-island visitors to choose from when their time for shopping was limited. My timing was bad near the end of my tour when a couple of VIP friends severely depleted my stock--I was forced into a crash shopping program to get enough quality grapes to take home.

As my tour drew to a close, little did I realize that my next tour would be back in Marine Corps Headquarters as G-l (Manpower), up to my collar stars with personnel problems and their planning. As to my ability to solve the GAO-reported readiness problems in 3rd Marine Division, my fitness report of 1 April 1964 (April Fool's Day?), written by Major General J. M. Masters, Sr., Commanding General, 3rd Marine Division, stated:

> Preeminently qualified--attitude, production, all around manners and method of operation leave nothing to be desired. Tireless, yet always cheerful--positive, demanding, yet always considerate of the viewpoint of others. Uncanny perception, unusual ability to anticipate; swift and sound in reaction. A real leader in every sense of the word who is constantly pedestalled by his juniors and rightly so. Potential unlimited.

Later, on a Special Report submitted on 26 June 1964 for my duty as "Commander of more than 6,000 men of different nationalities in an exercise in the Philippines to test the capabilities of the military forces of the Southeast Asia Treaty Organization (SEATO)" Rear Admiral J. M. Lee, U.S. Navy, Exercise Director, Combined Task Force 490, and Commander, Amphibious Group One, stated:

> SEATO Exercise "LIGTAS," Brigadier General Davis commanded the Landing Force (SEATO EXPEDI-TIONARY BRIGADE) and simultaneously acted as Troop Exercise Coordinator. He was faced with welding an international and interservice force, additionally complicated with numerous specialized elements of individual services into a coherent and effective whole, giving his Brigade a sound instructive and stimulating exercise plan and training them to readiness and finally leading them in executing the resulting highly complex, special forces/airborne/amphibious landings and operations ashore. It required the highest order of leadership, force, tact, intelligence, professional stature, diplomatic skill and competence in the field. In this demanding assignment, General Davis' performance was in every respect superb, and won him the profound admiration of all participants and observers. He is highly qualified, to an exceptional degree, for the highest Marine, joint, and international assignments.

It gives one a nice feeling to look back to such written statements about accomplishing missions in a tour of duty in the field. Somehow it all went together to lead right back to yet another tour of duty in our Nation's Capitol, at the Commandant's own Headquarters U. S. Marine Corps!

Ray Davis with Major General Jim Masters, Commander, 3rd Marine Division

Meeting with Secretary of Navy, Paul Nitze

CHAPTER 21. G-1 (MANPOWER), MARINE CORPS HEADQUARTERS

THE SECRETARY OF THE NAVY, WASHINGTON

The President of the United States takes pleasure in presenting a GOLD STAR in lieu of the second LEGION OF MERIT to MAJOR GENERAL RAYMOND G. DAVIS

UNITED STATES MARINE CORPS

for service as set forth in the following

CITATION:

For exceptionally meritorious conduct in the performance of outstanding service as Assistant Chief of Staff, G-l, Headquarters, United States Marine Corps, from 3 March 1965 to 15 March 1968. An extremely competent and resourceful leader responsible for formulating vital plans, policies and programs relating to Marine Corps manpower and personnel matters, Major General Davis displayed outstanding leadership, unique managerial abilities, and extraordinary professional skill in the development of manpower plans during a period of dynamic expansion of the Marine Corps, Although the environment of his tenure was characterized by a constantly increasing tempo of operations and expanding complexity of manpower issues, Major General Davis applied a vigorous objective thrust to the solution of a myriad of complex and critical manpower problems. The magnitude of his achievement is evidenced by the rapid expansion of the Marine Corps from 190,000 in 1965 to today's strength of over 300,000, the second largest Corps in our history, Concomitantly the budget for military personnel was increased from $765 million to $1.4 billion in the same time span. Major General Davis devoted countless hours to the development of sophisticated automated data models and processes to obtain ever improving managerial tools to exploit the modern computer in the achievement of optimal use of manpower assets during this period of turbulent growth. Despite the problems of rapid expansion, the accelerating tempo of operations in Southeast Asia, and strict policy constraints in the face of limited trained manpower availability, Major General Davis constantly provided a sure, firm guiding hand to the manpower managerial process while ensuring the preservation of those human factors which have been the hallmark of pride to the Marine Corps throughout its history. By his outstanding leadership, sound judgment, and inspiring devotion to the fulfillment of his responsibilities, Major General Davis was an inspiration to those who served with him. His performance throughout this critical period upheld the highest traditions of the Marine Corps and the United States Naval Service.

For the President,

/s/ Paul R. IGNATIUS, Secretary of the Navy

In a nutshell, the citation from SecNavy spells out the guts of my tour in Marine Corps Headquarters between my pre-Vietnam and Vietnam command billets. However it was not that cut and dried. First I reported in December 1964 to be Assistant Director of Personnel under Major General Jeff Fields, who had been 1st Marine Division G-3 (Operations) back at Peleliu at the time when I was Commanding Officer of Chesty's lst Battalion. I was to spend four months in the very bowels of Headquarters, Marine Corps, immersed in the actual ordering of Marines worldwide. It was of interest to me that for many years the Director of Personnel who managed the details of personnel management was a general officer's billet, while the G-l (Manpower) of the Corps who did overall manpower planning was one for a senior colonel. This meant that oftimes personnel operations did not actually bring about what G-1 had planned and programmed in response to policy and budgeting in Marine Corps manpower and personnel matters. That initial four months alerted me to the need for complete staff coordination during three years upstairs in the manpower management office.

My primary concern was providing manpower support for the Marine effort in Vietnam. That concern drove the whole effort, right down the line. When we started out, the Corps was very short of general officers, compared to the other services. We were required to fill a lot of joint billets in Defense Department activities which bled off the available general officers and aggravated the shortage. But that got resolved very quickly and very effectively on the basis of a single relationship.

Lieutenant General Chapman, the Chief of Staff, Headquarters, Marine Corps, had launched me informally to see what I could do. My first stop at the Pentagon was to sit down with an Air Force brigadier named Byrd in Department of Defense Manpower. We had worked together on a number of projects at manpower meeting conducted by civilian "Whiz Kids." As a uniformed minority, we stuck together in efforts to get military manpower requirements adequately funded. I gave him the general guidance Chapman had given me: To upgrade our General Officers from 61 to 75. In about 15 minutes Byrd had typed up a request for 14 additional marine generals, I signed for Commandant of Marine Corps "By Direction," and then Byrd walked it through OMB (Office of Manpower Budget), and set up a hearing in Congress in a week!

It happened so fast that I was truly embarrassed by it. I went back to Headquarters, Marine Corps and told General Chapman what was going on. General Greene (the Commandant) was away on a trip and before we could get him adequately briefed with all the backup material to support this increase to 75 and a necessary change in the law, Mr. Lemon, subcommittee chairman in the House set up a hearing. The Department of Defense (DOD) papers had been walked over to him with such urgency that he set up an immediate hearing and called for the Commandant to come over and justify it. This happened before we had completely developed the details and briefed General Greene on his testimony. The Marine Corps Commandant was livid because of our lack of backup data. He demanded endless charts and history to show to the committee. The Commandant, naturally, liked to go fully prepared, when he testified on the Hill, but we were caught short by this speedy transaction. We got together some rough charts and I rode in his limousine with him heading for

Capitol Hill to testify, handing him a statement he literally had never seen before. But I knew what the questions would be and I had the answers ready to pass to the Commandant. When we returned to his office and before we heard the favorable results he blasted us out of his office throwing some papers after us. Even though we got the general slots OK, General Greene laid down the law: No more fast deals!

By the time we got to the full Armed Services Committee, the Commandant had data and charts that were overwhelming. Meantime, Brigadier General Byrd had taken me to the congressional staffs and paved the way with written modifications to the law, etc. We got General Officers from 61 up to 75 in a couple of weeks total time! Chief of Staff Chapman said, "Ray Davis can do anything!" and put something like that on a fitness report. I really lucked into a fast start as G-1! We got the spaces, but I don't think General Greene ever forgave me for feeding him into that situation. (However, Lieutenant General Chapman later moved up from being Chief of Staff, Headquarters, Marine Corps to becoming Commandant)

Another major manpower problems was, of course, money. As the Vietnam War started, $11 billion was needed for DOD supplementary budget to pay for mobilization and deployment, but we were going to get only $1.7 billion. This meant that everything had to be gouged deeply and cut to try to keep the cost down, and the major cost is always manpower. Manpower is very expensive and we had a terrible time selling the needs for an adequate training, travel and casualty pipeline. As we committed the units into Vietnam; their support was essential. But we could not convince the bureaucrats in the Pentagon that we are going to have X number of casualties, this size of pipeline, this training cost. Things that, in our view, we had well documented, but the inexperienced civilians in charge were not convinced.

In fact, when Mr. Nitze was Secretary of the Navy, I sat across from him at one time and he questioned our casualty factors. I documented for him and in great detail how we arrived at them, and concluded with "That's the best military estimate we can possibly come up with and we've got to stand on it. Those are the casualties that we anticipate." And Secretary of Navy said: "Well, I'll accept that as your best advice, but I'll have to assert my authority as Secretary of the Navy and say that we are going to cut that by twenty percent," and he did. He was under pressure from his boss, to get this cost factor down. And that happened on all parts of it; the training base was chopped, the pipeline was chopped, the

184

casualty estimates were chopped, and that's the reason we had such a difficult time maintaining our rifle strength at the end of the line.

Also, there was some lack of communication and some mismanagement involved between Marine Corps Headquarters and Fleet Marine Force Pacific headquarters in Hawaii. When there was a shortage in the rifle units in Vietnam, the command in Hawaii would set up special training programs and grab people out of the pipeline in various basic skills and transfer them over to another which required retraining. Our Personnel Department was over a barrel as their training outputs were being warped. I made a trip out to the Pacific (including Vietnam) with an inspection team for six weeks to examine the manpower problem and we came back with a raft of recommendations. The most serious problem that I had observed out there was the fact that in running manpower from Fleet Marine Force Pacific Command in Hawaii, there was a lack of communication between there and manpower folks. It hurt to the degree that a battalion could be assigned a combat mission and suddenly find it stripped of many of its people by dictate from Hawaii. So, there was a communications breakdown, but it all got worked out.

Overall, I felt that there should have been a better manpower management team in General Walt's headquarters in Vietnam and less back in Hawaii. It could have been better handled if Washington and Danang (III Marine Amphibious Force Hq in Vietnam) had the main effort, with Hawaii doing more monitoring than managing. But there was a lesson learned from all this: the entire system needed to be mechanized; our records were totally inadequate. General Chapman was an ideal man to have as the Chief of Staff, and a great proponent of modernizing the system. He was pushing for computers and they had a special attraction for my engineer's mind. We immediately got busy and led the Marine Corps Headquarters in a move to a manpower management computer system.

I found Sam Jaskilka in a deadend job on some kind of a review panel in the Navy Department in Department of Defense. Sam, as a Major returning from service as a rifle company commander at Chosin, had gained experience as the 03 (Infantry) monitor in the Personnel Department; so he had basic personnel experience. He had also been my G-3, and I needed a "doer"--Sam was that. I got him into G-1; put him in charge of getting our computer system going; Sam knew little about computers, but soon became such an expert that, after I left, the Chief made him Head of the Marine Corps Headquarters Computer Division. Sam was on the escalator. (And later, how fortunate that he was there as Manpower

Head, three stars, to help salvage the Corps from some faulty policies of the Cushman/ Anderson era). Eventually Sam was to become the Assistant Commandant of the Marine Corps.

The biggest positive factor for Marine Corps Headquarters was Chapman--a leader of great intellect and total integrity. There was no shading the truth, no cover-up, no half truth--everything was up front, above board. He always gave the whole truth and nothing but the truth with Secretary of Navy, Joint Chiefs of Staff, Department of Defense, Congress, media, subordinate commands, etc. Plus he gave approval for a 3-star Manpower billet as Deputy Chief of Staff. Up until then, the Director of Personnel Department was always senior to G-l and at times ignored G-l plans and designs for manpower needs. Result was undertraining in some areas, over in others. Schools and career patterns were off kilter. Too many jobs seemed to be more important than riflemen in fire teams, for one example.

However our big personnel management problem at the beginning was the "GIGO" bit: Garbage In, Garbage Out. We had a room full of "garbage in" people, literally. As they opened the doors and started hiring to get the original punch card room opened up, I was told they hired untrained people to come in and operate the machines. We had sometimes 30 percent error input in the system, and couldn't figure out what was wrong. We could not live with that, so we launched big effort to move towards optics scanners and the like, to upgrade accuracy. The goal was to be that when the First Sergeant makes his report on a printed form, the optic scanner will get that information into the system correctly from the start. Millions of dollars could be saved.

Realize that with the computer data errors it's nearly impossible in a 200,000 Marine organization to know precisely where every Marine was at any moment in time. Uncertainty hurts the budget and many other money considerations, since the analysts always take the "worst case" to determine the dollars approved for the Corps. I don't think that this caused major problems in terms of effectiveness in a given unit, but in my time as G-l (Manpower Coordinator), the limited capabilities of machines to analyze the overall system made good planning impossible.

As a result of this tour, after previously serving in the G-2 (Intelligence) business and G-3 (Operations and Training) shop, and overseeing G-4 (Logistics) problems as Assistant Division Commander, 3rd Marine Division, I had a great feel for staff responsibilities and capabilities, and I was ready to go to Vietnam. A billet request for a Deputy to the Army Commander of the Provisional Corps in the northern part of South Vietnam came into our Headquarters, and I told General Chapman I had the ideal man for the job: "Raymond G. Davis!"

A glance at a typical fitness report by Lieutenant General L. E. Chapman, Jr., Chief of Staff, Marine Corps Headquarters, Washington, D.C. stated:

> As principal Marine Corps coordinator and advisor for personnel planning, programming and budgeting, Major General Davis' outstanding abilities have been powerfully evident over many backbreaking months. He is calm, determined, very intelligent, selfless and wise--an able negotiator and speaker, and he has created imaginative automated approaches to our many personnel planning and programming problems. A thorough gentleman, and a top-flight Marine with a great future.

Following this, General Chapman honored my request and ordered me into combat in South Vietnam!

Back to the field!

Knox and Ray Davis pin 2nd Lieutenant Gordon Miles Davis' brand new bars!

CHAPTER 22. DEPUTY CG, PROVISIONAL CORPS, VIETNAM

In the early 1960s, North Vietnamese communists guerrillas (Viet Cong) entered South Vietnam in increasing numbers. By 1965 the communist main-force regiments and battalions posed such a threat that the U.S. launched forces into South Vietnam to assist in defense. A very gradual buildup of forces failed to provide the security needed and led to piecemeal operations, more and more casualties, with little progress to show for it. It took four (4) years to position the needed forces into Vietnam. By then, people in the U.S. had given up. Our forces were withdrawn, and South Vietnam was surrendered to the communists. I arrived in Vietnam one year before our withdrawal.

"Destroy the enemy--this is the only correct role for military forces!" Certainly this is what Chesty Puller taught back in Basic School days. Once again in March, 1969 I found myself enroute to war, my third, determined to carry out this dictum. In the '40s, it was World War II; in the '50s, it was Korea; and now in the '60s, it was Vietnam. I had visited Vietnam before, as a brigade commander for 3rd Marine Division and again as G-1 (Manpower), Marine Corps Headquarters, so I knew where I was going and what I hoped to do. And before long, my son Miles, who was a student in The Basic School, would be on his way to Vietnam, too, to his first war.

Naturally I felt well-qualified for any duties that I might assume over there, since I had commanded on just about every level, and had served in the personnel, intelligence, operations, and logistics worldwide. Thus, I had the prior experience, plus the luck of the draw, in that I had been on great terms with Lieutenant General Bill Rosson, U.S. Army, who was commanding the Provisional Corps in the northern I Corps area just to the south of the demilitarized zone. While serving as General Chapman's G-1, I was happy to hear that Rosson was asking via the grapevine for me to be his deputy.

We had attended the National War College together, where we were very close friends, plus our paths had crossed a couple of times since. Bill was, in my view, the ideal type of commander who was really out with the troops, getting the most out of his forces all the time, day and night. While I was to spend a relatively short time as his Deputy Commanding General, I spent most of those initial days just with him. He gave me a helicopter to follow him around, for the better part of a month. It was an ideal way to get oriented and attuned to the entire situation so that I could assume command if anything happened to him.

Bill's primary effort was in orienting me towards something similar to what I had done in the 3rd Marine Division on Okinawa in 1964, that is, in terms of the readiness of forces and the effectiveness of forces. I was just getting involved in the details when I got word that I was going up to command the 3rd Division at Dong Ha along the demilitarized zone. It was like a musical chairs where General Bill Van Ryzin was going back to be Chief of Staff in Washington, and Rathvon "Tommy" Tompkins was leaving as Commanding General, 3rd Marine Division to succeed Bill as deputy to the senior Marine Commander at Danang. Tommy had come out as an emergency measure when Major General Hochmuth was killed in a helicopter crash, so he hadn't been out there very long when he was moved south to the headquarters.

I've been asked many times if my assignment as Rosson's deputy was because of my having known him at the National War College. That certainly was a contribution, because when your name comes up for assignment, it's checked out with many senior commanders. Bill later told me that when he heard my name, he went to bat to get me out there. That's one of the great advantages of the National War College. Not only Army, Navy, Air Force, but State Department, CIA--meeting so many people when you're there. You are together for the better part of a year, arguing with one another, discussing things, making trips to the various parts of the world; it's a very fine relationship and to me, a main gain for the time spent in the College.

When I arrived in Vietnam, Military Assistance Command (Forward)--MACV (Fwd)-- was in transition, as General Abrams was moving it back south, and leaving Provisional Corps, or XXIV Corps, up in the northern area, in which also was located the 3rd Marine Amphibious Force (III MAF) headquartered in Danang. The senior Marine Corps command, III Marine Amphibious Force, eventually became the boss headquarters over XXIV Corps, but there was no way of short-circuiting the direct channel between Abrams in Saigon, and Rosson, because many things from Saigon were in support of the Army units up north. This was the Army's support channel in the same way there was a lot of direct channel dealing between 3rd Marine Division and III Marine Amphibious Force in Danang for Marine support purposes, even though I was to be under the operational command of XXIV Corps when I went to the Division. Complex though the responsibilities were, I really can't pinpoint any serious problems.

I did not see having a senior army command in the Marine zone as a vote of no confidence on the part of Gen Westmoreland vis a vis Marines at Danang. The Army had put its best and most important forces forward when they deployed the air cavalry and the airborne divisions and other divisions. These were the best the Army had, and they were in an all-helicopter posture. They had not previously fully committed all of these kinds of forces to combat, so I can see how the Army would be ticklish about turning them over to Marines.

Along with the 3rd Marine Division, Lieutenant General Rosson had the 1st Air Cavalry Division and the 101st Airborne Division, the Army's best. They had the best material support, a full allowance of helicopters, the best commanders. And Rosson pushed them, pressed them, and kept them out after the enemy. That was the key. I could feel that Rosson was concerned about the immobility of the Marines in Quang Tri Province. One time when the North Vietnamese invaded through the demilitarized zone with two regiments just above Dong Ha, he was somewhat disappointed the Marines didn't really apply all forces to the situation. And I agreed with that. I tried to understand that when forced into a defensive situation involving the manning of strong points for so long a period, one can become less aggressive in the pursuit and destruction of the enemy.

I kept remembering that the Puller outlook on war was one of total dedication to the proposition that you go out and find the enemy or guerrilla and destroy him. He never once thought about trying to protect an area or strong point and displacing people or winning hearts and minds. All that was totally secondary. I really believe that if we had started with that premise in Vietnam, it would have been over very quickly. Instead we ended up in total disaster.

I learned a lot during those few months with Rosson. The most important thing was air mobility. I was at Quantico after World War II when one of the answers to the atomic battlefield was the helicopter. You might say that Marines "invented" the troop-carrying helicopter, but we failed to exploit it fully. The Army came along with the large numbers of helicopters and had greater air mobility. They could really exploit the mobility of the helicopter, combined with the highly mobile air power and artillery and engineering equipment. Being oriented towards helicopters already and watching this with Rosson, I learned the lesson of operating with helicopters on high ground as opposed to the way the Marines had been doing it in flat landing zones. Out in the mountains in the western part of Vietnam there were no flat landing zones, so through necessity the Army started knocking off the tops of hills and hummocks and making places for helicopters. This was an entirely different concept, and I picked it up immediately.

As I recently told a leadership symposium at our Marine Corps Command and Staff College in Quantico, I sent my aide, Captain Dick Camp, now retired Colonel Dick Camp (and author of the best seller "LIMA 6," which included his day by day experiences as a rifle company commander in the Khe Sanh defensive operation) to visit with 1st Air Cavalry Division, 101st Airborne Division, and the Marines, and to propose an article for the Marine Corps Gazette, an illustrative problem on the Marine Regiment in the Heliborne Assault, highlighting the lessons learned by combining Army and Marine concepts.. We worked it over, and co-authored the piece.

Strangely enough, the editorial board of the Gazette turned it down; said it wasn't "real." I called Lieutenant General Bill Van Ryzin, Chief of Staff at Marine Corps Headquarters, who had just returned from Vietnam, and said: "Bill, you know what's real, those guys don't!" So they published it. It became the bible for the first few months of my oncoming 3rd Marine Division command--but I'll get to that in a moment.

In defense of the Marines, the situation was changed from the Korean War or World War II. We are somewhat a victim of our circumstances and our capabilities. In World War II it was kind of a shoulder to shoulder situation. In Korea we had a little more mobility but still were confined by our ability to move over the ground, walking or in jeeps, and so forth. Here comes a highly mobile force with everybody in a helicopter; the Assistant G-3 (Operations) had his own helicopter in this Army. There were just unbelievable numbers of helicopters, and with these, you can, as we found when enough helicopters are available, fight the battle quite differently. I presume that the Army was looking at what the Marines were doing as their helicopter lift was developed. Our CH-46A troop carrier helicopters had the tail come off a couple of times and we had to stand down, rebuild them. They were reduced from lifting a rifle platoon of three squads to only one squad. Possibly Army was looking at this while designing their own capabilities to move forces by helicopter with a different concept, thus were somewhat critical of how Marines were doing it. There was never any criticism of the Marine way once we got the helicopters and got going.

It was not a matter of commanders or personalities. Bill Rosson thought very highly of Tommy Tompkins, who was under his command. He lamented the military posture that we were in, however, and I had to agree with him. When we could, we needed to drop our primarily defensive strategy. It was such a defensive posture that on one of my visits up there initially with Rosson, we observed a situation involving a heavy action the night before. The Marine troop units had considered that their primary mission was to break off contact with the enemy and get back into the battalion position before dark. That's the way the thing was designed. As a result, we had some extra casualties in breaking off before dark instead of whipping the enemy--you always have less casualties if you whip him and stand on the battleground when it's over. Then you control all of the wounded, yours and his.

Thus I served with Rosson for the better part of two months--out with him every day, directly involved and actually participating in these high-mobility operations that the air-cavalry and airborne division were conducting. I had reviewed their writing and observed their lifts of a couple of Marine battalions at that time. It was interesting to me that the Marines were beginning to participate in this kind of a high-mobility helicopter operation, which they really hadn't done before. We had our operations usually tied to selecting an ideal place for a helicopter to sit down as opposed to sitting down where you can best defeat the enemy. In the past helicopter landing zones had been an overpowering requirement too often.

I saw what was happening up in the Marine division and while participating in Rosson and Westmoreland conversations, I came to feel that it was not necessary to have so much of the force tied down to fixed positions. We had something like two dozen battalions tied down, with little exception, to these fixed positions. The situation demanded otherwise. So when the Army moved into Operation Pegasus to relieve the Khe Sanh operation they applied forces directly responsive to the enemy's dispositions and forgot about real estate--forgetting about bases, going after the enemy in key areas--this punished the enemy most. Pegasus demonstrated the complete decisiveness of high mobility operations. The way to get it done was to get out of those fixed positions, to get mobile and go out to destroy the enemy on our terms--not sit there and absorb the shot and shell and frequent penetrations that he was able to mount. All this led me, as soon as I heard of my assignment to 3rd Marine Division, to do something I had never done before or since, and that is to move in prepared in the first hours to completely turn the command upside down.

During this brief, but very illuminating, tour with Lieutenant General Bill Rosson's Provisional Corps, I returned mentally to my The Basic School days with tactics instructor Chesty Puller, when he related the details of the minute-by-minute, day-by-day, week-by-week campaigning on the trail, the actual combat in places like Nicaragua, which were, in essence, mini-Vietnams. I found that his manner of teaching was the best way to find out about the war business: to listen to (and read about) the people who have experienced it. (Which Marine Commandant General Al Gray caused to be done throughout the Corps).

But now, thanks to Bill Van Ryzin finishing his Vietnam tour, and Tommy Tompkin leaving the billet of Commanding General of the 3rd Marine Division, I was now moving back to the same organization of which I had been the Assistant Division Commander just a few years before -- and I was really ready for it. I had enjoyed a great tour with Bill Rosson, and had experienced both a jungle war in the Pacific and a mountain war in Korea.

CHAPTER 23. CG, 3RD MARINE DIVISION, VIETNAM

Recently, Bill Davis received the following from my former aide, Dick Camp:

Dear Bill: As you know, I was General Davis' first aide in Vietnam--serving from the end of March until I rotated home in July, 1968. During that time he was Deputy, Provisional Corps Vietnam and then Commanding General, 3rd Marine Division. (I also served with him upon his return home to command the Education Center and then Marine Corps Development and Education Command). Looking back over the years I have come to realize what a tremendous individual he was. I think you will agree that he had a superb tactical ability--probably the finest division commander the Corps has ever had. I was fortunate enough to have seen him remotivate an entire Division so that it became a winning team.

One small story: Prior to assuming command, General Davis told me to pass the word that he would address all key staff officers and regimental commanders in the Division conference room immediately after the change of command. He began his talk by waving a copy of the High Mobility article (published by the Marine Corps Gazette) and announcing that from this point on, the Division would use it as a guide. He told the assembled officers that no longer would infantry guard fixed installations--that they would be protected by their tenant units. There was no doubt in my mind that he meant exactly what he said. I stayed in the room after he left to judge reactions--as a junior officer I was amazed at the almost unprofessional reaction of the august senior citizens. "Who does he think he is?" "Wait until he finds out what it's really like." were typical of the statements.

Less than a week later, the South Vietnamese Army briefer mentioned to the General that elements of a North Vietnamese Army battalion had been identified just north of Dong Ha in the so-called "Square" area. Before he could proceed, the Old Man stopped him and asked several questions which served to more fully bring out the situation. The South Vietnamese reaction was something to behold. I think in all the years that he had briefed the Division no one had ever asked any questions. The General turned to me and requested that his helicopter standby in order to take us to the Army of the Republic of Vietnam 2nd Regimental headquarters. Before I could let them know we were coming--it was only a two minute flight-- we landed in their compound. It looked like we had disturbed an anthill--South Vietnamese soldiers running everywhere. Colonel Giai ran out and escorted the General into his headquarters. He confirmed the report and added several other pieces of information. At the end of the conversation, I asked him if his 2nd Regiment could support an operation against the North Vietnamese Army. He said he could furnish two battalions. We flew back to the Division compound and then walked to the 9th Marines' command post.

You could see a very skeptical look on the Commanding Officer's and Operations Officer's faces--previous to this they couldn't scare up a reinforced rifle squad (their infantry were guarding fixed installations). They were asked to take charge of the operation, and before they could reply, the General told them of the two South Vietnamese battalions, a battalion of Marines would fly in from Khe Sanh, one would move across from Con Thien, and another would move down the Cua Viet--a multi-battalion encirclement. Needless to say, this action started the ball rolling--plus the arrival of a fresh helicopter squadron in the Division Zone. By the way, General Homer Dan Hill was specifically assigned to Marine Air Group-39 to ensure that the Division did not hurt their helicopters. What the Wing Commander didn't know was that the two generals got along famously.

While I had not known that Dick and Bill had carried on correspondence, that certainly rings true. The change of command took place at 1100. At 1300 I assembled the staff and commanders. Before dark, battalion defensive positions had become company positions. It happened just that fast. Serving as Rosson's Deputy gave me the opportunity to observe the situation, to become a part of it. I had enough time to stake out exactly the way it should be. At the meeting I didn't ask or plead with them. I ordered: "Before dark, these things will happen." I laid out the scheme, what were later called my "before dark dictates."

I already had permission from my commanders to violate the McNamara Line concept.

McNamara's brain trust had come up with a defensive concept of putting manned strong points across the demilitarized zone, with all these megabuck sensors in between, to keep the guerrillas out. Well, we weren't fighting guerrillas. We were fighting North Vietnamese Army divisions. So the concept was faulty. The strong points were too far apart to protect the line, and it was a tying down of forces.

I directed that each of the four or five forward positions where we had a battalion holed up--or hiding out, as I called it--would now have only one company, and the other three rifle companies and the headquarters would deploy as a mobile force to seek out the enemy. The result of this was that we moved out on the offensive. The 3rd Division had become too defensive minded. Even when the Army was moving brigades around Khe Sanh, there was still concern about the role the Marines were playing and a reluctance of Marines to participate. They seemed convinced that they couldn't break out of there, take this hill, and run over here and take that hill, as they were invited to do. They did and it worked, but there was a reluctance.

I was in on the talk about it up at Khe Sanh and they could not visualize the Army concept. Having been there all this time--there were five Marine battalions pinned down at Khe Sanh, almost completely immobilized, plus the five so-called strong points in the demilitarized zone--the relief of and closing down of Khe Sanh was a major change. When asked by the newsmen: "How can you abandon Khe Sanh after you paid so much for it?" I told them that I can manage that whole area with a couple of mobile battalions better than it was being managed with five fixed, in place, battalions. I also wanted to bring back unit integrity. I couldn't believe what I found out there. In the Marine Corps, even though we had fixed regimental organization in our organization tables, we had a shambles as far as organization on the ground was concerned. This whole business of rotating units in and out of fixed positions just served to disrupt the organization, all under the guise of flexibility. The regimental commander didn't know his own regiment at all. With four of my regiments, half their battalions belonged to them and the other half were down at Danang.

When I reduced forward positions to company size, a mobile force of several battalions was organized. It became easier to put the regiments and battalions together with the engineers, artillery, communications, and everything that belongs together. Unit integrity is essential for high-mobility mountain warfare--very complex, very fast-moving operations where you must depend on people knowing each other and being able to respond. It was crucial to the kind of war I wanted to fight.

To make the unified forces more effective, I also started the Division on greater mobility. Fortunately, I arrived at a time when our resources were fully generated: the new model of the CH-46 helicopter was becoming available, with greater power and lift capacity. Soon we were knocking the tops off little mountain peaks, putting our forces up there to move down against the enemy.

When I was in ROTC at Georgia Tech in the thirties, I did a presentation on Stonewall Jackson's valley campaigns in the Civil War. The thing that impressed me about Jackson was his mobility: he would mount his horse and ride to the sound of the guns. I thought of that in Vietnam when we finally got enough helicopters. The division commander could mount his horse, so to speak, and ride to the sound of the guns. The Army provided me with a super-powered helicopter so I could operate in those mountains with safety. I would fly out to firebases and forward units in the field every day.

I learned from traveling around that the troops were delighted by my orders. They had been holed up for months, and now they were doing what Marines were supposed to do. So they took to it. And pretty soon the North Vietnamese accommodated us by launching down in there to get themselves clobbered. In my area we destroyed five North Vietnamese Army divisions in four months. They didn't realize the force we had in terms of Marines with helicopters and mobile firepower, so they just ruptured themselves. We intercepted radio reports from these units as they marched back up toward Hanoi. They were reporting complete destruction: all the officers and non-commissioned officers killed, weapons all lost, no supplies. Not one of these five divisions came back south for the next two years. We had butchered them. We were out looking for the enemy--as Chesty taught us--and winning!

General Abrams taking over as the Commanding General of the U.S. Military Command in Vietnam also helped us. Abe was my kind of guy. I guess we had initially stuck to the position defense and McNamara Line because the forces were inadequate for effective operations. But now that the forces were in place and we had the capability to do things differently, the whole attitude changed. I remember I was flying around up by the demilitarized zone with Abrams. I was complaining about the fact that up there were 162 North Vietnamese Army cannons which could open up on us anytime, and I wasn't permitted to do a thing. His answer was, "General, don't you worry. We're not going to let them s--t on us anymore."

196

With that, General Abrams accepted a design, a new generation of computerized fire direction and control. He even had college professors out there working on it. With every enemy cannon that would open up, the computers would tell our eight-inch guns where to shoot. In thirty or forty days we had air reconnaissance pictures showing that every cannon that fired on us had been turned over or knocked out.

The result was that the North Vietnamese said: "Let's have a cease-fire across the demilitarized zone. If you don't shoot at us anymore, we won't throw rockets into the cities." Well, we had just captured 3,500 of their rockets in the mountains so they didn't have any rockets. But the politicians watching this were so anxious for some sort of agreement that they grabbed at it. On October 31, 1968, the U.S. announced the cessation of bombing of North Vietnam, in return for a pledge by the enemy not to attack South Vietnamese cities or violate the demilitarized zone. We gave up our advantage and let them up. This is unmilitary. It was not pursuing success, as you do in the military. It hurt our ability to pursue the war to a successful conclusion--namely, defeating the enemy.

Once those divisions were destroyed and we had seized all their bases, we were able to destroy the Main Force regiments of the Vietcong that were supported by the North Vietnamese Army. Then we were able to go into the villages and get the Vietcong out. Eventually we had total pacification. In the early days since we didn't have enough forces to protect the villages, we ended up in a major displacement of the population into smaller areas where they could be protected. That was backwards. Lewis Puller taught me that you spend your full time, day and night, pursuing those guerrilla forces. That's the way to pacify the countryside. You don't sit around trying to protect the population. The guerrillas can only work when they are supported by main forces; the only way to get guerrillas is to destroy main forces and their bases of support.

When we went back and cleaned out the villages, Quang Tri Province became totally secure--so secure that I felt safe in any village out there, day or night. That was my challenge to the newsmen, to get them used to the idea that this place was secure. In the helicopter I would say: "You can point anywhere in this province, day or night, and we'll land there and I'll take off my pistol and we'll walk around there alone, to show you how secure it is." I said many times that Quang Tri Province was much safer than the streets of most American cities.

To keep the enemy out, and to collect intelligence for the mobile forces, we had sixty four-man reconnaissance teams throughout those mountains. Twenty of them would be on the ground all the time; the others would be getting ready to go or they would be coming out and getting refurbished. Every day at our staff briefing, my officers knew I would ask the same question: "How many patrols do we have on the ground?" If we had less than twenty, they would have until noon to get twenty on the ground. That's how we kept track of hundreds of square miles that we were responsible for. We kept people in key spots all the time to report on enemy activities, and when they located supplies or concentrated forces we could go and get them.

The mode of operations of these reconnaissance teams was purely stealth. In this large area we had to know what was going on in those mountains. The North Vietnamese Army had established logistic bases about ten miles apart. They had high speed trails, some with hand rails, so that at night, porters could carry supplies from one logistic base to the next, and hide from our air during the day. We kept the reconnaissance teams in all the key places where activity was suspected so we really knew what was going on in our vast area. Where we found activity we went in and smashed them.

Late one day a special request came from one of the patrols, "Send a large helicopter for emergency liftout". I approved quickly when I heard that a tiger had attacked a member of the patrol. The patrol leader had killed the tiger and wanted to bring it out.

We measured the tiger to be near eleven (11) feet from nose to tail tip. It had slipped through the high grass, grabbed the Marine and jumped 15 feet into a shell crater. A buddy chased after them; the tiger was startled and released his prey long enough to be killed. The large helicopter ramp was lowered for the Marines to drag the tiger on board. The tiger skin was placed on display in the Recon headquarters and attracted many visitors.

Incidentally, this tiger turned out to be an old female, missing a fang--this saved the Marine from suffering serious damage. The victim of the tiger attack was Richard P. Goolden who was subsequently medically retired as staff sergeant

There were a lot of enemy supplies and men over the border in Laos, but I was not permitted to go over and get them. We had an ambassador in Laos who was committed to protecting the "neutrality" of Laos, as he called it. Hell, the place was full of North Vietnamese troops and trucks by the hundreds were coming down the trail at night with ammunition to kill Americans. He screamed like a stuck pig when a rifle company got over into his territory during Operation Dewey Canyon. But the North Vietnamese didn't know where the border was and didn't care.

Let me speak to Dewey Canyon for a moment. In the '89-'90 School Year of the Marine Corps Command and Staff College (MCCSC) in Quantico, which in past years you remember I had attended then headed, they held a leadership symposium for these field grade officer students on our biggest, most successful and really typical operation against North Vietnamese Army Main Force troops and supplies. Dewey Canyon was kind of a graduation piece for any number of like operations on a lesser scale throughout the mountain area. The 9th Marine Regiment had captured many caches of supplies before; they were not new at this. They had built many firebases before, also. In fact, the 9th Marines was called my "Mountain Regiment," my "Strike Force Regiment."

Thus, the Marine Corps Command and Staff College faculty set up an entire day devoted to this operation, some two decades after the actual events. They brought onto the stage six participants: The Corps Commander, Lieutenant General Dick Stilwell (General, US Army, Retired), Rosson's successor; the Division Commander, Major General Ray Davis (General, US Marine Corps, Retired); the Regimental Commander, Colonel Bob Barrow (General, US Marine Corps, Retired, 27th Commandant of Marine Corps); one Battalion Commander, Lieutenant Colonel George Smith (Major General, US Marine Corps, Retired); one Company Commander, Captain Wes Fox (an active duty US Marine Corps Colonel, who earned the Medal of Honor on this operation); the Regimental Air Officer, Lieutenant Colonel Stan Gatz (Colonel, US Marine Corps, Retired).

In this order, each of the participants in the original operation explained the planning and execution of that regimental helicopter-borne operation from the perspective of the billet he filled at the time. It was fascinating to hear and see the six levels, actually five levels plus the overall air operations for those levels. Realize that without air support, there was just no way that this multifaceted operation could have succeeded. Each of these officers took almost exactly thirty minutes per presentation in the morning, then the afternoon was spent in the student group conference rooms answering any and all questions, much the same as the system I had set up years before when I was the Director, Senior School.

Essentially, my part was to bring the students up to a point of how we got situated to go into Dewey Canyon, most of which I have spoken to in this chapter: The demilitarized zone, Khe Sanh, the high mobility mode, our recon teams. Then I had to get into our air support problems and how we solved them, because the "normal" Marine Air--Ground Team concepts just were not doing the job when I first became Commanding General, 3rd Marine Division. Normally, each Marine Division has a Marine Air Wing of some 300 tactical aircraft providing its air support. In Vietnam, we had one wing supporting two divisions. The wing itself was in the Danang area, in the vicinity of the III Marine Amphibious Force and 1st Marine Division. We were in the northernmost area of South Vietnam, many miles away. To alleviate this, the Wing Commanding General placed a helicopter Group (the air equivalent of an infantry regiment) in my area, because of the time and danger of helicopters flying all the way up from Danang.

One day, assistant wing commander, Brigadier General Homer Dan Hill, appeared on the scene. I placed him at Firebase Vandegrift with my Assistant Division Commander, then Brigadier General Carl Hoffman, who headed Task Force Hotel. With him, Brigadier General Hill brought authority from the Wing Commander to not only offer professional advice to me, but to run our air operations. And this is very important when you are totally dependent on air. You get troops in a helicopter, you get half of that unit out on a hill, the weather closes in or something else happens, and you have to make choices. Without the Wing Commanding General's authority, the ground Commanding General can't require pilots to fly an extra hour over what the Chief of Naval Operations has said they can fly. You can't have them fly in situations that are not "normal." But with the Assistant Wing Commander there, he can see our plans taking place and respond to them and to us. That way we knew that he knew what we wanted to do, so we would be supported. Ultimately, this became a fixture for all of our operations. The Air Wing supported two Marine Divisions; the Division "up front" had the Assistant Wing Commander there to employ the air resources (while III Marine Amphibious Force and 1st Marine Division in Danang had the Wing Commanding General close at hand).

Homer Dan Hill (who later headed the Division of Aviation in Marine Corps Headquarters) gave us great flexibility. For example, during Dewey Canyon the weather closed in totally. Resupplying the troops out in the mountains approached impossibility, but we worked this out: We established three major areas, Firebase Vandegrift, Quang Tri Air Base and the Army's Camp Evans, all with helicopters ready to go with supplies. Then if on Dewey Canyon's firebase weather opened up the slightest bit, for a couple of hours, one of those three logistic bases might send off its helicopters immediately. Usually one of those three would also be open, so resupply was done. When all was closed down completely, then airdrops were made to Dewey Canyon, much like those made to Fox Company back south of the Chosin at Toktong Pass when my battalion was moving cross-country through the snow. The biggest difference was that this was pure jungle, triple canopy.

As we relived Dewey Canyon that day, through both the words of the multi-level participants and TV news recaps of the operation at that time, it really took me back some two decades to just how we performed and the many lessons learned which hopefully these students would pass throughout the Corps in their future billets as major, operations officers in ground and air units, and lieutenant colonel, commanding officers. We were really pushing the lessons I learned from Chesty to another level.

One major change that we made was in the infantry assault. We did not storm up every defended pinnacle. An example occurred on a visit to the battalion commander. We sat down and talked the thing over, sent small scouting parties up to get enemy defenses specifically located, then put air and artillery on them to grind them up. We did this for two days until there was not much up there to kill Marines. We got the job done with practically no casualties, whereas if we had gone with a blood and guts attitude of just assaulting it, we would have had 25 or 30 people killed. Conversely, I found that when Marines are in the defense, and the situation requires it, they can really dig in with carefully designed final protective fires, etc..

We all know about the ability of the North Vietnamese Army-Viet Cong to organize the ground, their knowledge of the terrain, their ability to dig, their ability to fight at night, their ability to fight with a lesser logistics support base, fewer supplies. I think that they are brought up with this kind of existence at home. I've seen reports on North Vietnam, where they've tunneled and dug, I mean that every hill and every place else was tunneled out and dug out. I believe that this is a part of that governmental system of keeping them busy. If you keep them working hard, they think that they are getting something done.

The enemy was forced to do it to survive, but where we had to dig in, like Khe Sanh and some of those hills around there, we had some pretty fancy, substantial digging done by Marines when the pressure was on them. Some Marine commanders got themselves involved in building a perfect defense around a hilltop. They had cleared fields of fire and had covered holes with shooting slots. It was amazing what Americans can do when they put their mind to it. You could hardly tell that a defensive position was there, yet they had 80 or 100 Marines along the area with good secure positions. It's an art we'd lost, in large measure from World War I.

Major General Ray Davis (right), Commanding General, 3rd Marine Division, escorts Lieutenant General Henry W. Buse (center), Commanding General, Fleet Marine Corps, Pacific, at Cam Lo in northern I Corps of Vietnam

Laying corner stones for a children's hospital sponsored by 3rd Marine Division, Vietnam, 1969

CG, III MAF Herman Nickerson was my mentor in Vietnam, Korea, and Senior School. (With Lieutenant General Lam, CG, Vietnamese I Corps)

Another longtime mentor with Nick and Ray Davis: General Lew Walt, ACMC and former CG, III MAF

APO 4895, 14 February 1969
Major General Ngo Quang Truong
Commanding General, 1st Infantry Division
11th Tactical Area

Republic of Vietnam
RVN Armed Forces
1st Infantry Division
11th Tactical Area

No. 65 /VPTL/SD1

TO

Major General Raymond D. Davis
Commanding General
3rd Marine Division

Dear General Davis;

    A year has passed and we are again in the season which is dearest to the Vietnamese people - TET. I am sincerely grateful for the support rendered to the 1st ARVN Infantry Division, and the Regional and Popular Forces of the 11th DTA by the American Forces during the past year. With your help, we not only defeated the enemy at every turn but have been able to rid our area of responsibility of the Communist aggressors and provide security for the people of Quang Tri and Thua Thien Province to a degree never reached heretofore.

    As a result of the sacrifices you have made, the Vietnamese people in the 11th DTA will be able to celebrate this traditional day in safety. Without your help this would not have been possible.

    Therefore, during this special season, and on behalf of the Vietnamese Armed Forces in the 11th DTA, I take this opportunity to extend to you my most immense thanks and my wishes for a happy and successful Lunar New Year to you.

Sincerely,

Truong

Major General Ngo Quang Truong

A letter of commendation from Major General Ngo Quang Truong, Commanding General, 1st Infantry Division in 11th Tactical Area, Vietnam, 1969

Twice Ray Davis presented Purple Heart to his son Miles Davis

Ray Davis presents captured rice to a village chief (400 tons from Operation Dewey Canyon)

lst Lieutenant G. M. Davis is receiving 2nd Purple Heart from his father, Major General Ray Davis, Vietnam, 1969

Ray Davis and Aide Dick Camp visit Fire Support Base.

Reverand Billy Graham visits Ray Davis in Dong Ha.

Incoming! This is the enemy gun my sergeant got to Quantico, based on my one-paragraph letter telling him to do so!

Outgoing! These are friendlies firing from Firebase Razor during Operation Dewey Canyon.

As I visited with Dick Stilwell, I thought of the great support Army gave us throughout; helicopters when we needed them; anything we asked for. I'd get on the phone and they'd launch an Army brigade up there to help me if necessary. I knew they would never leave me out on the end of a limb. And of course Marine support was always there. But I cannot stress enough that the tactical situation required an air commander on the ground with the infantry commander, as we had in Homer Dan Hill. When you put Marines out on those pinnacles, you can't walk out to them, supply them, get their casualties out without air support. This was really an air-ground war we were fighting up in Quang Tri Province. And we made it work--together.

One thing we did learn was that if the Assistant Wing Commander could not overrule restrictions from the Wing Commanding General, at least you knew about it, as the tactical situation developed. There was firsthand information from the air commander what he was going to be able to do and what he wouldn't be able to do. Then you could translate what he could do into some positive action. Being with Bob Barrow reminded me that when we got his forces implanted out in Dewey Canyon area and the weather closed in for 10 or 11 days, that was real trouble! With total reliance on the air for support and supply, and all of a sudden the weather is such that under any kind of normal instructions from an air command they would close down all flight operations. In such challenging situations you must have somebody who's there and has the authority to make exceptions to those ironclad rules and restrictions.

As an example, when one of Barrow's units started reporting: "I've got a hole in the sky right now," and Camp Evans would say the same, then add: "I predict that it's going to last for a half-hour or so," somebody had to have the authority to say: "Helicopter, you go there, you pick up this and you take it there," when the helicopters are sitting back in a place where they had been told not to fly. Also, as a ground commander, I realize that Marine aviators have all the guts in the world. Maybe the commanders were reluctant to risk their resources but the aviators were never reluctant to fly into danger; they did that all the time!

As for fixed wing support, remember that in World War II and Korea we had air support on station, literally overhead as we advanced on the ground. When we planned to jump off in the morning, we wanted four Corsairs on station for a certain time, at a certain time, and they'd be there. Now you can't do that with jets. They don't have the time on station that we had in the old airplanes. And so we lost that kind of flexibility, because when they're on station up there, and the situation on the ground changes, you could call on them to do what needed to be done.

Also we had the problem of Korea's Joint Operations Center and Vietnam's single management problem for air operations which removed Marine Air from our direct control. The net effect of those systems was that more Marine air went in support of Army. I do not disagree with Army infantry getting supported, but I think that the Air Force needs to plan for adequate support for the Army divisions, so that it won't be necessary to use so much of our Marine capability.

As the Dewey Canyon battalion commander, George Smith, and company commander, Wes Fox, talked in the symposium, it took me back to the rationale for mounting out that operation. My whole concept of getting out on the offensive and the use of fire support bases was a result of the enemy situation. We had discovered that his logistics system was designed to support not only his main forces, divisions and regiments, but also his local forces through prepositioned supplies. He would start down through Laos or the demilitarized zone and establish these concealed bases about every 10 miles. He brought supplies as far as he could by truck, and when he was exposed to our air, he moved them by hand. Each of these bases was prepared with bunkers and tunnels and hideaways, so that his porters could leave their supplies and dodge our air attacks.

When our 4-man reconnaissance teams were scattered about, they would discover and monitor these high speed trails. By moving our forces on top of pinnacles near these key places, we quickly tore up his entire logistics system for 30 or 40 miles throughout the area thereby denying his people needed supplies. They ran out of ammo, radio batteries, food, everything that had been coming down this channel. Thus, the firebases were the answer on the mountain tops and in the isolated areas, because that was where the enemy effort was. Then when we discovered that he was positioning what ultimately turned out to be a division supply dump just on the border of Laos and Vietnam, we mounted out Dewey Canyon, employing a reinforced regiment, 9th Marines (Reinforced).

We knew they were moving trucks down the Ashau Valley, where I had been with earlier Army's operation to observe that the enemy had built roads and totally camouflaged them. Now we were to discover in the northern part of our area that they had trees and bushes planted in wooden pots which during the day they could pull out in the middle of the road and make them look like trees and bushes. When they moved trucks at night, troops stationed along the road would pull the "trees" out of the road. We picked some of this up by infra-red aerial photography, but it did show how much ingenuity and determination they had. When we plotted out some of the key choke points on the road, we employed large bombs to totally knock the roads out. To be sure we checked out both from pictures and flights over there in a helicopter. However before the next morning, they had repaired the road! They had mobilized hundreds of peasants and repaired that point and were running trucks over it. It was just unbelievable.

Our reconnaissance teams discovered that about every 50 to 100 yards down those roads they had individuals stationed who were apparently road repairmen. Anytime a truck would break down or the road was damaged, they'd assemble from everywhere and give it a push or fill up the road; they had enormous manpower support in their logistics effort. But we did not reach a "stalemate." We totally whipped them throughout Quang Tri Province and ran them off. They had no capability of doing anything in that province in the middle of '69.

Another concept that we worked out was following up B-52 "Arclight" bombing strike with our ground forces. The B-52s were under such a centralized system that it was more important to dump tons of bombs per day than to affect the immediate enemy situation. I finally made an inroad into that system on two occasions. We convinced them that we could, if the Arclight went into an area at a specific time, launch forces in there and get much more out of the Arclight. Because, if there are any enemy forces there, they were dazed, they were hurt, they were disrupted, but could soon recover. Whereas, if you send Marines in there, then you destroy the remaining force. Yes, we did demonstrate that the B-52 Arclight strike can be coordinated with ground maneuver. The point is that whatever weapon system you have, it is more exploitable to use it in a precise way to get maximum benefit from it.

As for becoming helicopter-qualified, where senior ground officers attempted to act as copilot riding in the front seats, I was against it. I was a commander in a helicopter and I was in and out all of the time, which is hard to do from the front seat. Plus, in the back seat, I could carry my own secure communications with me, thus work with my staff officers and my aide. I wanted to command from back there, and be free to get in and out often and quickly. Also, at times they let me down in very rough terrain, where they couldn't even touch down, just hover enough for me to climb in and out. You can't do that easily from up front. And when you are in rough weather or close combat, you need two pilots up front. I think it was a serious mistake for a commander to take a front seat. In fact, I ran into this one time when General Cushman came up and we were going out in the hills. We couldn't go out in his helicopter because he had only one pilot and you needed two pilots. He liked to ride in the front seat, so he had limited his ability to operate in a combat arena by not having two pilots in his craft. We got over in an old beat up cargo helicopter and it looked like hell, but it had two pilots and we could go where we needed to go.

In this age of the helicopter, I could know where my troops had a problem, then go out there and influence it successfully. You can talk to people on the radio all you want, but you are not going to get a precise indication of what's going on and what you could do about it without going there. That's the thing that takes commanders to the scene of the action. I don't mean you seek out a rifle company in the middle of a firefight and go sit down on top of a company commander. But you could go up and see where it is and what it is and get to a nearby place and sit down and talk with his adjacent units or his battalion commanding officer and see what you could do to influence it.

Sometimes there is a conflict: maybe you've got three companies going at once, with reports coming in all reading exactly the same. But you get out there, you see that one is much more serious than the others, and therefore you can shift the artillery resources and the other things to the most serious place. That is, to me, the essential part of command.

This Vietnam war was not just a small unit war. For example, once I got unit integrity back in the regiments, the key to the success of Dewey Canyon was Bob Barrow as regimental commander, because he was out there with them. He eventually had four battalions out there. The tough part on the battalion and regimental commanders was lack of helicopter command ships. I saw companies more often than the battalion commander, because I had access to them with my helicopter. I had a helicopter "strapped on my back" to go at any time. The battalion commander had difficulty getting one to go and see his company commanders, except when I gave him a lift.

I do believe that this war demanded totally outstanding superior quality commanders even more than Korea or World War II. There were just too many near impossible things that had to be done. In other words, the very good to excellent officer can perform most things, but when you've got Marines' lives at stake, you need an excellent to outstanding officer who can ensure that the task gets done with least casualties. I'm not proud of this, but I guess I relieved as many battalion commanders as anybody, perhaps five or six of them, but it was never because of any flush, immediate judgment. It was because of performance over a period where they were getting too many Marines killed, not responding to the kind of operation that we wanted to conduct, or some other good substantial reason.

I had an announced "law" that nobody could lose a skirmish with the enemy. There is no such thing as ending up the next day not having won the skirmish, because we would pile on the support and troops and whatever it took to ensure that we won the skirmish. We had to win, and always win at no great sacrifice. Any time an outfit got chopped up pretty bad, the first question that I wanted to know from the battalion commander was how many rounds of artillery they fired, and if they didn't shoot enough, then he was criticized. When a unit is in trouble, the way to get it out is to pour on the support to get him out.

Again, Lewis Puller and The Basic School back in the late '30s had prepared me well for "counter-insurgency." There was just no way to manage the people in this area so long as the enemy had free access to them, with the capability of installing his cadres in there with threats of death or kidnapping people if they did not do as they were told. People are going to respond to the guy who's in there at night telling them how to react. These cadres could move in at night because there was a base nearby from which they operate and be supplied and supported--batteries, ammo, communications, etc. They were supported by an organization, a company or battalion, and that's supported by major installations, which are in turn supported by a division or security regiment. And where we missed the main point of the whole thing, I thought, was that the locals can be cleaned up very quickly once you get rid of the support. Once we got enemy divisions gone and his regiments ineffective and the logistics system torn up, we could go in and clean a village out and it would stay cleaned out. That's what happened in northern I Corps and that's what happened in many parts of Vietnam after South Vietnamese Army General Truong moved from our area to below Saigon down in the Delta. So, late in the war, we started to experience what it took to handle an insurgency situation and we could have easily won that war with very little effort after that.

Let me offer this on the large-scale Dewey Canyon operation to clean out a North Vietnamese Army division supply dump. Sure, it was great to capture over 1,200 machine guns; 4,000 bicycle tires; over 2,200 big rockets; two big (122 mm guns) cannons; plus unlimited amounts of ammunition. But the big lesson learned was that we could operate in the most

THE CH-46 SEA KNIGHT...

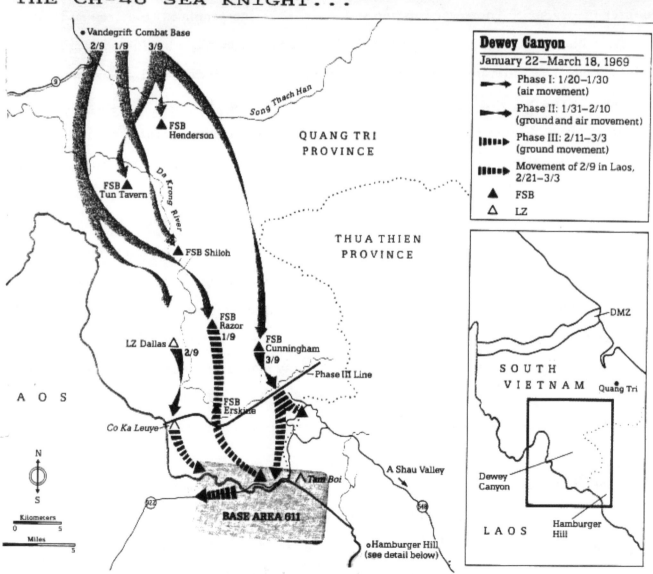

Vandegrift Combat Base
2/9 1/9 3/9

Song Thach Han

QUANG TRI
PROVINCE

FSB
Henderson

FSB
Tun Tavern

Da Krong River

FSB Shiloh

THUA THIEN
PROVINCE

FSB
Razor
1/9

LZ Dallas

2/9

FSB
Cunningham
3/9

Phase III Line

A O S

FSB
Erskine

Co Ka Leuye

Tam Boi

A Shau Valley

N

S

Kilometers
0   5

Miles
5

BASE AREA 611

Hamburger Hill
(see detail below)

Dewey Canyon

January 22–March 18, 1969

→ Phase I: 1/20–1/30
(air movement)

→ Phase II: 1/31–2/10
(ground and air movement)

|||||▶ Phase III: 2/11–3/3
(ground movement)

|||||▶ Movement of 2/9 in Laos,
2/21–3/3

▲ FSB

△ LZ

DMZ

S O U T H
V I E T N A M   Quang Tri

Dewey
Canyon

Hamburger
Hill

L A O S

214

Nurses went everywhere, braving the jungles in Vietnam.

adverse conditions that anyone can dream up! On that we gained more than we went for. We didn't expect those kind of conditions, perhaps a couple of days of bad fog. Even with eleven straight days of complete fog, we wiped out all enemy forces and got every bit of supplies he had on this side of the Laos border. I was a little bit put out because some of the supply dumps we found went right up to the border, and we were not permitted to go and get those on the other side. Overall, this was the culmination of Bob Barrow and the 9th Marines being together as a TEAM for the better part of a year. It was just an absolutely superb performance based on experience, experience, experience!

Another air-ground lesson we learned is that we really need a scout ship, which is a one-man flying platform. We once tested one called the STAMP program, and we got it going with Williams Research, but either the Navy (who funds Navy and Marine aircraft) or the Corps diverted the money to a ducted-fan deal in Texas, which was an entirely different concept. Although the Army is pursuing the idea, we still do not have this little one-man flying platform. It is a jet engine that fits inside a platform and the pilot flies it by leaning one way or the other. A very simple little machine that can do the scouting. It goes down inside the canopy and flies over a trail. We were working on it with the Williams people when the Mayaguez Incident took place. Two big helicopters went down and 40 Marines were killed when they went into a heavily armed camp of enemy. But had we put say four of these little scout ships in a big helicopter, opened up the tail door when near enemy forces, and the four pilot/scouts could fly out on these platforms and find where the enemy is, or more to the point in that operation, where he is not. We could have saved a lot of lives then and in the future, because these scouts could move so much faster than our ground-bound recon scouts.

When I was in G-3 (Operations) in Headquarters, Marine Corps years back I used to say that we should rename the helicopter and call it a "truck." The problem was that every helicopter you put into the inventory was counted as an air frame and we were working against Pentagon people who were oriented towards numbers of air frames. So, if the Corps was going to have 1,500 air frames in the inventory, every time you put a helicopter in, you take out a fighter. This kind of a syndrome was detrimental to the air-ground effort. So I was talking about taking our recon ground troops, equip them with these flying platforms without letting them become more air frames. And Williams found that they could take a guy off the street and train him to fly these STAMPs in one-third the time it took to fly a helicopter. I'm still pushing for this program after all these years. Experience, lessons learned, they stick with you!

Another question I still get at my talks concern the Viet Cong and North Vietnamese Army troops that the media presented as outstanding fighters, invincible jungle fighters who could slip silently through the jungle wearing only black pajamas and rubber tire sandals. In Quang Tri Province we took this "giant" from eleven feet tall down to a midget. He just didn't exist when we finished with him. Again, because we soon learned how to apply our superior mobility, flexibility and fire power, and he had no way of defending himself, as hard as he tried and as determined as he was. In fact, for example, there was a radio intercept from the North Vietnamese Army 320th Division commander, where he was telling somebody that he had reassured his superiors if he were given one more try, he would show that his division could destroy us. So at least the division commander was serious about coming down and trying to operate in South Vietnam, but he just could not hack it. Everywhere he went, he found Marines on top of the hills coming down after his forces, which soon got scattered. He lost contact with them. He couldn't shoot his artillery, because he didn't know where his troops were, so on and so on, just totally unable to operate against, not our numerically superior forces, but our superior equipment, superior doctrine, superior fire power and mobility. A lesson to be learned from the enemy in a positive sense, sure, he had a great ability to survive, to dig in, to endure great hardships, but our people can do all of these things even better if they have to.

There were a few negative moments during this tour, too. I got in trouble because some press guy quoted a private conversation of mine saying: "It makes me sick to sit on this hill and watch those 1,000 trucks go down those roads in Laos, hauling ammunition down south to kill Americans with." I just could not believe our policy would demand that of us--like not crossing over into Laos, into the enemy's sanctuary--but it did. This young guy had been up with me a number of times and we had a lot of conversations "off the record," but he put this out and it hit the press hard. It had even become a total "no-no" for anybody to even suggest the word "win" or "victory." I still feel that the American people, somehow and at sometime, need to know what caused the problem in Vietnam, and why we got in such a mess, and why we had such a disaster out there

I didn't go to serve in Vietnam reluctantly at all. I went happily because I'd been out there and I knew many of the Vietnamese people, and I knew that they were going to be

217

destroyed by the Communists. I believed in what President Kennedy said, that where liberty is threatened anywhere in the world, we've got an interest in it

So I didn't go out there feeling that this was none of our business. I know that Generals MacArthur, Shoup, and Shepherd made the point at various times that we should never be involved in a war on the Asian mainland, that it would swallow us up. But that was not the situation here at all. That is the reason that it is important to expose the fact that our defeat in Vietnam was a political one and not a military one, because, as far as I'm concerned, my Marines in Quang Tri proved to me and proved to anybody who came to take a look that we could easily destroy the enemy forces which could not stand up to us at all. It was a one-sided, one-way affair and we were on top.

I challenged an editor from TIME named Christopher who came out and expressed to me in the strongest terms during a full day of visits around to these fire bases his total amazement at what we had done. He could not believe that this was totally contrary to what he had been led to believe and what he thought was going on. I took him to all the villages where the people had gotten themselves organized and were rebuilding; they were working, they were totally devoted to their local government and their national government. I finally told Christopher: "Well, you could make a major contribution to our nation if you would somehow go back and convince your peers in the publishing industry that this is what's going on out here instead of the reverse which I read in your pages every week, and you could turn this whole thing around. We could establish a free and independent South Vietnam very quickly and very easily if we were permitted to do it." He said: "Oh, you expect too much of me."

When my audiences tell me that this was not a popular war, well, I don't think that any war can be popular. It certainly wasn't in World War II, it wasn't popular to many people-- the fanfare blew people into it. You certainly couldn't stay home in World War II because everybody else was gone. You would be like a sore thumb. However, that didn't make it a popular war. And I wonder if we could have survived in Korea--actually, we gave way at the end of the Korean War. But I wonder if we could have survived as far as we did if we had the television cameras taking the pictures that they wanted to take and putting them in our living rooms at home. The distorted pictures that they wanted would have ruined us the way they did in Vietnam. In fact, I told some of the news people out there that this is the first war where we had no censorship and it ruined us. They totally failed, the news totally failed. They had, I thought, some pretty astute observers out there in the early part of the war. Of course, you couldn't expect them to stay there, but many of the guys that turned up in the end just didn't have any concept of what it was they were looking at. They asked the most stupid questions. They just had no valid ideas.

One saying I heard was that the Marines use helicopters as "ships"--to get to the battlefield--while the Army uses helicopters as horses--to move around the battlefield. My concept of operations bore this distinction out. Under my use of air mobility, we would advance slowly into the mountains with CH-46 helicopters first bringing artillery and ground troops to establish fire bases on the edges of the operational area. These bases were constructed to provide overlapping "artillery fans," a common practice, so that none of the area was beyond the reach of artillery protection from at least one fire base. From there our rifle squads, even entire battalions, would move on foot to search the area thoroughly, slowly moving to the edge of artillery protection. Then a second phase would follow, including the construction of new fire bases and permitting a deeper penetration into the operational area. Slowly, methodically, largely on foot, but never beyond the protection of artillery fans, additional phases could be carried out until the entire operational area had been searched for enemy forces and logistical bases.

Few of our fire support bases came under attack. Normally the high pinnacles with nearby artillery support were easy to defend. One exception. Captain John E. Knight, Jr., was awarded a Silver Star for his actions in Company H, 4th Marines' defense of Fire Support Base Neville which came under heavy assault from enemy forces. Our air and artillery finally drove the enemy off.

In this sense, I suppose Dewey Canyon was a major departure from most earlier American efforts, since the target of Dewey Canyon was enemy logistics, not enemy forces. There was no major enemy combat force down there. We knew that. Our primary target was to go in and ferret out this system--without any thought that there was a major force there. Ironically, it was enemy 122mm guns firing from Laos and a threat of reinforcement from there that gave Bob Barrow's troops a permanent threat and caused him to send Captain Dave Winecoff (son of the 1st Marine Division Operations Officer at Chosin) across into Laos. The strongest vote of confidence received came from General Abrams himself. When apprised of the purpose of the ambush, Abe reversed his earlier position and authorized a full battalion of the 9th Marines to enter Laos for the purpose of destroying the threat. Abe requested only that there be "no public discussion" of the foray across the border and informed the American ambassador in Laos, William Sullivan, only after the operation was underway.

Again, ironically, I was out of country when Winecoff went into Laos. Everyone serving in country went on 5 days of "Rest & Recreation" (R&R) usually past mid-tour, so I spent mine in Hong Kong with my son Miles. It was an interesting development that Miles, a Marine lieutenant, got into the 3rd Marine Division while I was in it. Normally, the policy is not to have two members of the same family in one Marine Division, but as I went out to Provisional Corps, Miles was just finishing The Basic School and had his assignment to the 3rd Division. I was not yet in 3rd Marine Division. Miles, from our tour in Paris, was language-oriented, so he had orders to Vietnamese Language School enroute, but still had orders to the Division upon its completion. Then I got assigned to 3rd Marine Division, so he was really assigned to it before I was, even though I arrived there before he did. And as he was about to go out, of course, the people in Washington became aware of this assignment and it was against policy, as they well knew. But they had to have a request from one of us to make a change. They couldn't just arbitrarily change it. And so Lieutenant General Nickerson, who is a very dear friend (I was his Executive Officer, 7th Marines after Chosin Campaign and his deputy at Senior School, as well as Commanding General, 3rd Marine Division while he was Commanding General, III Marine Amphibious Force), and a great man in every respect, made a tactical error in calling my wife, and getting her involved in the problem and decision.

I always have to laugh when I think of this: Knox just said to Nick: "You guys up there are just chicken. You're not doing your job. This is not a matter of decision for a mother and wife. This is a decision for menfolks and Miles is a grown guy, and if he wants to go, I'm going to put him on the airplane," and so off Miles came. He arrived and I met him and took him into my hooch there at the headquarters to have a little chat with him. The first thing he confronted me with: "Well now, Dad, I don't want you interfering with my assignment and career and so forth," you know, telling the old man to stay out of his business. And then he changed: "But, I do want a rifle platoon," so we had a conversation about that and I told him that there was concern on the part of his mother about him coming out there and being in a rifle platoon and both of us being over there at the same time--a kind of double exposure for her and so forth. But I said: "I'm somewhat of a fatalist in these matters in that the system has assigned you to the 3rd Division and circumstances have brought me to the 3rd

Division."

"I am not about to make a move because if I moved you, and then something happened to you, I'd feel that I had caused it, you are already slated for a rifle platoon, so I really don't have to do anything about that, either," and off he went.

Our overlap was for about six months. He had a rifle platoon out in the 9th Marines and was in a very active part of the war with Bob Barrow's high mobility operations. He had a great challenge on the trail with his troops, like everyone else. I had two opportunities to go out and walk the trail with him in areas where not too much was going on and just enjoyed his company for an hour or two. But the worst day of this, my longest day, started early one morning when Kilo Company, 9th Battalion, where he was assigned as a rifle platoon leader, had a clash with the enemy. Cryptic reports were coming in: "Kilo Company, fire fight, 1 killed, 2 wounded." An hour or so later another skirmish, one or two killed and a few wounded, and this went on out in heavy fog. I was scheduled to be at Colonel Barrow's headquarters at 8 o'clock. I wanted to be right on time because this was where this message was coming from. I could not permit the staff to call Barrow on the phone and ask him about Miles. I felt that I should let things go and hope.

I arrived to find a CH-46 sitting in the place where I normally landed on my frequent visits. So I landed over on the next finger and had to walk down a little draw to get over to Barrow's command post. As I came up out of that draw near the 46 (it turned out to be a crippled ship that put down there), the doors were open and coming out of it was my son Miles with his arm in a sling. He had been shot, obviously, but not seriously. That's the first time that I knew of his wound. His tale of the past few minutes of his life, though, was one that will always stay with us.

He was conducting his platoon in a firefight and happened to hold out his hand to motion to somebody to do something, and he had been shot right through the fleshy part of his hand. He continued his mission and finished the combat action. As things settled down, his corpsman told him he'd better have the wound taken care of because in the jungle you could get some very serious infections and lose a hand. He reported to his company commander who arranged for a chopper to pick him up. It was necessary to hoist him up on a string from below the trees, but as he reached the helicopter, it was hit by some kind of projectile--a rocket round struck just as he had gotten his body on board. It hit some fuel lines and fuel was flying everywhere. Of course, the pilot's reaction was to get the hell out of there.

He was hovering over a cliff, so he threw the helicopter down, down this cliff, to get up speed to get away from there. So--I can laugh about it now--Miles said he was just terrified beyond belief because he was convinced that that chopper was headed for a crash down the side of the mountain. The helicopter was damaged but pulled up and flopped down a few miles away in Barrow's command post. That was the chopper in my normal landing spot. Miles said he didn't realize how terrifying it could be--that helicopter being hit just as he was getting on board.

When I went back to my Division Command Post, I took him over to the hospital and got the wound checked on and dressed out. Because Miles was going to have a few weeks out of action--at a minimum a few days--and I was due for "Rest & Recreation," we decided to grab a few days. We got a ride on a small Navy jet up to Hong Kong for three or four days. We had a great time visiting and shopping and I had an opportunity to show him some of the sights. To visit with him was just ideal.

Soon after my return to Vietnam, the decisions were announced that we would withdraw U.S. forces from the War. I knew that this was premature. The South Vietnamese were not ready to take over the whole country. They couldn't expose their capital city to the threat from Cambodia, so they kept their forces down there and pretty much limited their effort up north. Even though we had total security when I left in April, 1969, we hadn't really tied up the loose ends enough to say: "We are going to turn them over to you." I could see the handwriting on the wall. Things were really going to fall apart.

But by this time it was too late. Our people at home had had enough. Three and a half years of suffering, and they were ready to quit. The only trouble was that our success came so late that Walter Cronkite and the press had already told us to get out, that we were beaten. Nobody was interested, and you can't fight a war without popular support. World War II had full support. In Korea we had full support until 1952 when we had our forces committed to a defense where the casualties were flowing with no progress to show for it. When you get yourself into this kind of situation, support at home erodes quickly. That's the situation we got into late in Korea and early in Vietnam.

From the beginning the United States made several "deadly decisions" that led right down the trail to the most tragic disaster in our history in Vietnam. I witnessed most of them: Not providing adequate funding. Failure to call up the Ready Reserve. Allowing the enemy sanctuaries. Calling bombing halts and cease-fires that allowed the enemy to rest and regroup. The enormous waste of the McNamara Line. Other decisions were only minor, as I discussed in Chapter 1 of this book, but all contribute to the idea of limiting our ability to win. The military decisions, of course, were influenced by the overall problem of having an inadequate force and operating under restrictive ground rules that favored the enemy. We were not permitted to destroy the enemy, which is the only correct role for military forces.

This was against my military education and training and experience through three wars in three decades, from World War II in the early '40s through Korea in the early '50s and here in Vietnam in the late '60s/ early '70s. But what were my choices? My choices were either make do or resign. What good would it have done to resign? I felt capable of making do better than others. I had a lot of war experience under my belt. I could have gotten incensed and stomped around and just resigned. But nobody cared. They wouldn't pay any real attention. So I'd make do.

We should not go to war unless our objective is to destroy the enemy and win. Otherwise the cost is prohibitive. The cost of winning the war in Korea would have been less than the cost of maintaining the Korean situation as we have since 1950. The Chinese didn't want to talk until they were whipped. The same with the North Vietnamese. I'm convinced that the agreement with the North Vietnamese came only because they had had enough. They would have agreed to just about anything. But at the this crucial time, we too had had enough.

There is no substitute to going for the jugular. If the military doesn't do that, there is no way to succeed. But in Vietnam we weren't allowed to do that. That is what defeated us. We carried out our orders, and the orders we carried out could lead to nothing but a tragic disaster.

Since we began this view of the Vietnam fracas with a letter to Bill Davis from my first aide in that two-billet tour as Rosson's deputy and as Commanding General, 3rd Marine Division, perhaps a nice way to end it would be another letter to Bill from Carl Hoffman, who served with me in the educational, intelligence, and combat environments:

Dear Bill: As Major General Ray Davis' Assistant Division Commander, I was given command of a new task force: Task Force HOTEL (phonetic alphabet "H" for Hoffman). Its mission: from a base at Khe Sanh conduct offensive operations against North Vietnamese Army forces in the northern I Corps area. Ray Davis gave me the assets to do the job. At various times this included two reinforced Marine regiments, a U.S. Army brigade, a Vietnamese regiment, and predictable artillery and aviation support. Given this amount of resources, Task Force Hotel could range far and wide: West to the Laotian border, north to the North Vietnam border, south and east as we identified fruitful targets.

General Davis exuded confidence in Task Force Hotel's capability to go anywhere and defeat the enemy. He frequently "suggested" operations for Task Force Hotel, always phrased in gentlemanly terms, but fully expecting prompt action. Since I had worked for him in Quantico and in Washington and understood his leadership style, I knew that he didn't make suggestions just to hear the sound of his voice. His "suggestions" were invariably carefully conceived courses of action that carried the impact of a directive. Now I don't mean to imply that the subject was closed once he made a suggestion. He would listen attentively to any thoughts I might have. And if I could persuade him that some other approach might be preferable, he would alter or condition his suggestion. But if I interposed no further thoughts on the subject, then he expected action. Since I knew him so well, I lost no time in starting things moving.

From his experience as Lieutenant General Rosson's Deputy at Provisional Corps Vietnam, General Davis gained a healthy respect for the U.S. Army's technique of establishing fire support bases where artillery could be employed to extend the distance that offensive operations could be supported. Ray Davis fine-tuned the concept for Marine Corps application. In Task Force Hotel's area alone, we established over a dozen fire support bases. The procedure in each instance was similar: first, select a terrain feature that would permit emplaced artillery to support extended offensive operations; second, use supporting arms to blast away enough of the trees and foliage to permit helicopter landings; third, by "choppers" move in security forces, engineers and equipment adequate to carve out a suitable artillery position; fourth, lift into the base the artillery pieces, associated fire direction gear, ammunition and supplies; and fifth, initiate offensive operations within the umbrella of the newly emplaced artillery.

Ray Davis often "suggested" locations for new fire support bases. I did not delay getting started in each case. I also knew that, if I didn't physically land at the selected fire support base early in its development, Ray Davis would be there first. Of course, Ray Davis is a very courageous Marine. Although never fool-hardy, he didn't let concern for his personal safety interfere with his drive to exert personal, dynamic leadership. If he felt any fear, he concealed it well.

--CARL HOFFMANN, Major General, USMC, Ret.

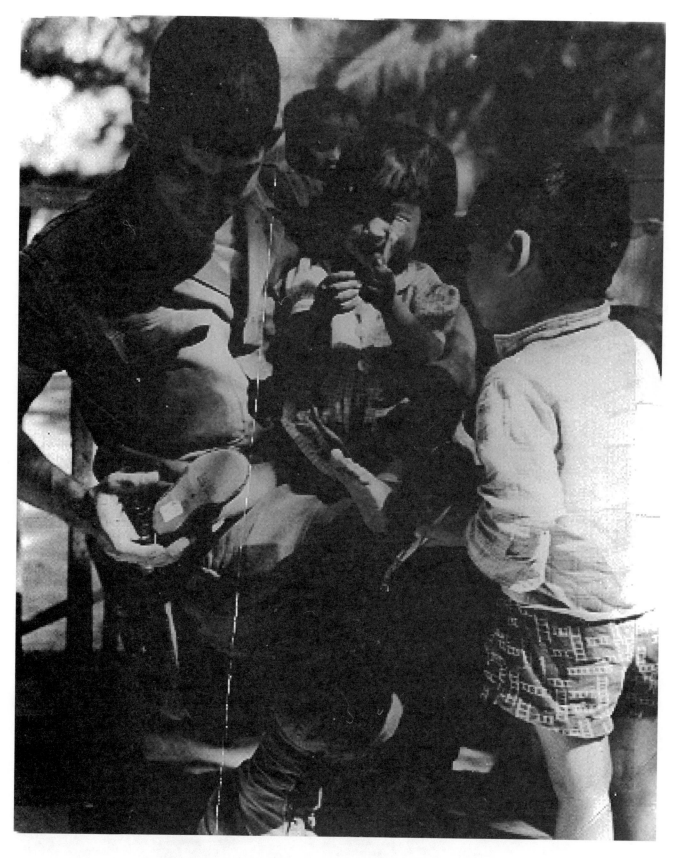

Warrior Marines love little children!!!

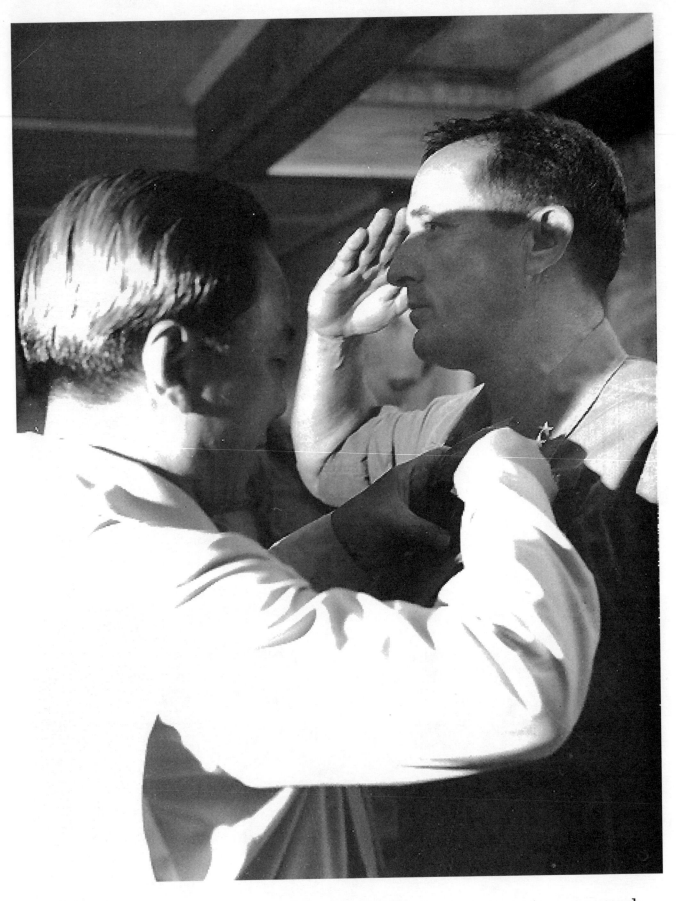

President Diem of the Republic of Vietnam presents an award
to Ray Davis, 1968.

Vietnam, 1968

This picture speaks for tiself.

Commanding General, Provisisonal Corps, Lieutenant General Richard Stilwell, presents Ray Davis with a model helicopter upon departure from the 3rd Marine Division.

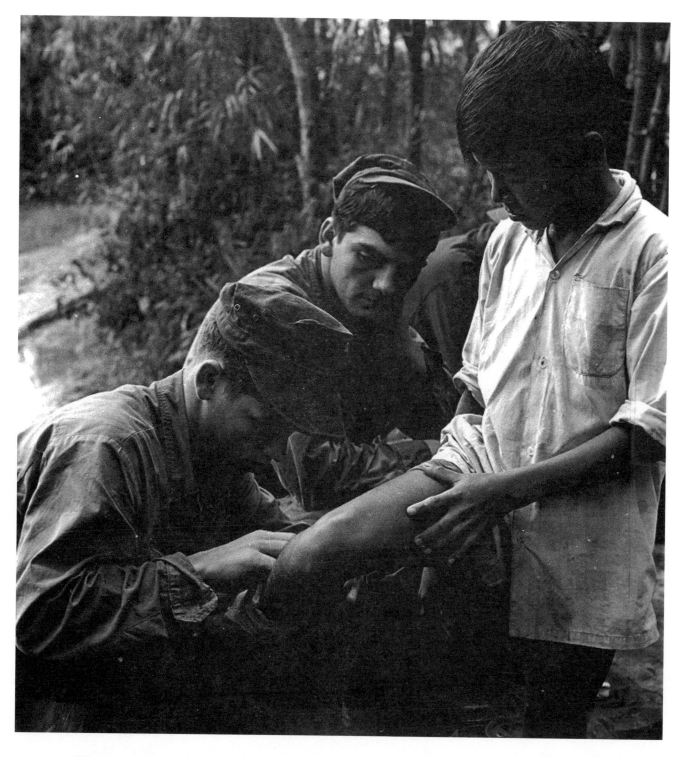

This is one of my favorite photos of Vietnam. A Marine patrol leader administers first aid. This was the most humane of my three wars! Marines like this would go 10 miles into the jungle to rescue hurt or sick civilians.

My departure message to my great, great Division:

Dear Marine:

You have done the Marine Corps, yourself, and your commander proud. For more than a year I have observed you march to the tempo of our times. Your steps have been firm and jaunty. As with your forebears, you have taken your place in the legend of Marines. The spirit, tenacity and steadfast loyalty to corps and country you have displayed have embellished and brightened the name "Leatherneck."

In your sacrifice of comfort and safety you have found glory. You will also have discovered the fuller meanings of manhood and camaraderie among men at arms.

Etched in the bronze of time you will find the chronicle of your exploits. The names of Dai Do, Lai An, DMZ Upper Ashau and Khe Sanh will join those of Iwo Jima, Guadalcanal and Bougainville to echo among warriors. With pardonable pride in your performance and with profound humility, I take leave as your commander. Godspeed Marine. May you always walk with a following wind.

Major General, U. S. Marine Corp

HAIL & FAREWELL!!! TO MY LAST COMBAT COMMAND

CHAPTER 24. DIRECTOR, EDUCATION CENTER, MCDEC

In May of 1969, once again I was transferred back to Quantico and the Marine Corps Development and Education Command (MCDEC) as Education Director, Education Center. I was deputy to the Commanding General who was Lieutenant General Jeff Fields of Peleliu and personnel department days. Having served in the old Marine Air-Infantry School, (now Amphibious Warfare School) and directed Senior School (now Marine Corps Command & Staff College (MCCSC)), it was a most logical move for the Corps to assign a newly returned from Vietnam Marine to be responsible for professional education and training.

I was most enthusiastic! I welcomed it as a great challenge, a response to the Commandant's forward movement in terms of developing a Staff Non-Commissioned Officer Academy, a Physical Fitness Academy, and upgrading all Marines' physical fitness-- General Chapman had many things like that going on. Plus there was added pressure to get The Basic School students completely combat-ready before they went overseas.

In addition to the programs of Generals Chapman and Jeff Fields, I had the personal challenge of educating Marines on the high mobility concept. To me, this concept was, in these circumstances, totally successful and in my view held much promise for the future of the Marine Corps. The Corps could provide worldwide amphibious (or airlift or whatever) readiness forces with a high-mobility concept. As I said in some of my writings about the sea-based concept, they could go into situations worldwide, with variations all the way from a four-man fire team for food relief up to the application of major forces launched from a sea base wherein it would not have to be necessary to wait for a logistic buildup. There would be no requirement to insert heavy installations in the midst of a civilian population. The Marine Corps continues to move in the direction of the requirement and development of this high-mobility concept with a sea base. I was so enthused about this that it became my main theme, effort and concern--the development, selling and fostering of this concept in the Marine Corps. That was my main interest at the Education Center.

I am not sure how much of a lasting imprint was made, but I described high mobility to each class of The Basic School, each class of The Officer Candidate School, each summer class of Reservists that would come into Quantico. With every one of them, I spent up to three hours, using large maps to walk them through the experience in Vietnam in great detail; a discussion followed for up to an hour and a half. I insisted on being there long

231

enough to thoroughly cover the Vietnam operations. If you appear long enough in front of bright, hardcharging youngsters they are going to ask you hard questions, and that was my scheme. I found no one reluctant to ask questions.

Later I instituted programs of having each unit in Quantico select one or two young lieutenants out of their organization to come with their wives to an evening discussion session in the library at Breckenridge Hall. There we sat around having cookies and coffee in a very informal fashion. I presented my general views on Marine Corps policies and conducted a two or three hour discussion with them, provoking them and drawing them out. Later we conducted a like program for the captains, then the majors. We had some complaints about not doing it for the lieutenant colonels, but we just did not get around to it before my departure. This was one of the origins (and they ran this in the Marine Corps Gazette) of exposing ideas and communicating with people through key select groups of junior officers and their wives. There were other similar programs developed through the Corps. I think that such input from them in the development of the total team and family effort is one of the keys to our continuing success as a Military Service.

During these meetings we explored questions regarding uniforms, assignments, drugs, beards, mustaches, and the like. We were particularly interested in those units that were deployed in the field, out in the hinterlands. There was agreement that in the field there was no concern with haircuts, because the troops found pretty quickly that hair was a bother, so they just cut it all off. It was so much easier to manage, to keep clean. Another view reinforced by my son, from his platoon in Vietnam, and many other junior officers and non-commissioned officers, is that there was no drug problem out in the hinterlands, because there was a self-policing of the troops themselves. Their lives depended on a clear head, and they would not permit anybody to smoke a marijuana cigarette or consume any drugs.

As for so-called "fragging", we did have a couple of instances, but it was not necessarily racial. We had a fine young lieutenant who had been my son's company commander at one time, who was killed by a couple of Marines. They said that they really didn't intend to kill him. All of our company administrative rear command posts were in the Dong Ha Combat Base or else back in Quang Tri. This company commander had gone back to take care of some company administration, and in the process had discovered two Marines who had gotten on a helicopter up front for an unauthorized flight back to the rear. He rounded them up and set them up for flight back up to the company in the field. Their response to this that very night was to throw a hand grenade into his "hootch", and they murdered him. They happened to be black Marines, but it really had nothing to do with race. It was a question of two Marines who were avoiding their duty and after being caught at it tried to beat the rap through violence. We had one or two other actions like this, but none of the others were so serious.

I did have a doctor tell me that 85 percent of some units were smoking pot. He happened to be a doctor whose duty was to interview the people caught with drugs. Those caught would say to him, 'Well, I was just one of many. Everybody's doing it,' He became convinced of the guilt of one unit that was positioned in an area where they occupied many bunkers. Some of these bunkers were used to hide and smoke pot. He became so convinced of this that I finally arranged with the Division Surgeon to move him over there, let him live with it, and check for himself. He came back convinced that the stories had been exaggerated and that there were only a few drug abusers.

However, at that time, anyone caught with as much as a half inch of marijuana cigarette in his pocket was given a discharge from the Marine Corps. They were tried, convicted, and heaved out. During my review of trials where there was no other evidence except this small piece of cigarette, I let the conviction stand, but recommended that he be given a year's probation and remain in the Corps if he performed satisfactorily for a year.

As for the subject of rehabilitation, I don't think the Corps should have set up any program, for this reason: If we are going to be truly an elite corps, we should be able to say to people, to parents, to everybody, 'If you want your young son or daughter to be in an outfit where they are not going to get into drugs, join the Marine Corps.' We should be able to make statements that indicate that we are, in every respect, a different, totally elite corps, and that includes no drugs. We need to get rid of alcoholics, we need to get rid of the drug addicts, and we need to get rid of the Ku Klux Klan types, the communist types, the racists. We should have some way of getting those who fail to meet high standards out of our system. They came out of society, let society rehabilitate them.

While perhaps it is true that nothing ever remains the same, that the Corps of the '30s and '40s is not the Corps of the '80s and '90s, various principles do tend to remain the same: the question of devotion to duty remains the same; the question of quality remains the same. There are claims that say we have a different kind of Marine Corps today, one in which some really fine officers are getting out early. I see a situation where there are two approaches to such a problem: If you are not happy with the way the Marine Corps is--this is the point I tried to make with young officers and their spouses--you have two choices. Either get out, or help change it. The good ones, the people who are truly devoted, won't consider getting out. They are going to put their entire effort in making it better. This is what sustains us. Everybody is bound to have warts. There is no way of having a perfect Corps, but you have to have that goal. Perfection is our goal, and anything short of perfection is not satisfactory. We have got to work toward that good goal.

In summation of my tour as Director of the Education Center, let me say this: The Basic School is a vast improvement over the small Philadelphia Navy Yard scene when Chesty was my company commander and small wars instructor. So is the Amphibious Warfare School in comparison with the old Marine Air infantry School, which was almost a squad leaders' course for aviators, to bring them up to speed for close air support of the Marine on the ground. And our Command & Staff College is doing what I wanted all along: using more seminar/conference instruction. The more senior the students, the more is gained from this exchange of ideas. We perfected the mechanics back in '58-'59. When each group has infantry, artillery, air, engineer, communications, tank, supply, other services, allied officer students, plus a mixmaster effort after the first few weeks of the course, the cross-fertilization is invaluable. It becomes extremely tough for a student to "hide out" for the school year; everyone was upfront at the round conference table, participating.

Let me add a few notes: Knox continued her interest in and support of the needs and aspirations of Marine Corps families. She maintained a schedule of work each week in "The Thrift Shop," for example. She became so experienced in the fitting of clothing that I was amazed on occasion to hear her describe someone we knew very casually by stating his or her clothing size. If a Marine came to the Thrift Shop asking for a size 42 and her estimate of him was that he was size 44, she would offer him 44's, saying to him that the used uniforms had been cleaned and had shrunk. Most times this expedited the fitting process.

She enjoyed the bridge club and wives club activities and sponsored tours and activities, particularly with the more Junior wives. One amusing incident came of this: the wife of one of our aides was expecting and Knox scheduled a baby shower for her at our Quarters #1. The expectant wife helped to prepare the invitation list to ensure that all of her friends would be included. Knox briefed the household staff on the importance of this event for the young wives and their guests, and admonished them that everything would go "first class."

Later, as gifts were being opened, one of the wives suggested that the beautiful bows and ribbons be saved and asked one of the stewards for some paper plates.

This tall, handsome steward who prided himself in his proper, correct manners responded: "No, Mam, no paper plates, we only go first class here!" Then he brought some fine china bowls. Knox could only grin and bear it!

Lieutenant General Lewis J. (Jeff) Fields, Commanding General, Marine Corps Development and Education Command, upon his retirement wrote in the fitness report rating me as his Deputy for Education:

> As Director of the educational programs of the Marine Corps, which included schools offering basic, graduate and postgraduate equivalent curricula for career officers located in Quantico, Virginia; additionally, the Editor-in-Chief of the Marine CORPS GAZETTE, a professional periodical with a circulation of 20,000; and the Secretary-Treasurer of the Marine Corps Association, a professional organization of 18,500 members, Major General Davis continues to demonstrate his capability for assuming increasing and greater responsibilities. He has made many contributions toward improving the education of our officer corps. During the period he has represented the Marine Corps most ably in many appearances before military and civilian audiences.

Probably as a direct result of Jeff's report, the Commandant of the Marine Corps, upon Lieutenant General Fields' retirement from active duty, ordered me promoted to Lieutenant General and assigned as Commanding General, Marine Corps Development and Education Command! So now I am Lieutenant General Ray Davis, commanding the base I love so well, and served at so often, and responsible for the development and educational functions, facilities and personnel therein!

CHAPTER 25. COMMANDING GENERAL, MCDEC

Since most long-term officer retirements occur on 30 June, which was the end of the old Fiscal Year, I was promoted to Lieutenant General on 1 July 1970. Realize that one-star (Brigadier) and two-star (Major) Generals are, in effect, "voted for" by Selection Boards held in Headquarters, Marine Corps, but three-star Lieutenant Generals are appointed by the President after receiving recommendations from the Defense Department, including the Commandant of the Marine Corps. There were eight such Lieutenant General billets at that time, and General Chapman had fortunately seen me perform in a myriad of tasks and missions over the past three decades, especially as his G-1 (Manpower) in Marine Corps Headquarters, and as Commanding General, 3rd Marine Division in Vietnam, where I luckily gained much favorable "mention in dispatches" from senior officers of other Services.

This tour of duty as Commanding General, Marine Corps Development and Education Command (MCDEC) lasted less than a year, but it gave me an opportunity to oversee not only the panoply of education and development for the entire Corps, but to right some old "wrongs" and to give more hardcharging young junior officers a chance to deal face-to-face with a three star general in semi-social settings, as I described when I was the two star Deputy.

When I consider my entire tour in MCDEC, I must say that when I finally left Quantico for the last time, I did not feel that I had accomplished everything that I had set out to accomplish. But then again, I don't think that anybody could feel fully successful because you do not know what your starting point is until you get up into the job.

However, that in itself was a key lesson learned, where two legends of the Corps, Merrill Twining and Victor Krulak, changed the major method of instruction in the Corps' high level school without possessing all the facts, which was one of the key teaching points at the Marine Corps Command and Staff College over the years. I am sure that General Krulak will recall that he gave me a few lectures on some studies made of a class of freshmen in some school up east. I believe it was Rensselear Polytechnic Institute (RPI) and a class in metallurgy for those freshmen. "The old professor" who lectured to a big group versus assistant professors who taught in smaller groups, and, of course, the old professor won. I'd told him that did not apply to what we were talking about: "You are talking about a freshman class in a technical subject (which I specialized in at Georgia Tech, not unlike RPI) and we are talking about 16 or 18 year veterans in an area of discussion of concepts and theories." But we just could not agree on that at all. He was under a higher directive to clean it out, so he just could not take any excuse or understanding. That is the position we get ourselves into at times.

Another lesson learned from General Twining was how not to do staff assignments. As previously mentioned, he put Jim Magee, a classmate of mine in The Basic School, as Chief of Staff, and he selected his other staff people junior to Magee. That meant with some 80 colonels and Navy captains on the base at Quantico that the 10 most junior ones were all the key staff officers to General Twining. This led to trouble not only because the inversion in rank gave you people with less experience, but they had less horsepower, less everything than people they were trying to coordinate and instruct. There were some deep feelings about that in all of us, but the younger ones try to prove their point, they try to establish themselves in a superior position with some of the outward appearances--selection of quarters, parking spaces, it just went on and on. So I knew many things that as Commanding General, MCDEC, I was not going to do. But let me get to some positive points concerning that tour for me.

It developed a chance to do something good for Chesty Puller. Tragedy struck Lieutenant General Puller and he was soon retired physically because of a stroke. He felt he was unjustly retired and for many years separated himself from every Marine activity. In 1970 I used my position as Commanding General at Quantico to round up a few officers who had been close to Chesty (ex-aides, junior staff officers, combat commanders) and sent them on a special mission to Saluda, Virginia, to visit him. One was George Dawes, one of my rifle company commanders on Peleliu, who carried my invitation for General Puller to honor us at some Quantico football games and to be our guest of honor as the next Marine Corps Birthday Ball. Chesty responded with obvious relish, and we were blessed with his great presence among Marines once more.

For me, this heroic warrior exemplifies another traditional role for Marine noncommissioned officers. Lewis Puller enlisted in World War I and was to become a gallant noncommissioned officer combat patrol leader in the Central America Banana Wars. He was awarded a field commission and subsequently rose to the rank of Lieutenant General. Traditionally, a major role for noncommissioned officers is to help fill requirements for commissioned officers whenever the Corps is expanded, especially in wartime, or in conflicts such as Korea. It is a role that they have filled with great success throughout, and I always think of Chesty as the perfect example of filling this important role.

In addition to the leadership requirements of the various schools in Quantico, I fortunately spent much time in the field observing and commenting on the tactics and techniques taught, especially at The Basic School, where I was always well-received, by Bill Davis the commanding officer who had countless opportunities to remind his commanders, staff and instructors on how Lieutenant Colonel Ray Davis had performed as his infantry battalion commander in the Inchon-Seoul and Chosin Reservoir Campaigns. In addition, I was impressed with what the Commandant, General Chapman, had caused to be done in Quantico. I am still all sold on the Physical Fitness Academy. Perhaps it could be done on a lesser scale, but we always needed a fountainhead place for developing and then closely monitoring ideas on achieving relative perfection in physical fitness. I'll never forget those days when we ruined a lot of Marine knees from duckwalk contests, and the like. We need true professionals in this important part of the education and training of all our Marines, from the youngest to the oldest.

There were other areas to be looked into as Commanding General, Marine Corps Development and Education Command. Radical groups in Washington had attracted the attendance of a few Quantico-based officers at meetings. Undercover federal agents reported their attendance. They seemed to fall into one group of officers at The Basic School--lawyers.

The day I heard of this I called for a meeting with the entire "lawyer" group with their instructors after work that same day. We met in a small auditorium. I had enough information about the radical group--it had some title like "Concerned Officers Society"--to discuss in some detail its composition, missions and activities. Then, after giving them some ideas on their Oath of Office, loyalty, dedication, devotion, I kept them there more than an hour extracting from them their questions, their ideas, their concerns. I never heard of another Quantico Marine attending "radical group" meetings. Another incident began with a report to me that an "old woman" was living in a shack just off the Quantico reservation, and that she claimed to be the widow of a Marine general officer. I immediately called the Chief of Staff of Marine Corps Headquarters to find out if such a widow existed and what her status was. She was indeed such a widow and well-known in the Headquarters, so I announced that we would do what we could to help. I sent an aide to investigate.

She was living in back of an abandoned store with two large dogs. Her story was that her husband's will provided so much for care of the dogs that there was nothing left for her. She had just received an electric bill for several hundred dollars even though she had only one small light. I talked to local power company officials and found that the store building had commercial power minimum rates and that her bill included some past due amounts. We moved her out and settled her power bill for a very modest fee.

For temporary lodging we moved her into an old recreation trailer in the training area. Water and power were available and the security patrols checked the area several times each day which provided us a way to keep track of her. Our chaplains visited her and from their sources provided some food and toilet items. I had aides bring her into The Thrift Shop where Knox outfitted her with some simple clothes. Then we had her up to Quarters #1 for freshening up and for lunch.

The Marines who found her initially took her on as a special project--raising funds, food and supplies. They also found an abandoned house and fixed it up. I got volunteer maintenance crews to oversee and inspect work on the house. In a few weeks she moved in. About this time I received a call from a reporter that was checking on a story that "the Commanding General was keeping a woman out in the woods in Quantico. "I asked him to hold the line a moment. I then got an aide and a stenographer on extension phones, and let the reporter know they were there.

I answered him truthfully and summed it up with the thought that we would take care of anyone like her found in our neighborhood, in addition I admonished him that if he printed any lies about me he would be in trouble. Nothing was printed. As wonderful and interesting as the story was, in my opinion the news media protected itself by printing nothing.

Let us leave Quantico with a few happy notes: Bill Davis received a letter from an active duty officer concerning what he saw as my impact on young Marines in Quantico:

> In November of 1970, I was a Second Lieutenant in The Basic School, and we were being introduced to our first Marine Corps Mess Night. Various dignitaries were invited, to include the Commanding General of MCDEC, Lieutenant General Davis. As a student who was doing well in my Class, I was selected to be his escort for the evening. He spent the entire evening making ME feel at home with him, engaging in conversation that would be of interest to a Second Lieutenant, and in asking those questions that indicated, that clearly demonstrated that he had not forgotten "the feel of the battlefield." We discussed my desire to go to Vietnam before our involvement there ended, and he expressed an opinion which has been very valuable to me ever since. He said that if I got only as far as Okinawa and was reassigned to the 3rd Marine Division rather than getting down to the 1st Marine Division still in Vietnam, and if I were assigned to a job as unassuming as Range Officer, that my goal should be to have the best Range on Okinawa.

Essentially he laid out for me an important point which has only become more striking in this age of rampant self advancement and careerism, that there are no bad jobs for Lieutenants, only Lieutenants who are less than sufficiently-motivated. As a wondering young officer, it was impossible not to be impressed by General Davis' decorations. I never understood why Marine Corps Headquarters wasn't smart enough to know that the only personal decoration General Davis didn't have was the Navy Achievement Medal. Of course he deserved a higher retirement decoration, but I'll bet he secretly wished that someone would have taken the unique opportunity to fill in "the missing square," rather than just another star on a medal he already had.

--Lieutenant Colonel Edward J. Robeson, IV--9 March 1988.

While I must admit that it is nice to see what a hardcharging young Second Lieutenant of Marines thinks about his Commanding General, so also is it nice to get the considered opinion of the Senior Marine in the Corps, General Chapman, who wrote the following in a fitness report:

Initially, overall Director of the Marine Corps education and development activities located at Quantico, Virginia. After transfer in March, 1971, the Assistant Commandant of the Marine Corps and promotion to the rank of full General. General Davis is a superior Marine leader--in and out of combat--and ONE OF THE FINEST MARINES OF ALL TIME. Can do anything, and do it superlatively well.

--General L.F. Chapman, Jr.--24 May 1971.

Secretary of the Navy Chaffee visits the Marine Corps Development and Education Command (Now a senator, he is a former Marine.)

The Spanish Ambassador to the United States delivers to Ray Davis a sword of "James The Conqueror" from King Carlos of Spain (who visited the Marine Corps Development and Education Command with his lady while Prince Carlos).

Four stars are pinned on me (Ray Davis) by the Commandant of Marine Corps, General Chapman, and my beloved wife, Knox.

And I received my official four star flag (plus my Congressman, Jack Flynt of Georgia).

CHAPTER 26. ASSISTANT COMMANDANT (4 STARS)

So it was that on 23 February 1971, I was nominated for appointment to the grade of General and assignment as Assistant Commandant of the Marine Corps. On 12 March 1971, after this nomination was confirmed by the Senate, I became General Raymond Gilbert Davis, a long journey from those days in The Basic School as 2nd lieutenant Ray Davis.

The immediate question that comes to mind after nearly 34 years of service: was I surprised at this selection? What were the circumstances? My answer: There was a most awful event that led to selection, in the illness of General Keith McCutcheon. Keith had been designated Assistant Commandant, and he suddenly found himself dying of cancer. I went out to see him, but I could not bring myself believe that Keith McCutcheon was not going to be able to serve as Assistant Commandant of the Marine Corps. This had a real dampening effect on the whole thing. I had no idea as to how I was selected to replace Keith. I certainly could not have been selected without the support of Generals Chapman and Walt, and they were as close to me as anybody. Those two had to have been keys in the decision. I fully realized the opportunity and certainly the great break that was mine. I had felt that three stars were unbelievable and four could never happen.

Since I had three stars as Commanding General, Marine Corps Development and Education Command (MCDEC) at Quantico, and 33 years of active service, I had originally thought of retirement after the end of my tour there. As I have said before, it was never my nature to sit around and review my aspirations towards promotion. I seemed to be consumed with the matters at hand most of the time. When I was MCDEC, I was trying to make that command the best possible, to solve all of its problems, to do everything I could, because I always thrived on accomplishment. That is my main instinctive drive: what can I get accomplished? Now, I cannot say that promotion never crossed my mind, because even if not of my own volition, there were people talking to me about my chances. Fortunately there were those interested in furthering my career or promoting my interest. You cannot be in the position that I was in among the senior group without somebody you've known along the way coming around in some way to talk about the prospect and possibilities.

As Assistant Commandant of the Marine Corps, I was in a position that I really enjoyed, with the trust and confidence of General Chapman. I had enough experience around the Headquarters to understand what was going on, but I also relished getting out of Marine

Corps Headquarters, too. I always enjoyed being with the troops. That is the thing that I am personally made of. That's me. When I arrived and talked at length with General Chapman about my duties and concerns, he readily agreed that I could spend a lot of the time on the trail, so to speak. I was gone at every opportunity; I was out with units on maneuvers, or in the civilian community. In fact, I still have a list tabulated for my civilian job interviews when I retired showing that I visited many educational institutions throughout the country all of the time, speaking to student and faculty groups, participating in exchanges with them. I also visited all kinds of civic groups.

My mission was to help build and sustain the Marine Corps image through appearances, speeches, visits, inspections--a great effort in this regard. During this period General Chapman was traveling a lot. When he was away, I had to be in Washington taking his place in the Joint Chiefs of Staff (JCS) and Department of Defense (DOD). As his term came to an end, he was gone more and more of the time, saying his goodbyes. Then I spent almost full time in the JCS and DOD arena plus testifying in the Congress. Understand that I did not see the position of Assistant Commandant as another layer in the Marine Corps Headquarters administrative level. I noted that it worked that way with General Anderson as my successor, but that was not true in my case. The Chief of Staff, Lieutenant General John Chaisson, was one of the most competent individuals that I know--we served together on Peleliu and the relationship between Chaisson and Chapman and Davis was such that there was no way that I was going to insert myself into the channel unduly. I tried to let John Chaisson be the Chief of Staff, Headquarters, Marine Corps, and run the administration of the staff with the Commandant. Since I was Acting Commandant part of the time, he had to keep me informed; I had total trust and confidence in that brilliant gentleman to do just that. Thus you would never find a pile of papers sitting on my desk waiting for me to OK them to go to the Commandant.

I understand that was the way one Commandant of the Marine Corps and Assistant Commandant of the Marine Corps operated. That explains one of the complaints that I heard from a number of field commanders who I knew closely and personally about the Assistant Commandant, and that is that they never saw him, and that he never visited their base. So, if he's in effect a super Chief of Staff, that explains why he could not get out of the headquarters. In my case, it was entirely different. Almost every minute that General Chapman was in the headquarters, I had scheduled myself to be out. I felt that it's an obligation to be out with the troops, and with the public, around the country and around the world as much as possible.

As Assistant Marine Corps Commandant, my schedule was really demanding. Just to demonstrate it, this is the one that "broke my back": I got involved to go out and speak to a college in Phoenix. And since I was going to be there, the Navy League had me speak at a luncheon, the college scheduled an afternoon speaking and symposium effort, plus that evening there was another group to talk to. A small jet aircraft was assigned to stay with me. Knox and the aides were along to help. The next day I was scheduled to be in Portland, Oregon, again to go through three sessions. The third day, in Los Angeles, again to go through several sessions, and the day after that, into Washington, D.C. for a Pentagon meeting. So here I am, flying into Phoenix, zip, zip, zip, changing clothing, off the elevator--I had a steward traveling along to help keep me in the right uniform--one Marine helping me take my coat off and the other putting another one on. I get back on the elevator, the aides hand me the paper that's involved in the next stop! I was completely out of breath before I got back to Washington on that trip. So, I told them: Never again! You've found my limit; I can't possibly be fully effective on a three-day trip making three appearances in each of the three places with that much flight time in between. I could succeed in this schedule primarily because of the outstanding performance of my senior aid, Dwight D. Weber, who as a colonel was Director of Command and Staff College.

But it was that kind of a stint, almost constant exposure, even at night. For example, we were asked by the Secretary of the Navy to entertain a group that he had coming to town and he had been unavoidably called away. Thirty people came out to our quarters at the Marine Barracks, 8th and Eye Streets, for dinner, then to the Evening Parade. After the parade they came in for coffee. Also, involved with this was somebody's son who was in a Scout troop. The Scouts came in after the parade and went up in the garret for ice cream. All these were people we didn't even know! That typifies the kind of constant pressures. Of course such schedules would be impossible under the present rules where they don't have enough stewards. We had adequate support to do those kind of things, but I don't know how valuable it really is. Certainly a plus for the people who came there and saw the life that we lived and attended the wonderful parade. That parade represents perfection, and that is always impressive. We certainly made friends for the Marine Corps out of those 30 people and the Boy Scouts.

So, the pressure applied both socially and in the travels and meetings. The pressures were great, but I thrive on that up to the point where they overdo it. The last part of my tour was in the "Tank" (the meeting room in the Pentagon of the Joint Chiefs of Staff) with the SALT I talks, the weapons mix, and budget problems and other such things. It was demanding, very difficult work keeping up to speed on a vast array of problems. It was a difficult personal chore for me to work through that endless stream of Joint Chiefs of Staff papers.

When I'm asked about how my retirement from the Corps came about, let me say this: I retired shortly after Cushman took over as Commandant, since he selected a Naval Aviator, General Anderson, as Assistant Commandant of the Marine Corps. He wanted his team in charge and I was certainly not one to stand in the way. It was made known to me that I could go down and take Lieutenant General Anderson's job as Commanding General, Fleet Marine Force Atlantic. That would not have been good for me nor for the Marine Corps. I just never appreciated people who would move around like that and just occupy the position. No, it was General Cushman's Marine Corps and he should have his own man down at Fleet Marine Force Atlantic and elsewhere. I just happened to be not one of his and it came as no surprise to me.

Let me note that I had been advised privately that the Pentagon was recommending me to be Commandant, but my hopes were subdued because I was aware of the personal relationship between President Nixon and Bob Cushman. Sometime earlier, the President had placed Bob in the CIA with three stars when otherwise he would have retired. The White House told the Pentagon not to submit any recommendations, so it was obviously to be Cushman as Commandant of the Marine Corps, and so it happened.

In earlier times Bob, when assigned as then Vice President Nixon's aide, was said to have saved the Vice President's life by shielding him from harm when radical demonstrators in South America attacked the official limousine. Later Mr. Nixon was, on occasion, a guest of the Cushman's at the Ranch House at Camp Pendleton. A close personal relationship existed over a number of years.

The appointment proved my theory about "cronyism" being bad medicine. The Corps took a downward spiral to become the worst of the military services in such things as unauthorized absences, brig population, drug and racial problems. Cushman was the only Marine Corps Commandant in recent history who was not permitted to serve a four-year term as prescribed in the statutes.

When people asked me to sum up my 34 years in the Marine Corps, my bottom line statement is this: "I wouldn't know how to do any better than I did." I have no serious misgivings of any kind. How could I, going from a poor country boy in Georgia up to four stars in the most elite organization in the world? The thing that we miss most is the people. The Marine Corps family is such a collection of totally outstanding people. Check off the people that I admire most, like Greene, Chapman, Walt, Chaisson, Puller, Craig, Masters, Buse, Nickerson, Barrow. I could just go on and on. Exposure to General Krulak was a gain for me. I'm not associated with those kinds of people anymore. Nowhere else have I found the quality of great family relationship that exists in the Marine Corps, both for myself and for my family.

That's what we really miss now that we are somewhat out of it. I gave it everything I had. I can't look back and see a single time when I took my pack off to coast. And the Marine Corps responded to that. That is why I am concerned that many people I meet today fail to recognize and appreciate the work ethic. I challenged my battalion, preparing to go to Korea--in the few hours I had to talk to the officers and noncommissioned officers-- with a theme and general direction that I have always gone and will always go: "When we are working, we are going to be the hardest working outfit ever. When we are playing, we are going to play harder than anybody, and when we fight, we are going to fight harder than everybody!" That is the kind of challenge I held up for myself at all times, and it obviously paid off with great, great dividends for me and my family.

As for retirement being difficult, I had an ideal transition in that I was retired from the Corps at 10 o'clock in the morning in Washington, and I was in my Atlanta office at 2 o'clock that afternoon in charge of the whole state for the Georgia Chamber of Commerce. However, to indicate the relative scale of effort, I was involved with a half-million dollar budget in Georgia, compared to the billions in Washington.

But no matter what the subject, or the phase of my Marine Corps career, since the day I was married, I like to talk about the Marine Corps and Knox Davis, the light of my life: Let me try to encapsulate her years in the service. You could almost put it into three segments of time. The first was the business of being totally the newcomer, just feeling her way along, and being imposed on, used and uncertain. I was away in World War II, to return to be with her for only two years before I went solo to Guam... Knox adds: "Now, you have to realize

247

that was because at that stage of the game, Ray was a senior officer, and I walked in as a senior officer's wife in a sociable place. Washington and Quantico are very social as far as the military is concerned. It's a sight..." That was a challenging two years for her following my 3 year absence in the Pacific War. Knox was to follow me to Guam six months later; and that was a very delightful tour with a close-knit group of people. You know, adversity builds character and close friends, and that's what that tour was.

In the following stage problems arose wherein we were in a more competitive atmosphere, where people seemed concerned about me being a strong competitor, because I had been fortunate or unfortunate enough to have been exposed to two wars, with the Navy Cross in the first war, and the Medal of Honor in the second war, plus a couple of Silver Stars. I had a chest full of ribbons going into this period of very competitive years. I guess it culminated when I got moved from the job as Director of the Senior School, after Twining had become my boss. He moved into Quantico, and moved me out of a very prime job.

We went to Washington and the third phase started for Knox. I moved into Washington with some very close friends and supporters--Walt, Nickerson, Buse and Masters--people who really were on my side. I landed in a good job as Assistant G-2 (Intelligence); then they sent me to the National War College which was a real plum; and then to Europe for duty. And on the way home from over there, I made my first star as Brigadier General, the most difficult step in the selection process.

So the last ten years of her Marine Corps life, Knox had great influence, in a totally different atmosphere, where she was, as she described, totally and sincerely interested in taking care of the families of the Marines. Her personality changed only in this light: Early on, she was kind of in a state of shock, and then in the middle she was somewhat embittered, then she was able to really reach out as she had always wanted to do, and what she was intended for in the first place, in these last 10 years.

Knox returns: "The only time that I really had to hold myself--and Ray knows it, too; he was mad at me--was when he was retired. We stopped in a little briefing room before we went to the hall where all the guests were, and many of our friends were there, some crying like everything. But anyhow, here we sat in that little room. I had memories of some of the great times. And I'll swear today, it took all I had to contain my feelings. Ray looked over and said, 'What in the world is the matter with you?' And I said, 'Ray, right now I can't take it.' Now, that's the honest truth. Then I asked them not to play 'Auld Lang Syne' because I knew I could not get through it without crying--with a flood of tears. And that song is traditional, really traditional."

"But Ray went right along with me. He said if you don't want it--because Ray knew I'd cry--he said if you don't want it, we won't have it played. So it was funny when the program was over, just at the time for

"Auld Lang Syne," the bandmaster played a Georgia song, "Georgia on My Mind" or something. No, it wasn't "Ramblin' Wreck."

Continues Knox: "I knew I could not take 'Auld Lang Syne,' that's about the only thing I ever changed in the military!"

But my military career did not end on a sad note. Perhaps a letter Bill Davis received from a past Director of the Amphibious Warfare School in Quantico will put my last days on active duty in perspective:

Dear Bill:

I am genuinely pleased that you and General Davis are getting together on his story. He is by far our greatest hero and leader. Circumstances, politics, and fate cut too short his service to our Corps.

As you know, I did not serve for the General in combat (Colonel/brigadier-Selectee at the time of his writing, Ron Christmas won the Navy Cross as a Rifle Company Commander in the Battle for Hue City) but was his Special Assistant when he was Assistant Commandant of the Marine Corps. Major (now Colonel) Dwight Weber was his Military Assistant at the time and is now Director of the Command and Staff College.

Both the General and his wife, Knox, were very special people to work for. They made Sherry, my wife, and I feel part of the Davis family. They were an inspiration and model for us in our years that followed in the corps. There is nothing we would not do for them.

A story about the General that might be told is his "Challenge to Youth Program." When he became Assistant Commandant of the Marine Corps, General Chapman charged him with "presenting" the Marine Corps to the Congress and the American public. He did the latter through this program. As you will remember, the early 1970s were not good times for the Marine Corps, or the armed services for that matter. We were part of a very unpopular government, or The Establishment, as the youth called it. "The establishment" was afraid to speak the truth according to the kids of the nation.

General Davis trouped from one end of the country to the other carrying the "facts" to high school and college audiences, which were not always friendly. But as he spoke, you could see the audience sway. "The Silent Majority," kids who didn't buy what their liberal friends were screaming, but kept quiet, began to speak up by the end of his address. It was magnificent to behold.

One instance worth mentioning occurred at a very liberal-based high school in Portland, Oregon. An assembly period --which was to address the high school had been organized by the school as an open, voluntary forum, for all the schools in the area. The auditorium was packed and I felt great apprehension when the student council president, dressed in wild clothes, introduced the General as "This here man from The Establishment."

As always, the miracle of positive persuasion and the General's sincerity and forthrightness prevailed. The unruly audience was swayed to the point that after the presentation a young girl, totally agitated and in tears, ran up to General Davis and pointed her finger in his face saying: "I know what you're trying to do; you're trying to change my mind!" Well, he had, along with 500 other students. I don't need to tell you, these appearances took "guts"--the same courage he has always exemplified.

General Davis is a GREAT man and I know you will do him justice. Knox Davis is the unsung hero.equally great in the supporting role. Please don't forget her.

--RON CHRISTMAS--29 Jan 88

Lieutenant General (1992)

With thoughts like these to tide us over, it was back to civilian life for the Davises, after a 34-year interlude in our Grand and Glorious Corps!

My final "Front and Center"
    in our Grand and Glorious Corps!!!
        1972, Washington, D.C.

War Memorial in Inchon, Korea, 1975

Knox and Ray Davis burn incense in honor of the fallen warriors at the Korean War Memorial in Seoul, 1975.

Ray and Knox Davis at a reception with Korean President Pak
Chung Hee and his daughter, Seoul, 1975

CHAPTER 27. EXECUTIVE VICE PRESIDENT, GEORGIA CHAMBER OF COMMERCE

Within four hours on the 31st of March, 1972, General Raymond Gilbert Davis became civilian Ray Davis, Executive Vice President of the Georgia Chamber of Commerce. An immediate transition from the martial splendor of the President's Own Marine Band playing at the official retirement at the Marine Barracks, 8th and Eye Streets in Washington to the quiet civilian surroundings of the new office in Atlanta, Georgia that very afternoon. From the second Distinguished Service Medal for service as Assistant Commandant of the Marine Corps to the unmedalled left breast of a new civilian suit, I was immediately at home in this new environment.

While I was still on active duty, I had many calls suggesting that I stick around to help with the transition of the new Commandant. But Knox and I had long since decided that retirement near our kids was the one sure requirement. Willa was attending Georgia Tech, Gil at the University of Georgia, and Miles looking at Florida. I owned farmland in central Georgia. Atlanta became a natural retirement target. A close friend as a contact was available in Atlanta in the person of Colonel Bill Ward. A phone call soon had interviews with a dozen key Georgia business leaders. Executive Vice President of the Georgia Chamber of Commerce had the most appeal: car, club memberships, credit cards, and $35,000 to start, not bad in 1972. I would run the Chamber; good, prime office space. The whole state was my province, with the elite of the elites as close associates. A good experienced staff was in place; the prior Vice President had died suddenly; a very sound membership and financial base was there.

All in all, it was ideal. I had a challenging position from which I could get reacquainted with my home state. I would enjoy a first name relationship with President, Georgia Southern Bell; Board Chairman, Georgia Pacific; Board Chairman, Delta Airlines; Chairman, Trust Company of Georgia.; President, Patillo Construction; President, Atlanta Gas/Light Company; Chairman, Georgia Railroad, etc. Even Jimmy Carter and Bert Lance called me by my first name, even though they both knew I did not agree with many of their programs.

Actually, I pretty much ran the Chamber the way I operated in the Corps. It so happened that my popular predecessor, Walter T. "Pappy" Cates had died in December 1971, after 20 years as executive vice president. I was able to work from a solid base by keeping his staff pretty much intact. H. G. "Pat" Pattillo, then chamber president, was looking for a new man, and I was looking for a new and meaningful career. I had stressed two vital requirements: One was a desire to return to my native Georgia; the other was that whatever I did must carry with it purpose, responsibility, and challenge. It wasn't really that easy, getting this particular position. Initially Pattillo was cold to the idea of hiring a retired general officer for the job.

He told me that he was very much opposed to it, and at first refused any suggestions that he see me. But one afternoon I telephoned him and asked if I could come over for a talk. After two hours of conversation, Pat later said that "it was obvious to me that this man was quality," which was very nice of him. Just as when I took over as Assistant Commandant of the Marine Corps, my first concern was to know the length and breadth of Georgia, and equally important, to let the chamber membership get to know me. I told my secretary to accept for me every speaking engagement that arrived in the office. And I made a lot of speeches all over the state.

I was aware that the staff that I inherited was a professionally competent one and I used it accordingly. Moreover, I continued to expand its operations. My basic thought was: if we cannot be of service to the membership throughout the state, then there is no reason for us to exist. I wanted us to be instrumental in providing the membership and the state with an enhanced quality of life. Again, as in the Corps, I operated with Task Forces, to accomplish a specific mission. One important one was the Employer- Employee Relations Task Force. They provided the means for facing problems with the combined talent of the entire membership without depending exclusively upon the chamber staff. For example, task forces were established to deal with the right-to-work law, equal employment opportunities, public employees legislation, workmen's and unemployment compensation, and occupational safety and health.

Each task force, drawn from the chamber membership, addressed itself to the problems relating to its area of concern. If, for example, exhaustive study indicated that the problems could be resolved through corrective legislation, a steering committee took over and charted the strategy and timing to be followed. And when other solutions were deemed best, they were followed just as thoroughly. There was nothing static about the task forces that I inspired. Each was tailored to confront a given problem. As the problems were resolved, the task forces were dissolved. And new ones were created with the recognition of new problems. One of the biggest was the establishment of an international department within the chamber. When the Atlanta Chamber of Commerce embarked upon the project of making Atlanta an international city, the Georgia Chamber of Commerce moved in the same direction insofar as the state was concerned. Native son Dean Rusk, with eight years as Secretary of State on the national scale, was enlisted in this endeavor, after I used a little personal persuasion on him.

The international spotlight had a broader focus than being restricted to Atlanta. This was emphasized with Governor Jimmy Carter's vigorous efforts to interest foreign firms in the state. Thus the stage was set for an expanded and more variegated commercial-industrial picture for Georgia.

Georgia has some 157 counties. Each one wanted a piece of my time. There'd be a dinner speech in Savannah, breakfast talk at Calloway Garden, a six-hour drive away--a schedule that I eventually tired of and retired again. But we made some real progress in upgrading the Chamber. My most extensive effort caused me trouble personally. We had top businessmen and lawyers working over proposed legislation, and they came down hard on some of Governor Jimmy Carter's favorite antibusiness bills. So hard that I got personal handwritten notes from him. This was preceded by an invitation to be Commissioner of Transportation (Highway Department) from the Governor. I received a report he was incensed when I turned it down. At twice Chamber pay, the job was just too political. I would be beholden to the political power brokers. In retrospect, the Chamber job was an ideal transition to becoming a Georgian again. Whenever I am asked if I considered entering politics, I always joked with those who ask: "My wife says that she could never sleep with a politician in the house."

Even though I've done much in many various service/veteran/church efforts, I have never considered politics. Too much duty in Washington for both of us to ever appreciate politicians. The effort was one of total scope in Georgia. Everything from tourists to industrial development, to the legislation, to the schools. The whole fabric of Georgia's well-being is involved in the Chamber of Commerce, and I was in charge of programs as the Executive Vice President. So that made the transition easy from a work viewpoint because I could get out on the circuit. I was in demand seven days a week everywhere in the state to come help out with a problem or speak to a group. That let me get acquainted and to get much support. And, my family is all here and I have some property that I bought way back as a second lieutenant. My son is nearby with a farm patch, a very big patch, with a herd of cows on his land. We have joined forces, and enjoy the great outdoors. As a family hideaway we have down in the country a house on a 12-acre fishing lake, where we often assemble the family, spend all night roasting a pig, and have many friends participating in the day's activities

Throughout my Marine Corps career there was more than just a family tie between myself and Georgia. True, my parents, Mr. and Mrs. Raymond R. Davis, lived in Milner, and my brothers were living nearby: Lloyd Davis retired near us in Atlanta and John Tribby Davis, a successful dairyman, was married to Dean Rusk's cousin Ellen. But in addition to this, I had always looked forward to returning to a 240-acre farm I bought when still a Marine lieutenant. I was in a tent camp in Quantico, Virginia, when my father telephoned to tell me a mortgage firm in Richmond was foreclosing a farm in Lamar County and I might be able to work something out. I did just that, but they wanted $100 down right away. In 1939 a lieutenant did not have ready access to an extra $100, but I managed to raise it and assumed the payments. I love it on that land, but I was not ready to just sit down and watch life pass by. During this time, and to get to our farm, the first stop was at the beautiful white-columned brick home we built in McDonough. We have now built a similar house near Conyers. This is where I live with my wife, the former Willa Knox Heafner, of Lincolnton, N. C. Our three children have lives of their own: Ray, Jr. owns a building supply brokerage business. Gordon (Miles) is a Vietnam veteran and a captain in the Marine Corps Reserve, and heads a law firm in Pensacola, Florida. Willa Kay married a Georgia Tech classmate, now a local dentist. We now have 7 grand children.

I like to think that the home in Conyers reflects the achievements of a prolonged and successful military career. There is a large den filled with mementos. If the situation requires, I have dress uniforms available. The farm was some thirty miles to the southwest. I had it fenced in by Georgia Tech students, to keep the cattle in. I don't actually 'take my ease' here. Between chores, improvements, new projects and the chamber's work, it is more of a command post right now. But we of the Davis clan do like to gather here, all of the families, just as I imagined we would, back in my Marine Corps career.

Chamber President Pat Pattillo summed up my work with him over the first year as "quiet competence." Almost like a Marine fitness report, he said that "He is personable and perceptive. He has depth and experience. He has an unusual way of understanding people, working with people, and talking with people. He has established a working relationship between the small towns and the metropolitan areas. It's amazing to see how quickly he relates to the small businessman and yet how he can come around to understand corporate problems. The only criticism I've heard of Ray is that he's not a hail-fellow-well-met. At a gathering you don't find him slapping backs. Instead, he's usually over in a corner listening to someone with a problem and trying to unknot the problem for the fellow. He might leave a gathering earlier than some because he's heard a number of problems and he wants to get back to his room to try and come up with solutions. I certainly can't fault him on that. Humility is an old-fashioned word. But to me, Ray is humble."

Jasper Dorsey succeeded Pat Pattillo; he concurred with Pat's assessment, and added that he feels that Georgia is fortunate to have a native son come back here and dedicate his life to making Georgia a better place. He says that is what he sees as my motivation. To me, I guess I feel that I am carrying on the same motivations for my home state that I did for over three decades for my beloved Marine Corps. But I couldn't stay in the Chamber forever. I guess you could say that I had some more civilian missions to accomplish.

After three years I retired, my family grew away from our farm activities so I sold it and put the money away for the education of grandchildren.

Exutive Vice President, Georgia Chamber
of Commerce, 1973

Ray Davis officially commissions USS CHOSIN, Jan, 1991.

After commissioning, Ray and Knox Davis watch the crew
bring USS CHOSIN to "life."

Knox Davis is smashing a champaign bottle in christen-
ing USS CHOSIN, Jan. 1991.

Living Medal of Honor recipients gather, 1993.

THE PRESIDENT   March 2, 1992

Dear General Davis:

Thanks for being at my side as we went to the American
Legion Hall outside of Atlanta. I thought it was a good
event. I like being with those Veterans and I thought
they gave us a very warm welcome. They certainly gave
you a warm welcome.

Barbara joins me in sending our best wishes.

                                    Sincerely,

                                    George Bush

A letter from President George Bush

Dorothy Sims Elementary School held its second annual International Day Celebration. Erin Kerr, grand-daughter of Knox and Ray Davis, represented Korea, wearing a pretty Korean dress. She holds a Korean flag and a Korean fan, May, 1991.

With my family at Christmas, 1989; three children with spouses and seven grand children; a friend is on the left.

Highway 42, Stockbridge to Locust Grove, Georgia gets a
new name, 1991.

Chapter 28. PRESIDENT, RGMW, INC.

In the Georgia Chamber of Commerce, as I did in the Corps, I went all-out in everything I did for the State of Georgia. And I combined it with as much as I could, time-wise, for my family. One reason Knox and I retired to Georgia was to be near our children, and their children, and all others of her family and mine, the Heafner and Davis clans.

Thus, it was best to "retire" again while both Knox and I were young enough to travel to those sites that we had dreamed about over the years. Following this, Knox knew that I would find another career in which I could once again honor the work ethic which had driven me while overseas and Stateside, in war and peace: to do whatever I could to improve the quality of life of my fellow man, whether in the Service of our country, or in my home State of Georgia.

Thus it was that RGMW, Inc., a family land development corporation, appealed so strongly to me. For me, this partnership has been ideal. We are indeed improving the quality of life of all those who come within the purview of RGMW, Inc. My partner is a national class land architect named Edward Alexander. He worked in Washington, D.C. on the Kennedy Center, White House grounds, Tidal Basin entrance; once had offices in New York and Florida's St. Augustine. He came home to Georgia to care for his mother and their family property. He stays busy: he is planning the development of a large plot of land along the Potomac River above Washington, D.C.; he is improving two mountain developments in North Georgia, totaling 8,000 acres.

Our immediate joint task has been 60 lots of two to four acres each with lake and park, streets, utilities, called "New Lake Estates," and that is just about finished. Beyond this is a design for golf club and community. Our target is a 36-hole professional course with 1,200 acres overall, with eight lakes, etc. As we complete New Lake Estates, we have chartered a Home Owners Association to run it. It will all be there: Neighborhood Watch, Women's Club, Civic Association, etc. I mark the accomplishment of my mission here. I have a minor role in the golf venture, even though I know it will be great (Atlanta is short 26 golf courses, especially pro-designed ones). I have more than enough to do otherwise: Reunions, conventions, speaking, boards (some back at Quantico), Korean War Veterans Memorial design for the past few years. Our well-stocked lake is ready for me to get back to fishing, and I have not played golf in 15 years! Knox and I were also ready for some serious travels, such as attending the 40th Anniversary of the Korean War in Seoul, Korea in late fall of 1990.

In addition to ongoing long-term projects, I am also a short-term doer when the occasion demands. One example concerned Jimmy Swaggart, about whom I wrote to a newspaper editor:

"Reverend" Jimmy Swaggart's confessed 'sin' was the lesser of two wrongs he reportedly has committed in recent days. His love fete with his friend, Nicaraguan strongman Daniel Ortega, in Managua, could have more far-reaching hurt than his alleged involvement with any prostitute. To say that "God loves" this chief of the Nicaraguan marxist slave master needs to be followed up with some admonitions. Could Swaggart not recall, for example, the words of Christ in Matthew 18:6, words which surely would apply to Ortega and the marxist denial of Christian experiences for children? "As for these little ones who believe in me, it would be better for a man to have a millstone tied around his neck and be drowned in the deep sea than for him to cause one of them to turn away from me."

The false philosophy which says that "friendship brings peace" generates confusion in all who follow that precept. If somehow Swaggart and others, including the Catholic and Methodist bishops, could lift their sights and see that freedom is the most noble cause of mankind, they would know that there is no lasting peace without freedom.

When this becomes the guiding philosophy of our nation, our objectives will become clear and our people can again come together in unified goals.

Above all, I see myself as a man of action. I never sit around and think about others doing this or that; I join a board to give birth to a Veterans Memorial, or write a letter to a strong organization trying to change one already built. I give speeches on leadership to military organizations, veterans clubs, service clubs, constantly. I am aware that as a holder of the Medal of Honor, I belong to this Nation forever, because of a combat situation where literally thousands of men's lives depended on the actions that I took when someone had to take action.

And I still seek action, even though I reached my late 70's and should be able to get out that fishing pole and a little flat-bottomed boat and row out on one of those famous Georgian lakes and "take my pack off." I've got the best of everything right now, I guess, and I'm still able to maintain active interest in things I'm devoted to. I've served as a trustee in the Valley Forge Military Academy, and Chairman of the Trustees for the Marine Military Academy, and on the Board of visitors of Berry College up in the mountains. These are all somewhat the same types of activity: education in a disciplined environment, which has all those attributes that you would expect. The students develop a self-discipline, they develop a sense of accomplishment. They can see that if they work hard towards an objective, they can get it done, and that quickly the iron discipline of a drill sergeant is replaced by a self-discipline, which means that it's a meaningful learning process.

Marine General George Bowman (Retired), who headed the MMA (Marine Military Academy) had evidence that the spread between his students' beginning test scores and their graduating test scores are the very best in the country. I'm interested in that and I spend some time with it. At the same time, I've maintained my interest in the veterans organizations. I've served on the board of The Retired Officers Association (TROA), and served as the president of both the First and Third Marine Division Associations. I speak to many small groups around Georgia, on things about community development, which I was exposed to in the Chamber of Commerce. More recently, due to my concern for the posture of our national defense, I'm out sounding the alarm nationally to every group I can. I try to limit that to two or three a month, but it's hard to say "No." Knox and I travel when we can. You see, it's a busy life right now.

When visitors tell me that I look as good as I did, if not better, than when I left the Marine Corps back in 1972, I laugh and reply that physically I am better. When I ended my tour in Vietnam, having ridden around for hours each day in that helicopter with an aluminum bar across my back, I developed some damage to the spinal column around my shoulder. I got where my hands would go numb at times, and I couldn't turn my head without pain. I came to Georgia and began riding a tractor with a plow or a baler behind which seemed to make things better. I also went to a doctor who put me through some physical therapy efforts. Now I can go all day with this machinery and turn my head all the way around with less pain. I've improved. Fewer aches and pains than I had when I retired from our Corps.

But an abiding truth is that whenever I carry on a conversation with anyone, no matter how long or brief, I eventually will turn to the favorite subject of my life: Willa Knox Heafner Davis, my bride of five decades. Right now my favorite story is this: When Knox gave birth to our daughter in 1950, news reports of the Korean War reached her saying "All were lost at Chosin," the area in North Korea where I was busy leading a rescue mission of a Marine rifle company with my infantry battalion. Then, 39 years later, on October 14, 1989, Knox christened a guided missile cruiser to be the USS CHOSIN (CG 65), and I was proudly there by her side.

The invitation to christen that ship came from James H. Webb, Jr., then Secretary of the Navy (and former Marine Navy Cross-recipient in Vietnam), who served on the staff of OCS (Officers Candidate School) at Quantico, when I was Commanding General at the Marine Corps Development and Education Command. Interestingly, CHOSIN is a 567-foot ship of the Ticonderoga class of missile cruisers--I first went to sea duty in a heavy cruiser USS PORTLAND--and is built to accommodate 37 officers, 33 chief petty officers, and 339 enlisted personnel.

I was really thrilled that this remarkable woman received this honor which she richly deserved. She has stood by me going through our fifth decade of marriage and three children and three wars. So while I am telling this to the members of the press, Knox is sitting in the study of our home overlooking our 15 acre lake, sewing new cuffs on my formal uniform, which I wear on the lecture circuit. Knox always says: "He's the one who was over there. I didn't do anything but be a military wife." Of course, that merely means that during our first 12 years of marriage, we were apart for six years. I was away from home for three years during World War II, 15 months in Korea, and some two years during the Vietnam War. So Knox had those three children all by herself for those six years.

Our daughter Willa Kay Kerr sympathizes with her mother. She told us that being a mother herself now, she can imagine how awful it must have been not knowing that your husband would ever make it home from each of three wars to see his children. But darling Knox credits Willa Kay with pulling her through the really hard times, because she had a baby to take care of in two of the wars, so she says she didn't have time to worry. And both Willa Kay and Gilbert, our oldest son born in World War II, said that Knox never let her fears show. Gil says that "Mom was tough! When things got tough, Mom got tougher!" And you realize that Knox, this tough young lady, is just over five feet tall, on a very petite frame. Gil also says: "Mom comes from the foothills of North Carolina and was reared in a large family who lived by the motto: 'Never let 'em see you hurt!' Willa always adds: 'I'm sure Mother was worried, but she never would let on to any of us.

Knox always explained it this way: "I coped by trying not to dwell on things. When you know you are going to live as a military wife, you have to learn to accept some things." And Knox not only had to care for the children when I was away, but when I was around it meant hosting dinner parties for such notables as the current king and queen of Spain, various members of Congress, the Secretary of the Navy, and others. And when she wasn't hosting parties, she was attending them, sometimes at the White House, once with Henry Kissinger as her dinner partner. Her role as a military wife took her from Guam to Madrid, from Paraguay to Istanbul, and dozens of places in between.

Between her social duties and traveling, Knox still made time to work with children. She was an elementary teacher when we first met, and also served as a Sunday School teacher, and a Scout leader. Knox has always been close to young people both while we were in the Marine Corps and since. She was always a leader in inviting young wives to parties and receptions, and getting to know them and to answer their many questions about life in the Marine Corps. And even today, 20-plus years after we left the Marine Corps, our closest friends are those who served with us as our junior aides and youngest assistants over those wonderful years.

For our 50th wedding year celebration we arranged ship tours to Alaska and to the Caribbean. In addition we took veterans groups to Moscow and China. I represented President Bush in celebrating the 50th anniversary of the Guadalcanal campaign in the Solomon Island. With our Korean War Veterans Memorial interest we also visited veterans activities throughout the U.S. By the year's end we felt a need to stay at home for a while!

CHAPTER 29. VISIT TO NORTH KOREA

I attended a historical round-table conference that took place in Pyongyang, North Korea, June 21 - 27, 1991. I found the capital to be a beautiful model city, excruciatingly clean, with modern skyscraper buildings and broad avenues. As true in the south, I found North Korean people that we met to be invariably friendly and courteous. Quite a few people that I met on the streets, particularly in rural areas, looked malnourished and hungry. The notorious campaign for "eating two meals" a day was launched while we were in Pyongyang.

Incidentally this conference marked the first time that Americans were allowed into Pyongyang for a conference not only with senior North Korean political officials but also with high-ranking North Korean military officers who took an active part in the discussions. The conference was co-sponsored by the International Security Council located in Washington, D.C. and the Institute for Disarmament and Peace (IDP), which operates under the umbrella of the Korean Association of Social Studies, effectively an arm of the North Korean foreign ministry.

Our delegation was headed by General Richard G. Stilwell (U.S. Army, retired), former commander of U.S. and U.N. forces in South Korea and former deputy undersecretary of defense. Included also were Dr. Joseph Churba, President of International Security Council; General Robert W. Bazley (U.S. Air Force, retired), former commander of U.S. Air Forces, Pacific; A. James Gregor, professor of political science, University of California, Berkeley; Vice Admiral James W. Nance (U.S. Navy, retired), former deputy assistant to the President for national security affairs; journalist and political analyst Sol Sanders; William R. Van Cleave, professor of strategic studies, Southwest Missouri State University, and senior fellow of Stanford's Hoover Institution: Colonel James V. Young, former defense attache, U.S. Embassy, Seoul; and (as an observer) Associate Professor Maria Hsia Chang of the University of Nevada, Reno.

The other delegation included (as conference co-chairman) Deputy Foreign Minister and President of Institute for Disarmament and Peace (IDP), Song Ho Gyong; Lieutenant General Li Hwal, former deputy commander of the air forces of North Korean People's Army (NKPA); Major General Kim Yong Chol, NKPA; IDP Vice President Kim Byong Hong; IDP director Li Hyong Chol, and several others.

Viewed from Pyongyang, the world was becoming an increasingly inhospitable place.

Alliances which had been for the most part reliable and predictable over the course of four decades were no longer firm. With the collapse of communism in Eastern Europe, North Korea, officially known as the Democratic People's Republic of Korea (DPRK), was left with fewer friends. A sense of isolation was paramount in the ruling elite that stubbornly, even defiantly, resisted change in its own country.

North Korea faced severe economic deterioration, food and energy shortages, and a huge defense bill. As a result, the government leadership began to seek rapprochement with Japan, and by cautiously making contact with South Korea and the United States. Japan in particular held the potential for badly needed foreign investment and economic aid. Concurrent with negotiations looking to the normalization of its relations with Japan, North Korea was seeking channels of communication with Washington.

Ironically, the very considerable success of U.S. policy on the Korean peninsula, which helped 45 million South Koreans to build a modern, industrial society, may have created a crisis here.

Harsh critics pointed out that mired down in a primitive combination of traditional regional despotism and a version of Marxist Leninism, North Korea's 18 millions are stalemated. Same critics also charge that the "Great Leader" Kim Il Sung, North Korea's only ruler since the Soviet army installed him in the immediate post-World War II period, is nothing short of George Orwell's Big Brother and that he would love to take over the wealth and prosperity of South Korea, which he failed to conquer during the Korean War in 1950.

North Korea keeps more than a million soldiers and reserves under arms. In addition, a huge armaments industry builds heavy weapons, as well as supplying small arms. It is this North Korean capacity for mischief which now preoccupies South Korea, Japan, and American policymakers. Washington believes it has evidence that the North Koreans are working on nuclear devices. The country has uranium in its treasure trove of metals. The Russians earlier supplied an experimental reactor.

Our conference got under way on the morning of June 21, 1991, in the second-floor conference room of the imposing and beautiful Koryo Hotel. Built by Japan's Mitsubishi, this hotel had many chandeliers and lights all over, but when we stayed there, much of lighting was usually turned off for saving electricity. The escalator was running only when someone stepped on the special stands on both sides.

In a pre-conference meeting the day before, Deputy Defense Minister Kim Kwan Jin assured us that his government encouraged contacts between Americans and North Koreans, adding that it would have been better if this military group had come to Pyongyang much earlier and (in an allusion to official contacts) in uniform.

General Stilwell replied that he and his colleagues had indeed been in North Korea much earlier, but that the climate was distinctly inhospitable! Kim spoke of the need for the reunification of the Korean nation, but as a confederation on North Korea's terms. He said that detente and collaboration should replace confrontation, but that could occur only if the United States changed its policies. North Korea, he emphasized, must be treated as an equal, not as a nation that could be dictated to.

Acknowledging that military expenditures were a burden on North Korean economy, Kim said that there had been a recent 100,000-man reduction, and that another 150,000 were dedicated to civil works. He showed his particular displeasure at the annual U.S.-ROK military exercise (TEAM SPIRIT). Cancellation of the 1991 exercise had been requested by North Korea as a precondition for the last scheduled prime ministers' session.

South Korea had, he alleged (inaccurately), been willing to cancel, but the U.S. refused and thus was responsible for the suspension of the high-level talks. Stilwell reminded him that he, Stilwell, had initiated the TEAM SPIRIT exercises in 1976 and that their sole nonprovocative purpose was to assure the U.S. capability to carry out its commitment to help defend against any further aggression from the North. Minister Kim replied that North Korea had not objected to 'TEAM SPIRIT' when it was of smaller scale; but now it had become a "reinforcement" exercise involving 200,000 U.S. troops. (This, too, is wildly inaccurate because the previous exercise involved 16,000 U.S. forces, the smallest number in the last decade.)

Stilwell added that stimulating North Korean efforts to search for the 8,100 Americans missing in action was high on the American agenda. Kim replied that he was not familiar with this issue but considered it manageable. Countering dismay at the lack of senior North Korean military officers at the conference, Kim expressed confidence in Major General Kim Yong Chol's ability to handle all matters, but said he himself would be available if needed.

Co-chairman Song Ho Kyong, at the outset of the opening session, quoted a Korean proverb—"better to see something once than to hear it one hundred times"—in welcoming the U.S. presence as a sign of changing times. He expressed the hope that the conference would heighten understanding of North Korea and its positions.

General Stilwell, responding, recalled that the two delegations had agreed to discuss, initially, North Korean and American perceptions of the global geopolitical environment, followed by a sub-session on the North Korean view of reunification. From the very first, however, the North Korean participants focused on reunification, with only cursory reference to the global environment.

Song went on to assert that the U.S. had shown no sincere desire to improve relations with North Korea. Nonetheless, he advocated frequent contacts between the two countries, aimed at paving the way for reunification of North and South Korea.

With U.S. and North Korean forces arrayed along the demarcation line, Song wanted to end the dangerous armed confrontation. The U.S., he said, was contradicting the global trend toward disarmament and detente by this continuing policy of confrontation. Instead, the U.S. should facilitate reunification of the Korean peninsula as rapidly as possible by reducing tension and establishing peace and security there.

He conceded that reunification was closely linked to broader international issues but argued that Korea never would have been divided in the first place had foreign forces not intervened. He reiterated North Korea's long-standing reunification proposal for a confederation based on the principle of one nation, one state, with two equal social, economic, and political systems and two governments ruling autonomous northern and southern regions. A Confederal Council with alternating chairmen from North and South would oversee common interests and policies, such as defense and foreign relations. Such a Korean state, brought into existence peacefully through negotiations, would be neutral and nonaligned.

At the same time, Song renewed North Korea's call for a formal declaration of nonaggression between North and South Korea and a peace treaty between North Korea and the United States to replace the existing armistice. Neither South Korea nor the United States had responded to these proposals, he said. U.S facilitation of a Korean confederation, involving the withdrawal of U.S. forces from the South as well as the creation of a nuclear free zone on the peninsula, would lead to a new era of peace.

For his part, General Stilwell focused his remarks on the international geopolitical environment as it relates to the Korean peninsula. He stressed that the American participants in the conference were in Pyongyang as private citizens who wished to further dialogue about ways and means of reducing tension and avoiding miscalculations in one of the world's few remaining regions of confrontation. Nevertheless, the members of the American delegation fully support the basic tenets of U.S. policy in Northeast Asia and the Korean peninsula.

Noting that many of the Americans had initially been involved in Korea as far back as 40 years, Stilwell identified several reasons for U.S. interest in the region. There is, in the first place, Korea's immutable geo-strategic location. Moreover, the deployment of large forces, primarily North Korean, along the demilitarized zone constituted danger of armed conflict that might not be contained. Most important, the United States was vitally concerned about the division of the Korean peninsula with its 70 million inhabitants, a people who share a common language, culture, and national heritage.

General Stilwell observed that international developments make this a propitious time to initiate dialogue between Americans and North Koreans. "The erosion of the balance of power at opposite ends of the Eurasian land mass poses both an opportunity and a challenge to international security," he said. Unrest in the Soviet Union and Eastern Europe, along with the collapse of the Warsaw Pact, the search for new collective security arrangements in Western Europe, and the increasingly complex environment in Asia heighten uncertainty and the possibility of miscalculation. All of this also enhances the significance of developments in Northeast Asia and has its effect on the Korean peninsula, Stilwell said.

He recalled that 20th century diplomacy had repeatedly failed to prevent war. The Gulf war against Iraq demonstrated how great the scope was for miscalculation, Stilwell added, noting that neither Iraq nor the United States and its allies had wanted an armed confrontation.

The alliance between the United States and South Korea and the U.S. commitment to defend South Korea against external threat remain the pillars of U.S. policy on the Korean peninsula, General Stilwell said. The principal aim of the North Korea government policy has been to erode that alliance and that commitment. But that will not be allowed to happen. For the U.S. will maintain its military presence in South Korea as long as both parties deem it necessary. "That presence constitutes the leading edge of the total array of U.S. military power that would automatically be invoked in the event of conflict," General Stilwell said, noting the resolve of the American President and Congress during the confrontation in the Gulf.

Describing the Pyongyang conference as "an idea whose time has come," Dr. Joseph Churba sought to reinforce General Stilwell's comments by noting that past attempts to challenge the existing balance of power had inevitably led to a crisis or general war because American, Asian, and European diplomacy had never successfully managed transitions in the balance of power. As examples, Churba cited the first and second world wars, the war in Korea, and the war in the Gulf where both miscalculated the other's intentions.

The Korean situation is particularly acute, he said, because 1.5 million men are deployed on a battlefield where hostilities could erupt without warning. A major confrontation on the Korean peninsula could destabilize the global situation. While it is for North and South Koreans to determine the modalities of reunification, Churba pointed out, the United States has many and complementary interests, and cannot view developments in Korea independent of East Asia as a whole. Referring implicitly to North Korea, Churba observed that no nation, particularly one of strategic importance, can live in isolation.

Major General Kim Yong Chol, one of the two North Korean military officers present— noted that the Soviet Pacific Ocean fleet already has been substantially reduced. On the other hand the United States and its allies, according to General Kim, are steadily building up their forces. U.S. forces, in fact, are being transferred from Europe to Asia to increase regional tensions. Security on the Korean peninsula and Korean reunification can be achieved, he maintained, only if U.S. policy is changed and U.S. forces withdrawn.

Vice President of Institute for Disarmament and Peace Kim Byong Hong argued that Korea as a nation predated both capitalism and socialism. He traced the history of North Korean reunification proposals beginning with President Kim Il Sung's call for a confederation in 1980, followed ten years later by more detailed proposals.

He said that North Korea had assured the United States from the beginning that the unified state would be neutral and serve as a buffer among the regional powers. Moreover, U.S. interests in South Korea would be guaranteed. Thus, he judged, the United States should be promoting the concept of reunification.

The conference co-chairman, Song Ho Gyong, noted that changes in Eastern Europe and the Soviet Union had sparked ill-founded hopes that similar developments would take place in North Korea. These hopes are without basis, he said, because North Korea has developed its own unique socialist system. Unlike the socialism of Eastern Europe, which had been established by Soviet tanks as a carbon copy of the Soviet model, North Korean socialism developed by itself, based on ideology and faith. That fact, and the principle of Juche, determine that the North Korean system is solid and will continue so.

Institute for Disarmament and Peace director Li Hyong Chol listed several principles, on the basis of which reunification would be achieved: it would take place on the basis of independence with no interference by external powers; the result would be a confederation; foreign troops must be withdrawn; immediate unification of the two different systems would be unrealistic; thus, there would be an interim phase following reunification during which the status quo would be maintained.

Song said that in the first phase of reunification, the existing governments in the North and South would retain full autonomy. Initially, each would have its own jurisdiction, while the federal government would "further the nation's development and prosperity" and exercise executive power over the armed forces in defense of the country against external threat, and over foreign policy. Gradually, the regional governments would transfer their powers to the federal government.

Dr. Churba noted an apparent contradiction in these North Korean statements: on the one hand, their system is invincible and, on the other hand, they envision the coexistence of competing systems in a reunified Korea. He noted that North Korean doctrine calls for the overthrow of the capitalist system, refuses to recognize private property and supports the establishment of a "classless" society. Does North Korea's reunification proposal, he asked, imply any change in these doctrines? Needless to say, the replies from the other side were very vague and evasive.

North Korean Foreign Minister Kim Yong Nam in a special session with us called for increased contacts. He said that his country has long sought to establish contact with the United States. In 1983, he recalled, the North Korean National Assembly wrote to the U.S. Congress in this regard. A year later, North Korea borrowed from former Secretary of State Henry Kissinger the idea of tripartite talks among North and South Korea and the United States.

The three parties, however, could not agree on how to conduct such talks or who should participate in them. In its letter to Congress, the North Korean Assembly made specific proposals for an agenda, the participants, and the modalities of procedure. The two principal agenda items would be the replacement of the armistice with a U.S.-North Korean peace treaty and a declaration of nonaggression between North and South. Although the political counselors at the U.S. and North Korean embassies in Beijing meet regularly, Kim noted, the U.S. has yet to respond to the North Korean proposals. He charged that the U.S. is "timid, narrow-minded, and indecisive "

Kim said North Korea was monitoring U.S. policy through the news media and visitors to the United States, for example, Ambassador Han Se Hae recently met former Presidents Carter and Reagan. Kim went on to criticize the "heavy-handed" policy of the United States which attached preconditions to an improvement in relations. He also charged that Japan wanted to improve relations but that the United States was blocking this, as was South Korea. Kim further charged—not entirely consistently—that Japan was demanding international inspection of North Korea's nuclear facilities as a precondition to improved relations because it wished once more to become a military power, specifically a nuclear power.

Responding in part to Kim's remarks, General Stilwell noted that the U.S. delegation came to Pyongyang at North Korea's invitation with the understanding that it wanted a frank dialogue. We assumed, he said, that North Korea's deteriorating economy, the loss of its credit rating, and its heavy defense burden might be influencing the country to adopt more flexible policies. But after two days in Pyongyang, General Stilwell said the Americans had yet to detect any change. Like North Korea, the U.S. has preconditions for an improvement in bilateral relations: these include renunciation of terrorism, signing of the nuclear safeguards agreement, an accelerated program for repatriating the remains of American MlAs, and a more responsible policy regarding the export of intermediate-range missiles to the Middle East. As for U.S. policy toward the Korean peninsula, Stilwell said its constancy does not reflect lack of courage but prudence—because the well-being of 70 million Koreans is at stake.

Churba asked Kim to comment on reports that, during his September 1990 meeting with then-Soviet Foreign Minister Shevardnadze, he (Kim) had threatened that North Korea would develop nuclear arms and support Japanese territorial claims against the Soviet Union if Moscow were to establish diplomatic relations with South Korea. Kim dismissed the report. If this is what Shevardnadze is saying, then he is "a shameful man." Kim charged that he is spreading such false rumors because North Korea refused to submit to Soviet wishes.

Toward the end of the meeting, Kim curtly dismissed General Stilwell's offer of 100 four-year scholarships in the United States for North Korean students who would be selected by North Korean government.

On the second day of the conference, on arms control, or measures to reduce the military confrontation, Stilwell emphasized the common understanding of the Americans and North

Koreans that the principal cause of tension on the peninsula is the large concentration of military forces on both sides of the demilitarized zone. He pointed in particular to the North Korean forces, which the U.S. accesses to be superior to those of South Korea, especially in offensive capability, and postured to attack without warning.

General Kim denied that North Korea has one million men under arms, but declined to give an alternative figure. He noted that a former South Korean defense minister estimated the North Korean strength at 800,000, but denied this figure also. At the same time, Kim stated that he had better data on ROK forces than the American delegation. He said South Korea has an active force of 800,000 and a reserve force of nine million. He said all active South Korean divisions, 80 percent of its artillery, 70 percent of its tanks, and 100 percent of its tactical missiles are deployed close to the demilitarized zone. He stated further that South Korea has twice as many armies deployed as North Korea.

I, together with General Bazley, expressed our interest in General Kim's disarmament proposals and noted that comments by the Americans were designed to make these proposals more realistic. Colonel James Young strongly disagreed with General Kim's assessment of South Korean strength and posture, stating that he could authoritatively describe South Korea's deployments as defensive rather than offensive. He noted that South Korean deployments are close to the demilitarized zone (DMZ) for the cogent reason that Seoul, the political, economic, and cultural heart of the Republic of Korea, is no more than 25 miles from the demarcation line.

An interesting aside demonstrated the North Korean preoccupation with masking the strength and deployments of their forces. General Stilwell, during the break in the first morning's session, showed General Kim a map with a detailed layout of North Korean army and air force major units and deployments, and asked for some corrections. Kim gave it a cursory inspection, but declined to accept it for corrections. The next day General Kim asked if he might have the map. In view of the rejection, General Stilwell said, no.

Recounting the history of the search for American remains: General Stilwell recalled that substantial efforts were made by both sides in the year following the signing of the armistice agreement to recover and return the remains of North Korean, Chinese and United Nations Command dead. Some 8,100 Americans are still missing on North Korean soil. Since 1954, North Korea has been asked repeatedly to account for 2,233 UN prisoners of war who were not repatriated immediately after the armistice. No action has ever been by North

Korea.

In December 1982, General Stilwell continued, the North Korean representative on the Armistice Commission was provided a map of POW Camp #5 and the adjacent cemetery where many who died in captivity are known to have been interred: in 1986, through the same channel, North Korea was provided with the locations of the several temporary United Nations Command cemeteries in North Korea, including one on the outskirts of Pyongyang, where the remains of 288 dead had not been recovered in 1954.

Additionally, the UN Command provided specific locations of 291 air-crash sites where some 300 air force personnel were lost. Finally, North Korea was provided with names and locations of the 14 POW camps immediately south of the Yalu River, where the 2,233 unaccounted-for UN Command POWs had been held. Search and recovery is not, as North Koreans profess, a binational issue. The remains are those of at least eight nations (Australia, Colombia, Greece, South Africa, Turkey, the United Kingdom, the United States, and the Republic of Korea).

In 1987, General Stilwell recalled, the U.N. Command recovered the remains of 25 members of the North Korean army and presented full documentation to the North Koreans. Incredibly, North Korea refused to accept custody of its own war dead for "procedural" reasons. Thus, the 25 were reinterred in the south, awaiting resolution of this matter.

On May 25, 1990, the North Koreans did transfer to U.S. custody several remains they had been holding for some years; Stilwell was present on that occasion. The U.S. side was given what were said to be the remains of five individuals, two of whom had been identified. Further forensic investigation demonstrated that the remains were of seven individuals and that the two had been, in fact, misidentified, to the great anguish of the two families concerned.

General Stilwell said that the Americans now seek a commitment from North Korea to undertake serious effort to search for war dead at the locations that have been previously identified by the U.S. side. Given such a commitment, and the development of a program for search and recovery, he was confident the United States would be willing to provide financing and technical assistance. As this is a multinational matter, the overall venue should be international. Stilwell suggested that this could be arranged through the International Red Cross or the office of the U.N. Secretary General.

Moving to broader issues, Li Hyong Chol said there is no reason for the United States and North Korea to remain enemies and called on the United States to enter into negotiations with North Korea without preconditions. The armistice agreement should be replaced by a peace treaty between the United States and North Korea. Such a treaty would enable the United States to withdraw its troops from South Korea under a timetable that would be negotiable.

Returning to the nuclear issue, which seemed to obsess the North Koreans, Kim Byong Hong asserted that the United States has 1,000 nuclear weapons in South Korea, including some 16 neutron bombs. Koreans do not want their peninsula to become the victim of nuclear war. Moreover, in view of the nuclear arms reductions agreed to by the U.S. and the Soviet Union, there is no remaining reason to emplace nuclear arms in South Korea.

Stilwell observed in passing that, in spite of their insistence on the dropping of preconditions for the improvement of U.S.-North Korea relations, North Korean participants continued to lay down preconditions of their own.

Van Cleave cautioned the North Koreans that the United States, and much of the rest of the world, take the issue of nonproliferation of nuclear weapons very seriously indeed. He denied that the U.S. opposes only horizontal and not vertical proliferation. With determination and some success, the U.S. has been engaged for two decades in negotiations to stop the vertical proliferation of nuclear weapons, Van Cleave said, noting the strategic arms treaty with the Soviet Union that would reduce strategic offensive weapons, and the agreement on intermediate-range nuclear forces in Europe. Beyond such agreements already accomplished, moreover, Van Cleave pointed out that in the years since the Nuclear non-Proliferation Treaty (NPT) was signed, the U.S. unilaterally removed some 8,000 nuclear weapons from its own arsenal and withdrew over 2,000 such weapons from Western Europe, before any arms control agreements on those forces were in existence.

Churba described the conference as "neither useful nor imaginative." The Americans had come to Pyongyang in the hope that they would find flexibility—the basis for better relations—but instead had encountered "malicious slandering of the United States and no spirit of better understanding."

Nothing said by the North Koreans during the conference was new. North Korean disarmament proposals are aimed at disarming the South and getting American nuclear arms removed. "That is not fair, not new, and it won't fly," he said. Similarly, North Korea offered nothing new on the MIAs. "Give me something to take back. Show me flexibility on a key issue, and maybe there will be negotiations," he said.

Expressing regret, Churba called on the North Koreans to review their situation and to determine clearly what they wish to do and what it is they want from the United States. Without that, there can be no progress in U.S.-North Korean relations. Churba warned that North Korea should understand U.S. resolve. The United States would not be intimidated or dictated to. Citing the example of Iraqi President Saddam Hussein, Churba said he was voicing not a "threat but reality."

He expressed the hope that the conference had served to clarify the U.S. position and noted that it had clarified to the Americans the position of the North Koreans, adding that he hoped a next conference could be held in a better spirit.

Churba's remarks were echoed by Stilwell who said the Americans had hoped for a more open exchange. The sole advantage of the conference, he said, was that the Americans now knew North Korea's position in greater detail and could confirm that it has not changed.

In his final remarks, Song said North Korea had not had high expectations from the conference but had hoped it would at least provide a clue for improved U.S.-North Korean relations. Those hopes had been dashed, he said. Song noted that the Americans brought nothing new to the conference table.

To set the record straight, Stilwell noted that the Americans had brought with them an offer for scholarships for North Koreans to study in the United States and to provide the resource for the search and repatriation of MIAs, and had attempted to work with North Korea to develop its disarmament proposals. "Those are genuine and substantial initiatives on our part," he said.

One comes away from Pyongyang with more questions than answers: does the lack of transparency in the North Korean policy-making process mean that the West cannot effectively negotiate with Pyongyang—even though Kim Il Sung appears to have made preliminary moves to break out of his diplomatic and economic isolation?

As we continue to grapple with the problem of disarming Iraq's nuclear arsenal after Baghdad was defeated in a war, the question of knowing whether North Korea is arming with nuclear weapons becomes even more difficult. In a country where one man has ruled ever since 1945, where there is every indication that he lives in a world of sycophancy and isolation from reality, can any effective negotiation be possible?

We were told that the system remains the same and that it will not change. Personal allegiance to Kim Il Sung is attested to by the colored enameled badge with his portrait that almost all North Koreans wear over their hearts.

Given the fact that the population has no way to let off steam, and the grinding poverty of the countryside will be intensified in coming months as the economic crunch worsens, violence seems almost inevitable.

We can only continue to try to penetrate the veil of secrecy and isolation in the hope that such a blowup can be averted or at least that North Korea will not turn into an international conflict.

A few episodes on our stay in Pyongyang:

Currency: Each dollar was exchanged for two "Wons" in our hotel; but we later found out that each dollar actually fetched 82 Wons in the black market. Since a high ranking government official told me that his monthly salary was 160 wons, it means that he is actually making about two U.S. dollars! Although it should be pointed out that prices for food, electricity, transportation, and housing were low because of government subsidy, living standards of the average people seemed very low indeed.

Airport: When we landed in Pyongyang airport, my friend, General Bazley told me to look carefully at the runway. It turns out that the entire airfield is made of octagonal concrete blocks, which can be dangerous if any get misaligned. General Bazley's explanation was that in case of bombing the repair would be easy and done quickly with stored concrete replacement blocks nearby.

Traffic: Apparently due to the extreme shortage of gasoline not too many people can drive cars. Even in the middle of main streets of Pyongyang there were not more than a dozen automobiles and trucks. No wonder Karen House of the Wall Street Journal who visited Wonsan from Pyongyang counted only seven cars in the entire trip. Indeed, Pyongyang is the driver's heaven.

Stores: I tried to buy some gifts and souvenirs for my grand children while in Pyongyang. But the stores seemed to have very limited items. Washing machines, refrigerators, TVs, etc are all limited to just one type. General Bazley had the misfortune of not getting his luggage until the day before our departure for home; someone mishandled them in the Kennedy airport in New York. He bought some Japanese-made underwear in the Koryo Hotel store. But even the king size was not big enough. The morning after he started to wear those underwears General Bazley came down to our breakfast, wiggling and twisting all over.

Air pollution: Since North Korea is not heavily industrialized, we expected to enjoy relatively clean air. But we were disappointed with a heavy smog hanging around Pyongyang. From the top of the Juche Tower, the air was full of hazy smog because of low-quality coal that North Koreans must use in generating electricity. High quality coal must be allotted for export, we were told.

This is Pyongyang's Koryo Hotel where our delegation stayed.

President Reagan has just appointed me to the Korean War
Veterans Memorial Advisory Board in the White House.

White House unveiling of the initial Korean War Veterans Memorial Model, 1988. (From left to right: General Ruchard Stilwell, President Bush, Ray Davis)

CHAPTER 30. THE KOREAN WAR VETERANS MEMORIAL

Beginning in 1987, I have been more than busy with the Korean War Veterans Memorial in Washington, D.C. I chaired the advisors' design-selection committee, which will acknowledge the contributions of veterans of all ages to the cause of freedom. (Let me note that the design selected was made by four architects from the faculty of Pennsylvania State University, Bill Davis' alma mater). Over $16 million has been raised for the monument, which will be located near the Lincoln Memorial, south of the Reflecting Pool, across from the Vietnam Veterans Memorial. Almost six million Americans served in the Korean War, and over 34,000 were lost. I recently received a letter from Representative James Florio (D-N.J.), who sponsored this legislation, saying:

"I look forward to a day not too far in the future when people from all over America will be able to stand before this long overdue tribute to the men and women who fought in Korea."

As Chairman of the Design Committee, I got together with old friend, Army General Dick Stilwell, the Memorial Advisory Board Chairman, to come up with this Board-adopted concept:

> The Korean War Veterans National Memorial has two interrelated purposes which constitute primary considerations for its design and siting. The first--and fundamental--purpose is to express the enduring gratitude of the American people for all who took part in that conflict under our Flag, those who survived no less than those who gave their lives. The second--and of equal importance--is to project, in most positive fashion, the spirit of service, the willingness to sacrifice, and the dedication to the cause of freedom that characterized all participants. As these patriotic virtues have been common to those who served their country at other times of national crisis--and must not be lacking in the instance of future emergencies--the Memorial must radiate a message that is at once inspirational in content and timeless in meaning. Both purposes dictate that this Memorial be unique in concept, designed for public use, located on a prominent prospect, and present renewable living aspects of hope, honor, and service.

Ironically, I became involved with the Korean War Veterans memorial as a partial result of my unhappiness with the Vietnam Veterans Memorial. Let me sum up my ideas on the Vietnam Memorial thusly: The only existing national monument honoring all American veterans of a particular war is the Vietnam Veterans Memorial in Washington, D.C. Its dominant feature is a black granite wall on which are inscribed the names of U.S. service personnel who died in Vietnam. The memorial has proved to be very popular with visitors to the Capital City, and has certainly contributed to the recent easing of the tensions evoked by the Vietnam experience. Nonetheless, and despite the careful preparation that characterized the project, the Vietnam Veterans Memorial has been the subject of some rather significant critical comment, much of which appears to derive from the fact that it was originally a design for a cemetery monument. In any case, consideration of some of the principal criticisms may prove useful in avoiding potential pitfalls during the planning for the proposed memorial in the nation's capital.

Not surprisingly, the Vietnam monument, as originally conceived, honored only the dead. No consideration was given to the hundreds of thousands who served with honor, and who survived. To correct that deficiency, and presumably the concern about impressions that death is the only reward for service and devotion to duty, a statue representing three troopers was added. Undoubtedly, the intent of the sculptor was to convey a sense of the hardship and suffering inherent in warfare. To many, however, the three figures, though great pieces of sculpture, appear slovenly and defeatist, and not at all representative of the dedication and professionalism commonly displayed by U.S. combat forces in Vietnam. Their demeanor has been compared, unfavorably, with the appearance and bearing of the Marines who are the centerpieces of the Iwo Jima Monument, the authenticity of which is confirmed by the famous photograph on which the monument is based. Portrayed are five infantrymen and one corpsman, who, after an assault landing and five days of the most punishing combat, remain properly uniformed and equipped, and are proudly raising their country's flag atop Mt. Suribachi. It was an act as inspirational to the thousands of Marines on the ground below as it has proved to be to the many who have visited the monument in the past 32 years. The Iwo Jima Memorial grows only more powerful as it ages.

In contrast, the Vietnam Veterans Memorial's failure to provide a positive and inspirational message, and its emphasis on the names of the fallen may, a few years down the road, limit its appeal to visitors. Once the friends and loved ones of those who are commemorated are gone, and the Vietnam experience has receded further into history, the Memorial, despite its current significance, could well come to be regarded as an anachronism.

In some local situations, veterans' monuments which emphasize the names of the dead have worked satisfactorily. In general, however, and particularly in the case of a national or major regional memorial, both of which draw visitors from broad, heterogeneous areas, a powerfully inspirational theme seems most appropriate. One of the most effective themes has proven to be the accurate depiction of live combat troops, striving to accomplish a noble task in a desperate combat situation.

It should be noted that my thoughts on the Vietnam Veterans Memorial and proposed changes thereto came to a dead end when the Congress put a "five year hold on any more changes." The driving force behind this was reported to be members of Congress, including Senator John Warner, former Secretary of the Navy and former Marine officer.

My involvement with the Korean War Veterans Memorial is based on my strongly-held views on the issues of our freedom and national security. I made the following speech on August 3, 1991 at Alpharetta, Georgia at American Legion Post 21 on the topic of "Old Soldiers Day."

"Thank you! You are most generous! My subject today is 'Peace Through Strength'.

Today's visit with you has a very special meaning for Me. Old Soldiers Day fits so perfectly into my recent activities with veterans. In fact, an old soldier was remembered in my early home town of Fitzgerald, Georgia recently where we re-dedicated a War Between the States veterans grave site - Albany's Marine Corps Band participated,

I conducted the ceremony, the entire town turned out. My wife and I have become particularly close to veterans in the past year--visiting more than 35 cities. This in relation to the Korean War Veterans Memorial in Washington. And, of course, the Persian Gulf war where we fostered efforts to support local families .

Marine families here were in great need of support because we had large numbers called up, but we have no Marine base nearby. Getting them into small groups supported by local churches was a great help.

On a recent visit to our Gulf of Mexico coast we commissioned the most powerful ship afloat -- USS CHOSIN. This modern missile cruiser represents in clearest form the validity of a most accepted principle -- peace through strength. The massive recovery of our military strength in the 1980s proved to the Soviets once and for all that their failing economy could not support continuing efforts to achieve military dominance.

For more than five years, the Soviet military kept pace and in many areas vastly exceeded our rate of upgrading. Since 1985, for example, they fielded more tanks and artillery pieces than exists in the combined armies of France, Britain and West Germany. In recent years, they have put to sea six new classes of submarines, four new classes of surface warships and three new types of naval aircraft, plus further building of large aircraft carriers--spending four times as much of their national wealth on weapons as we. But their people paid an extreme price in poverty and deprivation.

Our strength broke their back! The presence of our forces in Europe brought down the Berlin wall -- peace through strength ! ! !

Our presence in South Korea has helped to bring a prosperous peace there! Again, peace through strength. This proven principle must always be protected here at home, even as we hear uncertain trumpets and protests from those who have a different agenda -- the peaceniks, the quitniks, the freezeniks, the antis.

Their proclamations for peace have just the opposite effect. They seek peace through appeasement, through surrender, through enslavement. Now that peace through strength has knocked down the Berlin Wall, removed the Iron Curtain and destroyed Saddam's forces, can they not see the truth? Three soviet families living in a flat with a single bathroom? Controlled shortages in food supply? Medical systems which bend people's minds with drugs? Secret police who arrest innocent victims, plant evidence, convict them before night court magistrates and fly them out for Siberian work camps before morning? Every enslaved nation has polluted their streams, their land, their air to unbelievable extremes!

Leading Marxists now in Moscow are decrying their past breakdown in morality and consciousness --- how else they say could they, for example, have deliberately starved to death millions of Ukranian farmers who refused to heel? They now call for truth, for honor, for charity, for morality, for nobility, for conscience, all of which were missing before.

The Soviets are trying to move away from their peace of enslavement which existed for 70 years. The type of enslavement found in Iraq under Saddam. The same kind of peace of enslavement they brought to South Vietnam, to Cambodia, to Laos.

There in Vietnam we responded to the cry of protesters to stop the killing. We brought our troops home. Ironically, the Marxists killed more people in the next two years of their peace than had been killed in 13 years of war!

Our limited commitment in Vietnam led to the destruction of our national will. Our will came under attack again early in 1991--cries to cease fire and negotiate (we had 13 cease fires in Vietnam--all to the benefit of the enemy, at high cost to us). Again, cries not to send troops. We should not be there!

Let me quote from a great philosopher, John Stuart Mill: war is an ugly thing, but not the ugliest of things. The decayed and degraded state of moral and patriotic feeling which thinks that nothing is worth war is much worse. A man who has nothing for which he is willing to fight, nothing he cares about more than his own personal safety, is a miserable creature who has no chance of being free unless made and kept so by the exertions of better men then himself."

Those of Christian persuasion read from the scripture: "...My brothers, you were called to be free." These words undergird a foundation for my belief that "freedom is the most noble cause of humankind." Those who loyally serve freedom enjoy a great strength forged in a crucible of torment and heroic sacrifice. In our great bastion of liberty which God has provided for us, should He not expect us to serve as good stewards in the cause of freedom throughout His world? A determined few can make a difference!

The gallant defenders at Pearl Harbor, for example, served to light a bonfire of national spirit. Within hours we were fully committed to the defeat of our enemies and their unconditional surrender. Total victory was to be ours, except that we eventually gave away to the Marxists half of Europe, half of Korea and Vietnam and the land of many other free peoples throughout the world. Korea caught us off guard with our military in skeletonized formations. Even so, we persisted to help salvage freedom for South Korea.

Vietnam was a total disaster. Three nations surrendered to the Marxists; millions were massacred; and hundreds of thousands were forced to flee from their homelands. To repeat, our limited commitment led to the destruction of our national will to win .

In 25 years, we had gone from total victory to total disaster--not a favorable trend.

Then came the Persian Gulf...The world witnessed one of the great military performances in the history of warfare. A sudden, crushing defeat of a massive combat tested, totally equipped war machine. Done in record time and at less cost in American lives than was sustained in everyday events here at home in a like period. This miraculous feat did not just happen--not just luck or happenstance--it was by careful design.

The early 1980s found America's armed forces in low gear--inadequate weaponry, poorly trained, manpower deficiencies--unsatisfactory readiness. Our citizens at the polls mandated a turnaround. An upgrading program was launched. Fortunately, research and development efforts had been continuing even as our forces had declined. We had models of advance weapons on the shelf -- giving us a head start. An all out effort brought results. Our ground formations were equipped with a whole new family of sophisticated weapons--small arms, artillery, tanks, missiles. We nearly doubled the size of our active fleet with incredible advances in missile and air launch capability--247 ships up to near 600!

The most modern aircraft with stealth and stand-off smart-bomb and guided-missiles became plentiful. Most important of all, with an all volunteer force, we attracted the best qualified, highly motivated men and women in America -- the cream of our youth. Their training and readiness became top priority.

When Saddam struck we were ready. Leadership at the white house and in the pentagon was brilliant.

First, they clearly recognized the need for adequate forces. Quickly, forces were launched to protect Saudi Arabia. Before they were fully in place, the number being deployed was doubled. Then doubled again as allied forces joined a third American increment.

In four months we positioned more U.S. Forces in the middle east than we got into Vietnam in four long tragic years. The immediate insertion of this massive ready force was a key element in our success. Peace does come through strength--we must never lower our guard again.

Our modern sophisticated aircraft and missiles blinded Saddam by closing down his radar systems, communications and air fleet. Then his ground forces were decimated by constant pounding and finally routed by extremely deep penetrations and flanking strikes by our mobile ground forces. The enemy was given no sanctuary, no quarter.

Those experts who produced data to prove that we would suffer 10,000 casualties, missed it by 99.6%--they were totally wrong.

But with all the magnificence of the design, the planning, the strategy, the logistics, the technology, the smart machine and magic missiles--with all of these--the most important ingredient, by far, is and will ever be soldiers, sailors, airmen, coast guardsmen and Marines who lay their lives on the line for us. This included reservists and guardmen who were called up from throughout the country. They responded to the guidance of our superb field commanders .

Their great spirit and their gallantry, their dedication, their devotion to our cause; a do or die determination, no doubt buoyed by great support here at home, they got the job done--with unbelievable speed and effectiveness.

Their performance reminded me of like performance I saw in W W II, in Korea and in Vietnam when we were permitted to fight.

My good feelings for all veterans and warriors has remained true and has been enhanced time and time again. We have come to more fully appreciate the one common golden thread which runs through all our war experience--the service of veterans and warriors in the noble cause of freedom.

> *their gallantry in combat*

their compassion for the victims of war

their support of families and communities at home

their constant patriotism and loyalty

They are a major active force for good--a national treasure for America. I think it is safe for me to say that our soldiers, sailors, airmen, coast guardsmen and Marines are a different breed. To me, that difference is best defined as spirit.

Individuals join us who are of great personal spirit, but at the same time recognize the need to give way to their unit, their service, their country! In training, our exacting discipline is soon translated into a self-discipline--a spirit of one for all--all for one!

Our total spirit comes to us from those who have gone before--old soldiers--the spirit builds on our total commitment to always be of service: at work or play, on duty or off, active, reserve, retired. We never close up shop and go off to be something else. We serve now and forever. Above all else, our devotion to the noble cause of freedom generates a kindred spirit which motivates each of us in everything we do.

If we here assembled rededicate ourselves to a total commitment to the support of our troops and our veterans, and to a just and lasting peace, then this becomes indeed a hallowed tribute to those we honor today--those old soldiers of every age who have stood in harms way in the cause of freedom."

I would like to end this chapter by adding the text of my "Introduction to the Korean War Veterans Memorial" that I used in my briefings for many friends and government officials in a recent visit to Seoul, Korea.

I welcome this opportunity to explain a few facts about the Korean War Veterans Memorial. First of all, allow me to say a few words about myself and my background. I am Ray Davis, and I served in the Marine Corps for 33 years. Before retiring from the Corps in 1973 with the rank of a general, I participated in three wars: World War II as well as the war in Korea and Vietnam. I fought in the Peleliu, Guadalcanal and New Guinea campaigns, where I was awarded the Navy Cross, and in the Chosin battle in North Korea, where I was awarded the Medal of Honor. My last combat command was that of the Commander of the 3rd Marine Division in Vietnam.

I was appointed to the chairmanship of the Korean War Memorial Advisory Board by President George Bush after my distinguished predecessor, General Richard G. Stilwell, passed away in December, 1991. In the early years of our Memorial Advisory Board's exist-

ence, General Stilwell worked very hard with exemplary enthusiasm and devotion; we owe him so much for making this Memorial possible.

On June 14th, 1992 I accompanied and introduced President George Bush when he took part in the ground breaking ceremonies for the National Korean War Veterans Memorial in Washington, D.C. Present were more than 5,000 American veterans of the Korean conflict. And the ceremony was broadcast on national television. Since then, actual construction began on April 28, 1993. Now we are beginning our preparation for a big celebration from July 26 to July 30, 1994. About a month ago, I was designated the general chairman charged with this preparation for the forthcoming dedication. More details will be sent to all of you as they become available.

It was more than forty years ago that the United States of America signed the armistice agreement with representatives of North Korean and Chinese forces at Panmunjom in July, 1953, ending the Korean War. Since then, of course, the world has changed greatly. For one, the Soviet Union is no more, while democracy is on the march around the world. All in all, I am firmly convinced that the strong and decisive stand that we took in defense of freedom in the Korean peninsula not only stopped the spread of communist aggression in East Asia and elsewhere, but also started the long and often bloody chain of events that culminated in the ultimate demise of communism. Therefore, as Bob Hansen, Executive Director of our Board, aptly described, the Korean War "is no longer a forgotten war but in fact a forgotten victory which our Memorial will document and celebrate for all time to come."

The Korean War Memorial Advisory Board guided this Memorial project for six years, often undergoing tortuous studies, debates, and controversies. But we have persevered and finally you will see and enjoy the fruit of our hard work, which has brought together the inspirational sculpture of Frank Gaylord as well as the innovative stone-etched narratives of graphic artist, Louis Nelson. More than anything else, our magnificent memorial is going to express the enduring gratitude of the American people to our fighting men and women for their spirit of service and dedication to the cause of freedom. We will honor those who survived, no less than those who paid the ultimate price of being KIA (Killed In Action) or are missing.

The Public Law No. 99-572, which was enacted on October 28, 1986 by the United States Congress, authorized the Memorial to be built as a national monument to "honor members of the Armed Forces of the United States who served in the Korean war, par-

ticularly those who were killed in action, are still listed as missing in action, or were held as prisoners of war." Our Memorial will do just that and far more, I am happy to report. For our design in fact does honor all members of the Armed Forces. You should remember that there were at least 8 to 10 troops behind the lines, in support of each one on the front lines. Thus, our memorial will express our Nation's gratitude to those who came home as well as those who did not come home. It is a grand and glorious salute to all who served in Korea. Nearly 5.7 million Americans served in the Armed Forces during the Korean War. And many patriotic American as well as Korean-owned corporations have contributed over $14 million to bring the memorial to reality. Additional money has come from interest earned on the principal.

You will be glad to know that the Korean War Veterans Memorial is going to be a striking combination of sculpture, architecture, and landscape. The site stabilization, started in April, 1993, is going to be completed soon; thousands of pounds of dirt have been trucked to the site and many of the trees of the Ash Woods (the name of our Memorial site) are being replanted. The foundations and footings for the architectural setting will be constructed from April, 1994 until June, 1995. As President George Bush said, we welcome you to visit our memorial. When you do, you will agree with his remark that "Once this memorial, this fantastic memorial, is constructed, no American will ever forget the test of freedom our brave sons and daughters faced as they sought to stop aggression [in Korea]."

Our Memorial has three features; they are: l) a column of nineteen troops representing those who fought the war on foot, 2) a wall depicting the array of combat and combat support troops in operational mode, and 3) a commemorative area for those killed in action, missing, and POWs.

Like its universally admired companions, the Lincoln Memorial and the Washington Monument on our most historic Capitol Mall, the Korean War Veterans Memorial combines several design elements--inscriptions, narrative art, sculpture and architecture--to create an impressive memorial ensemble. The grandeur of the Lincoln building is widely acknowledged for the dignity of the 20-foot marble of the 16th President and the carvings of his two greatest speeches. While this Lincoln Memorial occupies the focal point of the west end of the Capitol Mall, the new Korean War Veterans Memorial is also going to be distinguished by its gentle landscape, the quietude of its circular pool and the majesty of the nineteen burnished steel warriors--all of which will present a striking and complementing harmony. Basic elements of our landscape design will balance intimate, tree-lined alcoves with attractive open vistas to the adjacent reflecting pool.

Nineteen troops in our Memorial are positioned in an open field with several emerging from the woods, giving the impression that there are legions to follow. The highly polished granite wall is 180 feet long and will have thousands of images etched into a mural that acknowledges, as Congress intended, the totality of the Armed Forces effort. A series of images, in operational mode--those of nurses, chaplains, air men, gunners, mechanics, cooks, helmsmen, among many others--symbolize the vast effort that sustained the foot soldiers. These thousands of faces will provide the basis for telling the story of the Korean War. Whenever you look at the mural you usually will see someone you may think you recognize. For that and other reasons this Memorial will live forever. It is a living Memorial for all time to come. The commemorative area is a suitably solemn tribute to our fallen comrades, those still listed as missing in action and the POW's. There is a still reflecting pool surrounded by a grove of trees and benches for visitors.

The Advisory Board and the American Battle Monuments Commission have also approved the installation of an interactive computerized video data-base of names and other details of all known casualties which will be accessible throughout the Memorial by all visitors. The visitor who wishes to do so will not only be able to see the name but also the details such as the date, time and location of the action that caused the death of warriors and possibly their photographs on screen. We are even working with the design team to see if there is a way for the visitors to take a printout of this information with them as a memento of visiting the Memorial. The system can be updated as new information becomes available and is verified.

Finally, it should be remembered that American fighting men and women joined in the Korean conflict under the American as well as the United Nations flags. It should also be remembered that our main ally in the war was the Republic of Korea and that its brave soldiers fought and died with our own warriors. With our help the people of Korea escaped the yoke of communist oppression. As witnessed by so many people from around the world through the 1988 Olympic Games in Seoul, our Korean friends have enjoyed many fruits of freedom and democracy accompanied by fantastic economic progress. The "Miracle on the Han" that the Korean people have achieved would have been impossible without our combined effort to stop the aggression by North Korea.

Therefore, it is fitting that many Korean-owned corporations such as Hyundai and

Samsung generously contributed millions of dollars to our Memorial fund. I am happy to report that I will be visiting Seoul again next month. I will contact many Korean dignitaries, including President Kim Young Sam. We plan to include many leading Korean groups-- musicians, dancers, painters, dramatists, scholars, journalists, veterans--in the grand opening of our Memorial.

We expect President Clinton and President Kim Young Sam to be with us as Honorary Chairmen of our Celebration. We also have plans to invite other distinguished guests, including several former U.S. presidents as well as representatives from those UN members that participated in the Korean War.

The Minister of National Defense, Byong Tae Rhee (in the middle), introduces me to President Kim Young-sam on June 25, 1994 in Seoul, Korea

I attended a memorial service at the National Veterans
Cemetary with other distinguished guests in Seoul, Korea on
June 25, 1994. It was my third trip of the year.

EPILOGUE
(By Bill Davis)

During the years this writer served in the "As Told To" mode, listening to the previously untold story of a truly authentic American hero, a source of constant re-motivation was sought.

It was found in THE NEUROPSYCHOLOGY OF SELF DISCIPLINE, a series of tapes by SyberVision Systems, Inc. Not only did it serve to continually motivate this retired Marine to plague General Davis with question after question over these years, but daily listening to these tapes caused him to realize that Ray Davis is not the acme, nor the epitome, nor even the zenith, but the very apotheosis of flesh-and-blood Self-Discipline.

As the three of us, Ray, me and you, the reader, re-live his career via mainly the billets he filled through over three decades, the essentials of Self Discipline exemplified demonstrate how all readers can accomplish their long-term goals in life.

Early in the course, SyberVision causes its students to grade themselves, from 1 to 7, in a Personal Assessment Form on the 10 Dominant Characteristics of a Self-Disciplined Achiever:

1. Do you have a strong Sense of Purpose?

2. Do you seek out positive Mentors?

3. Do you have a sensory-rich Vision of your life?

4. Do you have a positive Sensory Orientation? (i.e., Do you expect to succeed?)

5. Do you have a strong Belief in Self?

6. Do you have the ability to Plan and Organize?

7. Do you continue to acquire Learning/Skills?

8. Do you know the virtue of Patience (versus the "Quick Fix")?

9. Do you have Perseverance & Persistence (versus "giving up easily")'

10. Do you have a sense of Pleasure/Play in relation to "Work"?

If you are honest with yourself in answering the foregoing 10 questions, then you can ask yourself if you have it within you to perform at the Navy Cross (outstandingly) or Medal of Honor (Above and Beyond) level in your specific field of endeavor. Thus, by reading this book, from the examples set by Ray Davis throughout his early years, military life, then civilian life back in his home state, you will have learned how to conquer whatever fears you have concerning your ability to succeed doing whatever, wherever, beginning right now.

There are lessons to be learned from the lives of the great ones. Lee Iacocca put together two fine books about his life As Told To, which contained many examples of business savy that his readers can apply in their everyday lives. However, Ray Davis' brief autobiography will teach you much more in that you are literally enrolling in a lifelong course in the use of the master key to success: Self-Discipline.

It is ironic that this writer did not see all of this sooner, because the gaining of Self-Discipline is the essence of the Marine Corps experience. Whether in the Marine Corps Recruit Depot/"Boot Camp" (MCRD) or the Officer's Candidate School (OCS) and then The Basic School, the Drill Instructor/DI or the Officer Instructor in educating and training his volunteers to do one thing: Upon graduating from MCRD/ OCS/TBS--to possess and utilize to the fullest Self-Discipline; to be able to operate on his own in combat against any and all enemies. Alone, even when there is no non-commissioned or commissioned officer to lead him forward, as can happen in certain combat situations. Whether on liberty in Paris or fighting in the sands of the Middle East, he is on his own to survive with, or perish without, Self-discipline. The choice is his--and yours--in life.

Another current irony is that our major problem as a people concerns the growing lack of Self Discipline--Instant Gratification is the name of the game for most. While working with General Davis one day, I took a lined pad and easily ran down the alphabet with major problems: A=Abortion; B=Booze; C=Cigarettes/Smoking; D=Drugs... All 26 letters can lead you down the garden path, and almost every one is a matter of Instant Gratification and lack of Self-Discipline!

We all desire to be happy, healthy, successful. This story, with its examples from the life of Ray Davis, can serve as a master blueprint in your pursuit of those desires. Self-Discipline is the Master Key to Success. With it, you can focus your knowledge, talents and intellect into a tremendous power to organize your thoughts into matter, and matter into form. What now is abstract in our life will become concrete, and your ideas will become reality. Then, and only then, will you develop the inner will, drive and determination to achieve with excellence whatever you really desire.

Permit me one last quote, from another Southerner who fought World War II as a rifle company commander, then was captured by the Chinese near the Chosin Reservoir, and spent over three years freezing in Chinese Communist/North Korean prisons, yet survived to become Chief of Staff, Headquarters, Marine Corps and Commanding General, Fleet Marine Forces in the Pacific, Lieutenant General John R. McLaughlin, USMC, Retired:

> "Ray Davis may be the best combat leader the Marine Corps has ever produced, although my vision in this respect is limited by my own experience. However, I have served with Generals Lemuel Shepherd, Lewis Walt, Merritt Edson, Lewis Puller, and many other distinguished Marine fightingmen."

These Marine leaders were all great, and it is presumptuous to single out one Marine, but Ray Davis is the epitome of a "thinking combat leader."

In the Corps, as we prepare the lesson plan for a given class to be presented, we are taught to "Tell 'em what you are going to tell 'em; then tell 'em; then tell 'em what you told 'em!"

Hopefully, the foregoing pages of the life of Ray Davis did that for you, the reader. There is nothing left to say, but--

SEMPER FIDELIS!

Index

V

W

Y